Operation Torch

Operation Torch

By the Same Author:

Bloody Clash at Sadzot
Captain Cool
They Jumped at Midnight
Drop Zone Sicily
Agony at Anzio
Hitler's Fortress Cherbourg
Storming Hitler's Rhine

OPERATION TORCH

*The Allied Gamble
to Invade North Africa*

William B. Breuer

ST. MARTIN'S PRESS   *NEW YORK*

Design by Philip Denlinger

Library of Congress Cataloging in Publication Data

Breuer, William B., 1923–
    Operation torch. etc

    1. World War, 1939–1945—Campaigns—Africa, North.
2. Operation Torch. 3. Africa, North—History—1882–
I. Title.
D766.82.B74   1986   940.54′23   85-25142
ISBN 0-312-58685-X

First Edition

10 9 8 7 6 5 4 3 2 1

The job I am going on
[Operation Torch] is about as
desperate a venture as has ever
been undertaken by any force in
the world's history.
     —General George S. Patton

Dedicated to
JOHN HALL "BEAVER" THOMPSON,
who during World War II
earned the enduring respect and
admiration of thousands of
American fighting men by
reporting their ordeal from the
front lines on countless
battlefields. He set the standards
for those combat correspondents
who followed.

Introduction   ix

Photo sections follow pages 80 and 186

Introduction

In mid-1942, Adolf Hitler stood on the threshold of a quick victory over the Grand Alliance—the United States, Great Britain, and Russia. Through the ruthless and skillful employment of his war machine, the Führer had in two and a half years planted the swastika across an enormous swath of Europe and the Mediterranean. France had fallen. German territory stretched from the outskirts of Moscow and Leningrad—a thousand miles deep into Russia—all the way west to the Pyrenees on the Spanish-French frontier, and from the northern tip of Norway to the North African desert near the fortress of Tobruk in Libya.

At sea, Great Britain and the United States were suffering a calamity that threatened to bring both partners to their knees. German submarines had been inflicting enormous losses on Allied shipping, principally in North Atlantic waters, interdicting the supply lifeline between America and England. Under Grand Admiral Karl Dönitz, the U-boat wolfpacks had grown steadily in numbers and effectiveness, until in the early months of 1942, German submarines were sending an average of five Allied merchant vessels to the bottom every twenty-four hours. So daring had the U-boat campaign become that scores of Allied ships were being sunk within minutes of leaving port at New York, Boston, Norfolk, and Miami. Dr. Josef Goebbels, the diminutive Nazi propaganda genius, exulted in his diary: "The Führer is well on his way to his goal of world conquest."

Since being drawn into a global conflict by the Japanese bombing of Pearl Harbor on December 7, 1941, America had found itself almost totally unprepared. General John Dill, the senior British military representative in Washington, an officer whose country had been fighting the powerful German Wehrmacht (armed forces) for two years, wrote to General Alan F. Brooke, Chief of the Imperial General Staff:

"This country [the United States] is more highly organised for peace than you can imagine. At present this country has not—repeat not—the slightest conception of what the war means, and their armed forces are more unready for war than it is possible to imagine. The whole organisation belongs to the days of George Washington."

The predicament of the Army of the United States when the nation went to war with the Axis powers—Germany and Japan—reflected the mood of the American people in the 1930s and early 1940s. Most Americans had been preoccupied with their homegrown affairs. True, Nazi Germany had clamped an iron fist around much of Europe, and Japan was brutalizing and conquering China. But United States citizens were reassured by the two oceans that separated their country from the violence to the east and west. When Adolf Hitler invaded Poland on September 1, 1939, with 77 infantry and panzer divisions, 4,200 modern aircraft, and thousands of tanks and armored cars, the entire continental United States army totaled fewer than 130,000 men. To hold outposts from the Arctic Circle to the Equator and from the Panama Canal to Corregidor in the Philippines 8,000 miles away were only an additional 45,000 men. The United States did not have a single armored division, nor did a single airborne soldier exist. Only 17,000 widely dispersed air corpsmen were available to fly, service, and maintain some 1,000 aircraft, most of which were unserviceable or obsolete.

America had no military intelligence service worthy of the name, and no functioning secret service, which made the United States the only major nation in the world unequipped to covertly seek out a potential enemy's intentions. America's ingrained abhorrence over "spying on neighbors" was so intense that in the 1930s a horrified Secretary of State Henry L. Stimson had withdrawn his department's support of the Army Signal Corps's top-secret cryptanalytic service, which was trying to break the German and Japanese codes. Explained Secretary Stimson: "Gentlemen do not read each other's mail."*

Europe had been engaged in a savage war for a full year by the time the United States became alarmed over the inadequacy of its own defenses. As Americans awakened to the fact that only a beleaguered England stood between them and the Axis powers, a Gallup Poll showed that two-thirds of its citizens were in favor of some sort of arms aid to Great Britain. But beginning in the summer of 1940, some 700 citizen committees formed across the nation, stridently opposing America's "drift into other people's wars." The most conspicuous of these groups, with 60,000 members, was the America Firsters, one of whom was Charles A. Lindbergh, the famed Lone Eagle of 1927 and long a national idol. "Let us stop this hysterical chatter of [a German] invasion," he declared."†

Despite such outcries, in August 1940 a worried Congress authorized mobilization of the National Guard. At the same time, bitter clashes erupted in Congress over the introduction by Senator Edward R. Burke and Representative James W. Wadsworth of the Selective Training and Service Bill, which called for the first peacetime draft in the nation's history.

---

* Despite the apathy of the government, a brilliant American cryptanalyst (one who solves intricate codes), William F. Friedman, persevered. In early 1942 —too late to thwart Pearl Harbor—Friedman broke the Japanese cryptosystems. For the remainder of the war, American leaders knew of Japanese plans in advance.

† Later, in 1944, the War Department would ask Lindbergh to go to the Pacific to study the operation in combat of P-38 fighter planes. Although technically a civilian, he subsequently volunteered for and flew more than 50 combat missions, more or less incognito.

Isolationists inside Congress were outraged. "If you pass this bill," thundered Montana Senator Burton K. Wheeler, "you will be plowing one-third of our American boys under!" "Warmongering!" cried others. Yet a Gallup Poll in mid-August indicated that the nation was 71 percent behind the draft proposal. In September 1940, with Hitler's armies poised to invade Great Britain, the Selective Service went ponderously into operation.

The draft and the National Guard call-up were widely seen as stop-gap measures until the unpleasantness in Europe and Asia somehow would vanish. Congress specified that the one million new men entering the army could not be posted outside the western hemisphere, and duty tours were limited to one year.

With the Japanese attack on Pearl Harbor only four months away, and the army in danger of disintegrating with the conclusion of so many twelve-month duty periods, the House of Representatives passed, by a *one-vote* margin, the Selective Service Extension Act, lengthening duty tours and permitting all troops to be moved overseas.

By the summer of 1941 the Army of the United States numbered 1.5 million men—a majority of them reluctant draftees. Sagging esprit was depressed further by outmoded or nonexistent weapons, vehicles, and equipment. The general-issue Springfield rifle was a relic of pre-World War I days; many men trained with broomsticks in lieu of rifles. Machine guns and mortars were wooden models; artillery pieces were often long poles; old trucks with the word TANK painted on them were used for field exercises. Training was often conducted in ways calculated to avoid arousing resentment from the fewest citizen-soldiers and their families back home. For fear of newspaper headline blasts, officers refrained from keeping men outside in inclement weather or fatiguing them with body-toughening routines. As a result, America's citizen army was denied the intense, realistic training that pays off in combat.

Hardly had the smoke cleared from the surprise attack on Pearl Harbor than a privately elated Winston Churchill, the sixty-eight-year-old prime minister of Great Britain, brought a large entourage to Washington for strategy conferences with President Franklin D. Roosevelt and his key advisors. During these sessions a strategic policy was adopted by the two powers: Adolf Hitler and Nazi Germany would be crushed before the Grand Alliance turned its full attention to Japan. As a result of this decision, the United States, in January 1942, began implementing Operation Bolero, the buildup of American forces in the British Isles for the purpose of taking eventual offensive action against Germany. The soldiers in this vanguard of America's broomstick-trained army, disembarking in Northern Ireland, were relatively few in number, only partially trained, and, in many cases, poorly officered. The great bulk of the weapons, tanks, and equipment needed for offensive action did not exist. Most of the required landing craft had not even reached the blueprint stage.

With these raw GIs still trickling into the huge staging base that was the British Isles, U.S. Army Chief of Staff George C. Marshall and a then obscure subordinate, Major General Dwight D. Eisenhower, chief of the War Plans Division, called on President Roosevelt at the White House on April 1, 1942. There they presented a plan code-named Operation Sledgehammer, which called for an amphibious assault in the fall across the English Channel against German-held northwestern France. Roosevelt was delighted with the proposal. With the American people taking in a torrent of black news from the Pacific, he was anxious to take offensive action. Sledgehammer was approved.

In England, however, Winston Churchill and his advisors were stupefied on learning of these precocious American plans for a cross-Channel assault in September—only a few months away. Dug in on the French side of the Channel were 25 combat-tested, fully equipped, and expertly led German infantry and panzer divisions, backed by a potent and experienced Luftwaffe. "Sheer madness!" declared General Alan Brooke, the British chief of staff, on learning of the American proposal. Brooke, who was England's most decorated soldier since Wellington and Marlborough, warned Churchill urgently: "Any cross-Channel attack this year will meet with total disaster!"

The Allied situation soon grew from gloomy to black. In May and June the Russian army suffered more than 250,000 casualties in massive land battles with the onrushing Germans in the Crimea. Then the Wehrmacht launched a powerful offensive aimed at seizing the Caucasian oil fields. With catastrophe facing the Soviets, Premier Josef Stalin rushed Foreign Minister Vyacheslav Molotov to London to demand that the Western Allies open a second front—immediately—to relieve the enormous pressure on the Red Army. Otherwise, Molotov cautioned solemnly, Russia would collapse and Hitler would hurl the entire weight of the German war machine against England.

Molotov's desperate appeal was rejected by Prime Minister Churchill because England was facing its own military disaster: the British Eighth Army in North Africa was on the verge of being destroyed by the Afrika Korps, led by General Erwin Rommel, the famed Desert Fox, whose tactical skills had won him the fear and admiration of his Allied adversaries. On June 11—a day that would become known to the Allies as Black Saturday—Lieutenant General Neil Ritchie, commander of the Eighth Army, sent 300 of his tanks to assault Rommel's lines near the British-held fortress of Tobruk. Rommel had secretly positioned scores of high-velocity 88-millimeter guns along a low ridge outside the hamlet of El Adem, hoping to lure British armor into an ambush. In the ensuing clash, 234 of Ritchie's tanks were knocked out in less than four hours. Rommel, scarcely waiting for the battlefield smoke to clear, sent his panzers through disorganized British positions and seized the "impregnable" fortress of Tobruk together with its 35,000-man garrison. The Afrika Korps then drove eastward toward Cairo and the Suez Canal, nipping at the heels of a British army retreating in disarray. Ritchie's routed command did not halt for several hundred miles until it reached an insignificant Arab village known as El Alamein with only a handful of tanks. In two weeks, the Eighth Army had lost nearly 600 tanks and 75,000 men. In Cairo, near-panic reigned at British Middle East headquarters. Such quantities of secret papers were hastily burned in anticipation of Rommel's arrival that on a day to become known as Ash Wednesday, the sky over the Egyptian metropolis filled with black smoke.

Winston Churchill promptly sacked Ritchie and rushed Lieutenant General Bernard L. Montgomery to replace him. Abrasive, opinionated, at times infuriating to superiors, peers, and subordinates alike, Monty had a key quality Churchill was seeking—supreme confidence, the ingredient the prime minister felt was most needed to reverse the disastrous desert situation.

Adolf Hitler was jubilant over the British rout by the Afrika Korps.

It was one of the worst defeats ever inflicted on a British army. A grateful Führer promoted Rommel to field marshal, making the Desert Fox, at age fifty, the youngest German in history to hold that rank.

Having been rebuffed by Churchill, Foreign Minister Molotov hurried on to Washington to renew his plea for a second front. There his reception was quite different from the one he had received in London: President Roosevelt and General Marshall were alarmed by the Russian's gloomy recitation of the Red Army's plight. The president told Molotov to advise Premier Stalin that the Western Allies would launch a cross-Channel assault against France in September—only a few weeks away. Roosevelt then ordered General Marshall, Admiral Ernest J. King, and a trusted civilian trouble-shooter, Harry Hopkins, to fly to London and press for the thrust over the English Channel in the fall.

General Brooke's diary records his reaction upon learning the makeup of the American delegation: "It will be a queer party, as Harry Hopkins is for operating in Africa, Marshall wants to operate in Europe, and King is determined to stick to the Pacific." At almost the same time the Americans were boarding their aircraft for the flight, General John Dill cabled Churchill from Washington: "Unless you can convince [General Marshall] of your unswerving devotion to [a cross-Channel attack] everything points to a complete reversal of our present agreed strategy and the withdrawal of America to a war of her own in the Pacific, leaving [Great Britain] . . . to make out as best she can against Germany."

The stage would soon be set for a head-on collision between the highest leaders of the United States and Great Britain over the future course of the war. The worldwide forces that would put the spark to Operation Torch were already in place.

Part 1

Operation Torch Intrigue

1

"The Blackest Day in History!"

A TWA Stratoliner from Washington, D.C., cut through the gray and murky sky to a smooth landing at Scotland's bustling Prestwick airport. It was 5:19 P.M. on Friday, July 17, 1942. The large aircraft rolled to a halt, then disembarked United States Army Chief of Staff George Marshall, Chief of Naval Operations Ernest J. King, presidential advisor Harry Hopkins, and a galaxy of army, navy, and air corps brass. Faces were grim; there was no small talk. A sense of urgency prevailed.

President Franklin Roosevelt had rushed the delegation to London for what he considered one of the most monumental missions of the war: to "sell" the British, particularly Winston Churchill, on the need for a quick thrust across the English Channel to gain a toehold on the continent, relieve the pressure on the Red Army, and keep Russia in the war. It would be an extremely difficult sales task. England, at this stage of the war, would have to provide most of the troops, ships, and aircraft —and British leaders for many weeks had been adamantly opposed to the cross-Channel assault before the spring of 1943 "at the earliest."

At Prestwick, the Washington delegation boarded a waiting train sent by Prime Minister Churchill and sped through the Scottish Highlands southward into the English countryside. The no-nonsense Marshall, with crucial business at hand, had rejected an invitation from Churchill to stop over briefly at Chequers, the prime minister's home in Buckinghamshire outside bomb-battered London. Orders were issued for the train to bypass Chequers and travel directly to the capital for the looming showdown with the British chiefs of staff. Marshall had no way of knowing that his unwitting snub of Great Britain's top official would shortly trigger a violent outburst from Churchill.

Shortly after dawn, the prime minister's private train chugged into London's Euston Station, where the delegation was greeted by Lieutenant General Dwight D. Eisenhower, Marshall's protégé and commander of ETOUSA (European Theater of Operations, United States Army), by American ambassador John G. Winant, and by a host of British army and navy officers. Eisenhower was fifty-two years old, blue-eyed, trim, and possessed of an infectious smile, as well as a mule-skinner's vocabulary he had been honing since West Point cadet days. That Saturday morning he looked drawn and tired. Since the previous Thursday, Eisenhower had been working around the clock, preparing reports for General Marshall as ammunition for the impending debate with Churchill and the British chiefs of staff.

On Sunday, Harry Hopkins made a protocol visit to Chequers, where Winston Churchill had been pacing like an angry bear. "The Prime," as the Americans called him, was furious at having learned that General Marshall and Admiral King in London were already in informal discussions with the British general staff. As the homespun, friendly Hopkins, perhaps Roosevelt's closest civilian advisor, lounged quietly in an armchair, Churchill strode around the room, hands clasped behind his back, puffing on a cigar, lecturing the American on protocol. Speaking in vigorous tones, Churchill declared that *he* was the one the American delegation should have called on first, that *he* was the one the United States would have to deal with, and that the British army and navy were under *his* command. To dramatize his point, the prime minister pulled out a British book of war laws. As he read each page, he ripped it out and hurled it to the floor.

Hopkins listened until Churchill's anger had run its course. Then the American, who could give as well as take, counterattacked. The presidential advisor seemed to regard Churchill's explosion as merely another round in the ongoing slugging match which had erupted between the pair in previous meetings over the subject of a cross-Channel assault in 1942. Eventually, Hopkins's loud rebuttal lost its steam. Both men felt better. Another round of Scotch was consumed; the verbal adversaries warmly shook hands, wished each other well, and Hopkins departed for London.

That afternoon in a suite in Claridge's, a fashionable London hotel taken over by the U.S. military, generals Marshall and Eisenhower and Admiral King were intently discussing the final plan for Operation Sledgehammer to be pressed on the British. It called for a September attack on the Cherbourg peninsula, some 120 miles across the English Channel from Southampton. Lieutenant Commander Harry C. Butcher, a CBS radio executive in civilian life and now an aide and confidant to Eisenhower, noted in his diary that night, "The atmosphere [in the conference room] was tense."*

Even before the Marshall-King-Hopkins delegation arrived in Great Britain, Winston Churchill and General Brooke had agreed that some dramatic event would have to be staged, even if it met with disaster, to dramatize to an inexperienced American leadership the folly of a full-scale assault across the Channel in 1942. Better such an operation, Churchill believed, in which as many as 5,000 Allied troops might be sacrificed, than a premature all-out invasion effort in which tens of thousands of British and American soldiers, their weapons and equipment—and the war—would be lost. Consequently, Operation Rutter, a massive raid against the French port of Dieppe, was being mounted under the most intense secrecy. Rutter would be a frontal attack by sea involving 6,058 troops, mainly two brigades of the Canadian 2nd Division. In support would be a detachment of British commandos, a flotilla of 252 vessels of all types, and 56 squadrons of Royal Air Force fighters —more than existed at the time of the Battle of Britain in 1940. The ostensible objectives of the raid were to test both German coastal de-

---

* When the Western Allies had mustered sufficient power to attempt a cross-Channel assault nearly two years later, in 1944, they would strike at this precise locale—the Cherbourg peninsula.

fenses and Allied invasion techniques, capture the enemy-held port, destroy specified Wehrmacht installations, and then withdraw from the continent. Plans had been finalized, troop training was in its final stages, and commanders were waiting for the go signal. Only a handful of top British commanders were aware of the true purpose of the Dieppe mission.

In the meantime, the showdown over the contesting strategies opened at 10:00 A.M. on July 20 at the War Office. Hardly had the participants settled into their chairs when heated debate erupted over Sledgehammer. The principal antagonists were General George Marshall and General Alan Brooke—both capable, intelligent, and tough. Almost since their first meeting months before, friction had developed between the pair that tended to make each strategy session a tense confrontation. Marshall resented what he considered Brooke's patronizing attitude toward American generals—"newcomers from the Colonies." Brooke, for his part, felt that Marshall, who had never commanded so much as a platoon in combat, was largely a "political general." The British chief had confided to his diary that General Douglas MacArthur should have been the U.S. Chief of Staff instead of Marshall. Following an especially rowdy session the previous April, Brooke had penned in his daily log: "The Allies everywhere are holding on by their eye-lids. . . . In light of the existing situation [Marshall's] plans for [a cross-Channel assault] for September 1942 are just fantastic. . . . His strategic ability does not impress me at all."

The War Office sessions, then, were exhaustive, acrimonious, and prolonged. The Americans soon found themselves on the defensive, fighting a losing battle against facts ticked off by General Brooke. Personal vilification soon erupted. Brooke accused Marshall of "trying to assume the powers of the [U.S.] commander-in-chief, which are President Roosevelt's prerogative." In the hostile climate, Marshall shot back: "How do you expect to win the war—by defensive action?"

Brooke's grand design for victory over Nazi Germany was to bomb the Third Reich day and night, establish a naval blockade of German ports, keep the enemy off balance with commando raids and clever deceptions that would force Hitler to garrison some 2,000 miles of European coastline, strike at German morale with a propaganda blitz, encourage enemy rebellion from within, and conduct military operations on the fringes of the Führer's empire. Brooke proposed launching this strategy with an invasion of Algeria and Morocco, two occupied French colonies in northwest Africa. When these combined pressures indicated a weakening of German strength and morale, then—and *only* then—should the Allies launch a massive assault across the Channel and aim for the heart of Germany.

After four days of intense talks, the British carried the ramparts; on July 22, the Americans ran up the flag of surrender. French Northwest Africa, not northwest France, would be the locale of the Allied blow to relieve the pressure on the Russian army. The Mediterranean operation would be code-named Torch.

Torch was the brainchild of Winston Churchill and Alan Brooke, and they were delighted over acceptance of their strategic plan. Still they were not ready to celebrate their conference-table victory. It remained to be seen whether Franklin Roosevelt, commander in chief of the United States armed forces, would agree to support the drastic reversal in strategy.

Early the next morning, a glum General Eisenhower was having breakfast at a huge converted apartment building in London at 20 Grosvenor Square, headquarters of American forces in Europe. With him was tall, gangling, forty-six-year-old Major General Mark W. Clark, called the American Eagle by Winston Churchill after the youthful general's sharp nose and equally sharp mind. Clark commanded the II Corps, which, presumably, would spearhead any American offensive.

Conversation between the pair was subdued. Up from the basement, where the Marines operated a mess, wafted the pungent odor of boiled cabbage and brussels sprouts. Eisenhower had forbidden pessimistic talk or attitudes in his headquarters, but on this morning, after learning of the decision by the Combined Chiefs of Staff, he was unable to live up to his own directive. "Well, I hardly know where to start the day," he told Clark. "I'm right back to December 15."* Sipping a cup of coffee

---

* December 15, 1941, was the day Eisenhower had received an urgent summons from General Marshall to report to Washington and begin drawing up plans for an American offensive—Sledgehammer.

while dragging on an ever-present cigarette, the American commander in Europe expressed the fear that Torch would cause wide dispersal of Allied forces, particularly American. But what disturbed Eisenhower most was that the Allies would be fighting Frenchmen. Dramatizing his deep disappointment—shared by Clark—Eisenhower declared, "July 22, 1942, will go down as the blackest day in history!" The only hope was a Roosevelt veto of Torch.

On the evening of Saturday, July 25, one week after the American "showdown delegation" had arrived in London, a lively party given by Harry Hopkins and Steve Early, President Roosevelt's press secretary, was in full swing in a sumptuous suite at Claridge's. Guests from America included Kathleen Harriman and her father W. Averell Harriman, Mrs. Randolph Churchill, Anthony Biddle, William Bullitt, and Lewis Douglas, all in London for one reason or another. Heavily burdened "Ike" Eisenhower, who had been conferring with General Marshall in another suite, dropped by briefly for a drink. Eisenhower had distaste for such social functions, but he was beaming and vibrant. "I came," he quipped, "because I was 'commanded' to appear by Harry [Hopkins]."

Hopkins, in the words of one guest, had been bouncing around like a frog on a hot griddle all afternoon, ducking in and out of parlor and bedroom doors to handle an endless stream of callers while trying to be a convivial host. One of the people Hopkins talked to, by transoceanic telephone, was President Roosevelt in Washington. Hopkins was startled to learn that the chief executive had not received the cable from Marshall and King which detailed the tentative decision on Operation Torch by the Combined Chiefs of Staff. If Roosevelt rejected the Torch proposal, the American delegation would have to remain in London for further wrangling with their British counterparts. Otherwise, Marshall, King, Hopkins, and their entourage would head for the United States.

About 6:00 P.M., Hopkins darted back into a bedroom—President Roosevelt was calling. The president said that he had finally received the cable, had immediately convened his advisors, and had arrived at a decision on Torch.* Minutes later, Hopkins, who had been conducting

---

* Two days after the conference, Reichsführer Heinrich Himmler, head of Hitler's intelligence service, was reading a sheaf of intercepted transoceanic

international negotiations by transoceanic telephone while sandwiching in small talk with his guests, poked his head through the bedroom doorway and shouted: "Okay, boys, we're going home!" An Allied invasion of Northwest Africa was now official.

The following morning, a jubilant Winston Churchill canceled Operation Rutter, the reconnaissance in force against the old pirate stronghold of Dieppe. There was no longer a need for such bloodletting to show the Americans the folly of a cross-Channel assault in 1942.

When the resolute and optimistic General Marshall returned to Washington, he was shaken by reports of even greater disasters in the U-boat campaign against Allied shipping. On June 19 he had written to the chief of naval operations, Admiral King, "The losses by submarines off our Atlantic seaboard now threaten our entire war effort. . . . I am fearful that another month or two of this will so cripple our means of transport that we will be unable to bring sufficient men and planes to bear against the enemy in critical theaters to exercise a determining influence on the war." It was an alarming evaluation of the war situation by America's senior soldier. Now, six weeks after making that ominous assessment, General Marshall came home to an even heavier jolt: June had been the most disastrous month yet for the Allies at sea. Submarines had sunk merchant vessels at the rate of one every four hours, and the toll for the month reached a staggering 825,310 tons.

The architect of the devastating U-boat campaign was Admiral Karl Dönitz. On January 12, 1942, Dönitz had launched Operation *Paukenschlag* (Drumbeat), which was designed to knock the United States out of the war. Dönitz had selected 11 of his ace U-boat captains for the mission of cutting the American east coast shipping lanes. These lanes originate in the St. Lawrence River, cross the Gulf of Maine, pass New

---

telephone conversations. An SS general submitting the transcripts to Himmler noted: "The [London] conference will probably determine where the Second Front is to be established and when." Included were conversations by Churchill, General Mark Clark, Eisenhower aide Lieutenant Commander Butcher, and others. Long after the war, these intercepted conversations were found in Himmler's files.

York (where some 50 ships arrived and departed daily), and extend southward past the capes of Delaware, the Chesapeake Bay, and Cape Hatteras, into the Caribbean and the Gulf of Mexico.

The loss of Allied merchant vessels and hundreds of crew members along the Atlantic coast in the first half of 1942 was a national disaster comparable to saboteurs blowing up eight or ten of America's largest war plants. Worse, the carnage was inflicted by only a handful of U-boats; no more than 12 had been in action at any one time. And every month, Germany was building some 20 new submarines. Each U-boat carried 14 torpedoes, many of them a revolutionary electrically propelled type that left no wake of air bubbles. Often the first indication that a merchant vessel was under attack was the concussion of a direct hit.

In June 1942, the U-boats became bolder. Instead of attacking only at night, they now sank Allied merchantmen by daylight, often within view of shore. Thousands of curious bathers at Coney Island in New York City, Virginia Beach, Virginia, and Miami Beach, Florida, looked on as American and British vessels went to the bottom. German captains in those early days of the war allowed the survivors of mortally wounded merchantmen the chance to get away in lifeboats before surfacing and sinking the vessel with gunfire. The healthy, bronzed U-boat crewmen appeared to be enjoying their "field day" along America's coastline. Often they gave survivors in lifeboats water, cigarettes, and food, and sent them on their way with a standard joke: "Don't forget to send the bill for that ship to Roosevelt or Churchill!"*

It took three months after Admiral Dönitz unleashed his wolfpacks along America's Atlantic coast for Washington to announce that U-boat captains were being guided by lights and tall electric signs in coastal communities, and that this illumination would now have to be extinguished. When this basic defense measure was promulgated, there were protests from Atlantic City, New Jersey, to the top of southern Florida that "the tourist season would be ruined." Miami and its suburbs provided some ten miles of neon and electric lights against which the U-boats could see the silhouettes of north- and southbound vessels

---

* Later U-boat crews would refer to this period as "the happy time."

hugging the coastline to avoid the opposing current of the Gulf Stream.*

The catastrophic U-boat campaign along America's eastern seaboard stunned the Allied high command, which lacked means to counter the threat. Decades of American apathy toward its defenses had left the navy, like the army, ill-prepared for war. America's entire antisubmarine fleet consisted of three 110-foot wooden subchasers, two 173-foot patrol craft, a few converted yachts, and ten Eagle boats dating from World War I.

As General Marshall, Admiral King, and other high-level commanders in Washington fretted over the seemingly unstoppable U-boat onslaught, there was euphoria in Admiral Dönitz's headquarters some 3,000 miles away, outside Lorient on the Brittany peninsula of France. Reporting on the astonishing success of Operation *Paukenschlag* in a signal to the Führer, Dönitz pointed out that the enormous number of Allied sinkings since the United States had been at war had been achieved with the loss of only 26 U-boats. German shipyards were turning out seven 500- and 750-ton submarines every ten days.

Dönitz held a press conference. As German and neutral-nation newsreel cameras turned and photographers' flash-bulbs lighted the room, the admiral boasted: "Our U-boats are operating close inshore along the coast of the United States, so that bathers and sometimes entire coastal cities are witnesses to that drama of war, whose visual climaxes are often constituted by the red glorioles of blazing tankers."

In Berlin, Nazi propaganda minister Josef Goebbels spoke over the radio. "German heroism conquers even the widest oceans!" Indeed, the glow of burning ships, carried by the Germans to the beaches of the United States, was a most inauspicious prelude for the Allied invasion plan named Torch.

---

* It was not until June 1942, five months after the U-boats were unleashed off America's east coast, before the navy succeeded in getting a stringent dimout along the seaboard.

2

Patton and the U.S. Navy Collide

On the night of August 9, General Eisenhower was preparing to sit down to a dinner featuring chicken soup when the telephone jangled in his apartment. "Ike," exclaimed a high-pitched voice familiar to Eisenhower, "goddam it, I've just arrived in this goddam town. I'm holed up in Claridge's and don't know what to do with myself."

"Georgie!" Eisenhower recognized the voice of a longtime friend, Major General George S. Patton, Jr. "God, am I glad to hear from you! Come right over and have some godawful dehydrated soup."

Eisenhower truly was delighted that the irrepressible Patton had arrived in London. Since July 24, when President Roosevelt had blessed the Torch plan, Eisenhower had felt surrounded by a thick pall of gloom. Even he had begun to have private doubts over the North African invasion, and he needed a spiritual boost.

A half hour later Patton strode into Eisenhower's apartment, tall, ramrod straight, and immaculately tailored. The fifty-six-year-old Californian was flamboyant in his personal lifestyle, profane but at the same time deeply devout, and independently wealthy.* The silver-haired Patton had been one of the army's best-known figures since his days at West Point, where he had been a center of conversation among cadets since the day he had stood up between targets as his comrades blasted away on the rifle range. "Wanted to know what it feels like to be under fire," young George had explained. Just prior to World War I, Patton had accompanied General John J. "Black Jack" Pershing into Mexico, where he expanded his renown by tracking down a notorious Mexican outlaw, killing the bandit in a two-man shootout, and bringing the corpse back to camp strapped over the front fender of an automobile. In World War I, Patton's army-wide reputation as an aggressive fighting man and military innovator had gained further luster. He became the American army's leading expert on tank warfare and led a tank brigade in the bitter battles at St. Mihiel and in the Meuse-Argonne offensive, where he was wounded.

Now, twenty-four years later, George Patton had arrived in London, eager to have another early crack at "the goddamned Hun." A week previously, Patton had rushed to Washington from the California desert, where he had been training armored units. Chief of Staff George Marshall, who had supreme confidence in Patton, had summoned him to take command of the American task force that was to invade North Africa. Torch was still a vague concept, and a concerned General Marshall dispatched Patton to London to assess the situation there "personally and frankly."

During a few drinks and dinner at Eisenhower's apartment, the two old comrades had an intense discussion of Torch. Eisenhower's hope for a morale boost from the fire-eating Patton was promptly dashed. Patton himself quickly became bogged down in all-too-familiar apprehensions. He felt that the small number of troops—nearly all of them green and only partially trained—assigned to him by "those goddamned fools in Washington" would be insufficient to counter the hostile forces he expected to encounter.

---

* It was said that George Patton had long given his army pay to charity.

The party broke up and Patton returned to his suite in Claridge's, uncertain whether Eisenhower, the man who probably would be appointed to command Torch, was actually for or against the North African venture. Patton scribbled in his diary that night: "We both feel that the operation is bad and mostly political. However, we are told to do it and intend to succeed or die in the attempt."

George Patton remained in London for ten days on his fact-finding mission for the chief of staff. He encountered nothing but what he called "defeatism." Provoked by what he considered "the views of a bunch of weak-kneed sons of bitches," Patton was transformed into a staunch advocate of the operation, a sort of bright beacon amid the dark clouds of pessimism that hovered over London and Washington. He would become the supersalesman for Torch.

With Patton spreading the Torch gospel, General Eisenhower on August 11 convened the top United States Navy brass. The purpose: to convince that doubting service that Torch was the best operation that could be mounted at this time. On hand were Admiral Harold R. "Betty" Stark, the studious, even plodding, U.S. Navy commander in Europe, and several of his top commanders. Representing Vice Admiral Royal E. Ingersoll, who was in command of the Atlantic Fleet, was Captain Frank P. Thomas.

Captain Thomas did most of the talking for the navy; he painted a gloomy portrait of Torch, citing obstacles and difficulties, even hinting at disaster for the operation. George Patton, puffing on a long black cigar, glared at the naval officer in disgust. Aides noticed a surefire sign of deep anger—Patton's neck had turned red.

Captain Thomas alluded to the threat from one or two German aircraft carriers (the Kriegsmarine in fact had no vessels of this type). As Thomas went on with his litany of perils, Patton became increasingly exasperated—and more convinced than ever that "this may not be the best goddam show, but it's much better than nothing."

Finally, Patton challenged the navy officer's statements. One angry word led to another between the two men, until Eisenhower concluded the acrimonious conference by declaring firmly—while the red-faced Patton nodded in agreement—"Torch is an order from the commander-in-chief, the President of the United States, and the Prime Minister.

Whether we like it or not, it has to be carried out, despite any obstacles. If there isn't a single protective warship, my orders call for moving into West and North Africa and I am going to do it, warships or not—and if I have to go alone in a row boat!"

Only the following day, the Royal Navy unburdened its own pessimism on General Eisenhower. If anything, the British sealords were even more negative than Atlantic Fleet's Captain Thomas. In doleful tones, Admiral Bertram H. Ramsay, who would command Allied naval forces in the impending operation, told Eisenhower that the British navy expected to lose at least two aircraft carriers, a battleship, and three or four cruisers plus other vessels in any effort to land troops in North Africa.

Hard on Admiral Ramsay's heels, Eisenhower's British liaison officer, Major General R. H. Dewey, chimed in. Gibraltar, the British fortress on the enormous rock at the mouth of the narrows leading into the Mediterranean from the Atlantic, was in danger of immediate seizure once Torch was launched. Gibraltar and its crucial airstrip were within 300 yards of Spanish territory, Dewey pointed out, and either Hitler's unofficial confederate, Spanish dictator Francisco Franco, or the Germans themselves could pounce on Gibraltar within hours.

The disclosure that Gibraltar was so weakly held put new furrows in the Allied commander's brow. Reports indicated that the Vichy French had 500 warplanes in North Africa, and most of the American and British air strength to neutralize this potential hostile air fleet would have to be based on Gibraltar.

As General Dewey ticked off these discouraging facts, Patton sat by with increasing irritation. That night Patton wrote in his diary: "I'm the only true gambler in the whole goddamned outfit!"

A few days later, Rear Admiral H. M. Burrough of the Royal Navy called on General Mark Clark at Norfolk House, the planning center for Torch, located two miles from Grosvenor Square. A short time before, Eisenhower had appointed Clark as his deputy for Torch with the specific responsibility of planning the massive operation. Clark, who had been wounded as an infantry captain during World War I, had long been regarded as one of the army's brightest young officers.

Admiral Burrough was a husky, friendly, stern-faced man with an outstanding combat record and a reputation for courage. He had led a convoy through the Mediterranean to Malta earlier in the month. German planes and U-boats had been lying in wait for his 14 merchant ships, having calculated that the population of tiny Malta was nearly out of food and that the British would have to send a convoy to the beleaguered island. The Germans had decimated the Malta-bound convoy, sinking the aircraft carrier *Eagle* and the cruiser *Manchester,* and seriously damaging the carrier *Indomitable.* The Italians sank the cruiser *Cairo* and torpedoed the cruisers *Nigeria* and *Kenya.* Only five merchant vessels and tankers limped into Malta. When the North African invasion came, its ships would have to sail these same Mediterranean sea lanes. Thus Burrough, who would command a task force in Torch, had no illusions about what he would be getting into. "I figure that my job will be successful if we get half our ships through," he told Clark.

This recital by the resolute and experienced Burrough hardly fueled Mark Clark's optimism. The young general already harbored doubts he had expressed to no one. He knew that other leaders had similar concerns, and thought that Winston Churchill was the only person in London or Washington who was genuinely optimistic about Torch.

That night, General Clark had dinner with Lieutenant General Hastings Ismay, Churchill's military advisor. Ismay's line of questions on planning progress suggested that he, too, had reservations, notwithstanding the views of his boss. Outwardly, though, Ismay seemed enthusiastic. His chin was always up, and he lived up to his nickname, "Pug." During dinner, Clark felt twinges of disappointment. As he ate, a force of British commandos was conducting a raid on the French coast, something done periodically to keep the Wehrmacht on edge, capture prisoners for interrogation, and test enemy defenses. Clark could have been with this raiding party; Vice Admiral Lord Louis Mountbatten (Dickie to the Americans), the handsome, suave, forty-two-year-old commander of Combined Operations, had invited Clark along. The American general had eagerly accepted, but when Clark sought permission from General Eisenhower, it was promptly refused. The Oberkommando der Wehrmacht (German high command) would be delighted to get its hands on the Allied general planning an invasion, Eisenhower had observed. That is, if Clark survived the raid.

"Okay," Clark had replied. "But considering the fire I'm facing every day at the office, I think I'd welcome something as quiet as a commando raid."

The epidemic of apprehensiveness was spreading from London to Washington. On August 15, General Marshall cabled Eisenhower: "There is a unanimity of opinion of Army officers here that the proposed operation [Torch] appears hazardous to the extent of less than a 50 percent chance of success."

Before departing for his post in Washington, Patton called on Eisenhower, who only the day before had officially been designated as Allied commander in chief for Torch. "Listen to this, Ike," Patton said, pulling a piece of paper from his pocket. He read the document aloud. It was a draft of his demand for the surrender of Casablanca, where Patton's force, sailing directly from the United States, was to strike. Eisenhower grinned approvingly. Old Georgie, at least, was in tip-top form.

As invasion planning progressed, a top American officer, Brigadier General Lucian K. Truscott, Jr., was nearly fired from his post and court-martialed for a security lapse. Truscott was attached to headquarters of Combined Operations, the panel charged with planning and conducting raids. He had attended a conference in which broad strategy was outlined by Rear Admiral Louis Mountbatten, advisor to Combined Operations. Returning to his office, Truscott made notes on a scratch pad on the discussion, then cleared his desk (including the notes, he thought), locked up the desk, locked his office, and departed for the night.

Early the next morning the chief security officer, the Marquis of Casa Maury, called on General Truscott. Invited to be seated, the grim-faced marquis replied, "I prefer to conduct my business standing." The British officer took a piece of paper from his coat, unfolded it, and handed it to Truscott. "Did you write this?" the security chief asked.

Truscott, puzzled, said that he did; it was the memorandum he had jotted down the previous evening. He added that he could not understand how the marquis had gained possession of it. Truscott was shocked by the reply: The memorandum had been found in the courtyard in front of the building. The Englishman proceeded to lecture the inexperienced American general on the disaster that could befall Allied operations should Truscott's notes fall into the hands of German agents, who were known to be plentiful in London.

Mystified over how his notes got into the courtyard, Truscott accepted the rebuke. Casa Maury said that the commander of Combined Operations viewed flagrant security lapses so strongly that if he became aware of General Truscott's transgression the commander would contact General George Marshall and demand that Truscott be relieved of his post, called home, and disciplined. Truscott could only say that Casa Maury should not let the fact that he was an American general interfere with whatever action the security chief felt obliged to take. But Casa Maury responded that, in this instance, no harm had been done, that Truscott no doubt would never be so careless again, and that in the interest of Allied harmony the matter would be considered closed.

Only much later would General Truscott learn that his security blunder had not been an isolated episode, and that security-conscious British officers had been driven nearly apoplectic over similar transgressions by other high-ranking Americans—including those among the personal staff of Supreme Commander Eisenhower.*

Meanwhile, on August 12, Winston Churchill, General Alan Brooke, and the other British chiefs of staff had hurried to Moscow to explain to Josef Stalin why the western Allies could not invade France across the English Channel in 1942 and would instead strike at North Africa. Churchill's renowned oratorical powers would be put to the test of placating the besieged Russian premier. What good would an offensive on the periphery of Hitler's empire be to the Soviets with the triumphant Wehrmacht already knocking on the door of Leningrad, at the gates of Stalingrad, and less than 50 miles from Moscow? Stalin would want to know.

It would be the first meeting between the two steel-willed leaders. Moreover it would be a delicate one. Stalin was convinced that the United States and Great Britain had connived to let the German and Russian armies bleed each other into impotence before the Western

---

* Throughout the war, General Truscott used this episode of his own security violation to impress upon his officers the need to safeguard secret information.

Allies struck at Europe. Winston Churchill, for his part, did not trust the Russians and would have to choose his words carefully. Through intelligence sources the prime minister knew that while the two armies were slaughtering each other on the battlefields of Russia, there were clandestine contracts between members of the Soviet and Wehrmacht general staffs. If it served Stalin, Churchill knew, British and American plans would not be long in reaching Adolf Hitler's ears.

Meeting in a bar room in the Kremlin, Stalin immediately impressed the cautious British delegation as crude, cold, and calculating. Through his interpreter, the Russian dictator asked Churchill: "Why is Great Britain so afraid of the Germans?" Puffing on a long black cigar, the prime minister bristled at so direct an accusation and spoke for nearly thirty minutes on the "heroic" British battlefield achievements during the war. During this first session he explained at length the Western Allies' strategy of invading North Africa in 1942 and holding the Wehrmacht along the English Channel coast—and away from Russia—through deception stratagems and commando raids.

That night over drinks, Churchill told his chiefs he thought he had broken the ice with "Uncle Joe," (as Churchill and Roosevelt privately called him). Morning would prove him wrong. Stalin once again accused the British of cowardice, this time in even stronger terms. Churchill was furious and responded with a torrent of oratory, talking so rapidly that his interpreters could not keep up; all the Russian dictator knew was that the prime minister was hopping mad.

The following day, the two Allied leaders contented themselves with an exchange of memoranda. When the prime minister called at the Kremlin to bid farewell, Stalin received Churchill with warmth. They talked for six hours, far into the night; vodka flowed freely, and Stalin spoke glowingly of Torch and the valor of the British. Churchill should have been on his guard. Instead, in the fellowship of the moment, the prime minister spontaneously promised Stalin a second front in France in the spring of 1943. Grinning amiably and nodding his head favorably, Stalin replied, "I'll hold you to that promise, Mr. Prime Minister." It appeared that Stalin had gained with charisma (and vodka) what he had failed to obtain through his insults.

At dawn the next day, Churchill and his entourage flew to Cairo for consultation with his beleaguered generals facing Rommel's triumphant Afrika Korps. On the flight to the Egyptian capital, the British leader was haunted by an alarming thought: Would Stalin betray the secret of Torch to the Germans?

At the same time Churchill and Stalin were jousting in the Kremlin on August 15, hundreds of miles to the west German intelligence monitors along the Pas de Calais coast of northern France sent an alert to Wehrmacht district commanders: There had been a sudden and unaccounted-for change in the pattern of wireless traffic across the Channel in southern England. This was followed by a period of total wireless silence. Such patterns often indicated that a military action was being mounted by the British.

A short time later, the B-Dienst—the German code-deciphering agency—picked up a Royal Navy signal from the vicinity of Plymouth, deciphered it, and concluded that a large-scale movement of vessels in south England was imminent. Field Marshal Karl Rudolf Gerd von Rundstedt, the dignified Wehrmacht commander in chief in the West, believed he knew the significance of this activity: The Western Allies were ready to launch a blow of considerable strength across the Channel —at Calais, Dieppe, or Cherbourg.

Field Marshal von Rundstedt, sixty-seven years old and born of the nobility, was known in Germany as "the last of the Prussians." He was a brilliant tactician. Days previously, piecing together reports from agents of the Abwehr (German secret service), von Rundstedt had concluded that the British would strike soon. Evidence pointed to the old French port of Dieppe as the precise target. Abwehr agents in Dieppe had for several weeks been shadowing an official in the Todt Organization, the Wehrmacht's construction and engineering bureau. This Dieppe official, Abwehr agents discovered, had been working for the British secret service (MI-6) in London, and had been furnishing information on docks, installations, coastal gun batteries, and German troop deployment in and around the port.

If the British did strike there, von Rundstedt would be ready for them. Defending the Channel coast around the old pirate lair was a first-rate division (the 302nd), and Dieppe itself was held by a force of some 5,000 Germans. Backing up these coastal defenders were a regiment of infantry, a field artillery battalion, and, within a five-hour road march, a panzer division. Deployed at airfields all along the Channel coast were hundreds of Luftwaffe warplanes, ready for action on a few minutes' notice.

Bulwarking von Rundstedt's evaluation that the British were ready to smash at his French coastal defenses was the Führer's own assessment, gained from intelligence sources in Berlin, Luftwaffe reconnaisance flights over England, and spies infiltrated into Great Britain. Due to the sweeping successes of the Wehrmacht in Russia, Adolf Hitler declared, England would probably be forced to open a Second Front soon in order to keep Russia in the war. Hitler indicated that the landings would occur "along the Channel coast, in the area between Dieppe and Le Havre, or in Normandy, because these sectors can be reached by enemy fighter planes."

Indeed, the British were preparing to strike—and at Dieppe. Early in August, only a week after President Roosevelt had stamped his approval on Operation Torch, Winston Churchill had been advised by his emissaries in Washington that "certain influential American leaders" were again hammering away at the President to convince him that Sledgehammer, the cross-Channel attack in the fall of 1942, was still the best course of action. These "influential leaders" were Chief of Staff George Marshall and Secretary of War Henry Stimson. Learning that the American allies were now trying to undermine Torch in favor of Sledgehammer, Churchill and his chiefs of staff ordered that earlier plans for a reconnaissance in force against Dieppe be dusted off and the operation remounted. Now code-named Jubilee, the massive raid was hurriedly prepared under unprecedented security precautions. Not a word concerning Jubilee was to be put on paper—even by the British chiefs of staff. The Royal Navy high command was not told the reason for a request to supply 250 ships. There would be no rehearsals, no cover and deception plan, and it was hinted to the assault troops that they were preparing to raid Norway.

Thousands of men were unaware that they were to be sacrificed on the altar of Operation Torch.

3

Bloodbath on the Iron Coast

The night of August 18, 1942, was starlit and calm over the English Channel. It was nearing midnight when Major General John H. Roberts, commander of the Canadian 2nd Division, strolled out onto the deck of the destroyer *Calpe* to breathe in the refreshing sea air. Around him were the ghostly silhouettes of 252 vessels filled with 6,058 hand-picked assault troops, mostly Canadians, but including detachments of British and French commandos and 50 American Rangers under Captain Roy A. Murray.

Except for some of the commandos, none of the troops had ever heard a shot fired in anger. The armada was to cross 70 miles of mine-infested channel to attack Dieppe, destroy German gun batteries and installations along a 15-mile stretch of beach, then pull out on the afternoon tide. H hour would be 4:30 A.M.

Despite the limited scope of Operation Jubilee, the raid would have ambitious targets. Seven miles east of Dieppe, British Number 3 Commando was to assault and destroy a battery of 6-inch coastal guns, while Number 4 Commando was to knock out a similar battery seven miles to the west of Dieppe.

The heaviest weight of the assault would take place between these two flanking German coastal batteries. Some 2,500 yards east of Dieppe, the Royal Regiment of Canada and elements of the Black Watch would storm ashore, seize several enemy guns, and rush inland to blow up Dieppe's power plant and gas works. In Dieppe itself, the Royal Hamilton Light Infantry and the Essex Scottish would make a frontal attack over the beaches with tanks of the Calgary Highlanders. The tanks were then to drive four miles inland and destroy hangars and facilities at a German-held airport. Three miles west of Dieppe, the South Saskatchewan Regiment would knock out coastal guns, a radar station, and a fortified farm. Then the Cameron Highlanders would move ashore, pass through the South Saskatchewans, and join with the tanks of the Calgary Highlanders to destroy the airport. If time remained, the Calgary Highlander tanks were to drive inland for two miles and capture headquarters of the German 302nd Division, believed to be at Acques-la-Bataille. Overhead with the arrival of daylight would be the biggest air umbrella ever assembled by the British to that date—67 squadrons of fighters and bombers, challenging the Luftwaffe to come up and fight.

Tension gripped the soldiers in the holds of the Dieppe-bound armada. Would the Germans be lying in wait on the far side of the Channel along what was known as the Iron Coast? A month previously, several thousand men assembled for Operation Rutter had been told that the target was Dieppe before the operation had been canceled. Now the cross-Channel raid had been given a new code name, and within hours the Jubilee armada was sailing for the same target—Dieppe. Could that vast number of soldiers have kept their mouths shut?

Only a week previously—on August 12—British agents of MI-5 (the counterintelligence agency) had descended on pubs and other public places in the Shoreham area where large numbers of assault troops were garrisoned. Indiscreet conversation abounded. Canadians of the Calgary Tank Regiment were talking loudly in taverns of waterproofing their vehicles for an operation in which commandos would take part. Several of the loose talkers had been arrested and held until the operation was concluded. A Royal Navy lieutenant commander who left a copy of the Dieppe naval operation in a bar was taken into custody.

In the Dieppe sector, the month of August had been unusually quiet.

There had been no alert on land or sea. But Major General Konrad von Haase, commander of the tough, battle-tested, and full-strength 302nd Division, had the defenses fully manned from high tide each night to sunrise the next morning. On August 8, von Haase had ordered a *drohende Gefahr* (threatening danger) alert for 12 nights, until August 20. So far that month, Wehrmacht engineers had sown nearly 13,000 new mines along the beaches over which the Canadians would have to cross. At each end of Dieppe, the Gobes, ancient cave dwellers' homes perched on high cliffs, concealed scores of antitank and machine guns. Buildings had been razed to provide German riflemen and machine-gunners with interlocking fields of fire across the beaches. Miles of barbed-wire entanglements laced the beaches. That night, as General Roberts, commander of Jubilee, and his assault troops edged closer to the far shore, German troops were sleeping in position in their clothes.

It was 1:27 A.M. when General Roberts and armada commanders received an alarming signal from the British radar station at Portsmouth: a convoy of five or six German vessels, supported by warships of unde-termined size, was edging along the French coast near Boulogne and seemed likely to blunder into the assault fleet just before H-hour. Allied ships were under strict radio silence; General Roberts presumed that all had heard the warning from Portsmouth, but on the west flank, the escorting warships of Flotilla Group 5 (carrying Number 3 Commando) failed to get the signal. Roberts ordered the Armada to continue toward Dieppe.

At 2:32 A.M. the Germans became aware that something was in the wind. A *Flugmeldezentrale* (air warning center) along the Iron Coast flashed an urgent signal to Kriegsmarine West (Navy Group West) headquarters: Freya Radar 28 had picked up in its scope many vessels about 21 miles out to sea from Dieppe.

Nothing to be alarmed about, Kriegsmarine West quickly replied. It was only the Boulogne convoy which was expected to reach Dieppe at 5:00 A.M.

About 45 minutes before H-hour, at 3:47 A.M., the actual German convoy of five merchant vessels, protected by two subchasers and a minesweeper, which had been bound from Boulogne to Dieppe, bumped into Flotilla Group 5 carrying Number 3 Commando headed for the coastal guns 7 miles east of Dieppe. Chaos erupted in the blackness, a cacophony of colliding vessels, gunfire, shouts, and wildly blinking signal lights. Gunners at the Berneval battery had a bird's eye view of the sea battle offshore. Although on alert, German leaders at the gun position atop a high cliff did nothing, thinking that what they saw was merely a small-unit naval clash of the kind that erupted on occasion in the Channel. Even the nearby Ailly lighthouse failed to douse its illumination, despite the pandemonium offshore.

At headquarters of the *Oberbefehlshaber West* (commander in chief West) in suburban Paris, Field Marshal von Rundstedt was awakened by an aide at 4:26 A.M. and told of the "commotion" taking place offshore from the Berneval gun battery. He put in a call to Kriegsmarine West at Cherbourg on the Normandy peninsula, seeking more information.

"Nothing to worry about, *Herr Feldmarschall*," replied the confident voice of the naval commander. "It's just a customary attack on a convoy."

Von Rundstedt was not so sure that this was a minor sea clash. He ordered a full alert all along the northern coast of France.

In the predawn off the Iron Coast, grim-faced Canadians and British commandos, along with a few French assault troops and American Rangers, were slithering down rope ladders flung over the sides of transports and climbing into gently bobbing landing craft for the run to the Dieppe beaches over a smooth, glossy English Channel. Except for the muffled purring of boat motors, all was deathly still—even tomblike—as the first wave neared the shore. Were the Germans being taken totally by surprise?

Suddenly the eerie tranquility was shattered. Up and down the Dieppe coast, brilliant white flares went up and an enormous roar erupted as the waiting Germans poured shells and bullets into the invaders. As the first landing craft crunched onto the beaches, machine guns and antitank guns concealed inside the Gobes raked the soldiers as they leaped out. Bodies began to pile up right on the boat ramps. Men staggered a few feet forward before being cut down.

Eighteen Churchill tanks crawled out of the mouths of the landing craft in Dieppe itself, where concealed antitank guns put up heavy, flat-trajectory fire. Within 15 minutes, all 18 tanks were twisted, burning pieces of junk, their crews dead or captured.

At the Berneval gun battery, the powerful beam of the Ailly lighthouse was quickly doused, and when a small force of commandos and a few American Rangers under Commando Captain R. L. Wills stormed ashore and dashed for the foot of the chalk cliffs, they were met by withering automatic weapons and rifle fire from above. As bullets raked them, Wills's men clawed their way up the steep incline and prepared as best they could to attack the big guns, leaving behind many dead and wounded comrades on the outcroppings of the cliff's face.

Waving his men onward, Captain Wills charged a German position and was killed by a burst of machine-gun fire. Seeing their leader cut down, the commandos and Rangers wavered, then halted. Ranger Lieutenant Edwin V. Loustalot took over and led another dash toward the German guns, but he too caught a machine-gun blast and died instantly. The few survivors in the attacking force, hemmed in on three sides and caring for many wounded comrades, surrendered.

A short distance away on the Berneval beaches, other commandos led by Captain Peter Young got ashore with only minor opposition, and without being detected edged into position to hit another four-gun battery from the flank. Lightly armed and few in numbers, Young's force could not charge the German guns, which were protected by about 200 infantrymen. But the commandos deployed and for two crucial hours kept the enemy guns from firing by sniping relentlessly at the crews with rifle fire.

West of Dieppe another force of commandos and a handful of Rangers had scaled rugged cliffs and immediately engaged in a bitter firefight as they sought to reach the German guns. During the clash several commandos and a few Rangers charged a German trench network with bayonet-tipped rifles, killing five enemy soldiers and wounding others. In this savage fight, Ranger Corporal Franklin Koons may have been the first American to kill a German ground soldier in World War II.

A short distance away, other commandos were locked in a bloody encounter with German troops defending the big guns on the cliffs at Varengeville. The *Feldgrau* clung doggedly to their positions, and only after every German was killed did the British take over the guns. They promptly blew up the weapons and pulled back to the beach.

High above the carnage being inflicted on the invaders, the clear blue sky over Dieppe appeared to have gone mad. The greatest aerial battle since the 1940 Battle of Britain was raging between the Royal Air Force and the Luftwaffe. Among the thousands watching the aerial extravaganza was the U.S. Lieutenant Colonel Loren B. Hillsinger, who had come along as an observer on the destroyer *Berkeley*. Like other Americans in Jubilee, Hillsinger had never been under fire, and he was fascinated by the pyrotechnics and the sounds of battle around and above him.

Colonel Hillsinger was wearing a pair of Peel tank boots which he just had made and of which he was quite proud. Standing on the bridge, he looked up just in time to see a JU-88, which had been riddled by Spitfire machine guns, jettison its bombs. One of the bombs struck the *Berkeley* and blew Hillsinger off the bridge, severing his foot. He applied a tourniquet, fashioned from his handkerchief and necktie, to his leg. Looking down toward the water, he saw his coveted new boot with his foot inside it bobbing about. Cursing in disgust, he unlaced the other boot and pitched it into the water after the first.

Hillsinger was removed to a smaller rescue vessel, but refused to be treated until all other wounded men had been cared for. Once treated, Colonel Hillsinger, ashen-faced and weak from loss of blood, fought off efforts to take him below. He propped himself up and spotted enemy planes for the antiaircraft gunners, staying at his post until he collapsed.

Another American observer, Brigadier General Lucian Truscott, was intently taking in proceedings from the destroyer *Fernie*, which was alternate headquarters for Jubilee. The *Fernie* had been edging steadily closer to shore, and soon the big German guns on the cliffs began ranging in on her. Truscott heard an enormous rustling sound as the huge shells approached, and saw the geysers kicked up when the projectiles splashed in the water. He was peering shoreward through binoculars when a mighty crash rocked the *Fernie* herself. Truscott was knocked violently into the rail and nearly flattened. The general felt a sharp pain in one foot and heard something clatter to the deck. He picked up the object and saw that it was a nut torn loose from the superstructure by the blast. A shell had struck the after end of the ship, killing or wounding 16 men.

Despite extensive damange, *Fernie* navigated under her own power and headed for the concealment of a thick smokescreen. General Truscott, meanwhile, had regained his composure and now went below deck to the operations room. There were grave faces and heavy hearts. Over the radio, one report after the other was coming in from the beaches and from landing craft skippers. It was a litany of disasters, of entire platoons and companies wiped out.

At 11:00 A.M., the remnants of the Jubilee force were given the order to withdraw from the bloody beaches of the Iron Coast. Brigadier Mann, chief of staff of the Canadian 2nd Division, looked up wearily from a small desk and said to a grave-faced Lucian Truscott, "General, I am afraid that this operation will go down as one of the great failures in history."

A short time later the radio crackled again. A Canadian officer on shore was explaining, in a voice choked with emotion, why he was surrendering his decimated and surrounded unit. "I understand," Brigadier Mann replied sympathetically, trying to keep his voice from betraying his own anguish.

"Good-bye to you all," the voice from shore called out. "Please take a message to—"

Then all was still. The raid on Dieppe was over.

Recrossing the English Channel, *Fernie* was a grim vessel. She had taken aboard so many wounded that blood-caked, bandaged men were lying shoulder to shoulder on decks, in wardrooms, in cabins, and even in the galley. There were not enough pharmacist's mates or medical supplies aboard to provide more than first aid, nor was there enough morphine to ease the pain of grievously wounded and dying men.

General Truscott picked his way through the bloody disarray of men, agonizing because he was powerless to help relieve their misery. Almost unconsciously, Truscott took out his sack of Bull Durham tobacco to roll a cigarette. As he lit it, one wounded British youth lying on the deck called out, "I say, old fellow, you wouldna have another 'un about ya, wouldya now?"

Truscott crouched and placed the cigarette in the youth's mouth. He saw that the boy had been badly wounded in the stomach, but an opiate injected by a medic had temporarily relieved his suffering. Now the American general became aware that other eager eyes were staring at him, so until the Bull Durham sack was empty, General Truscott rolled and lit cigarettes for wounded men.

The raid on Dieppe had indeed been a disaster. Sixty percent of those in the assault—3,623 men—were killed, wounded, or captured. Of the 4,963 Canadians involved, 68 percent became casualties. For days afterward, bodies from the Jubilee force washed ashore in Dieppe and for ten miles to either side of the port. The Royal Air Force had suffered the destruction of 106 badly needed aircraft and the Royal Navy lost 550 men plus a warship and 33 landing craft from a flotilla of 252 vessels of all types.

German losses were relatively light—591 casualties, 46 aircraft. At 5:38 P.M. on the day of the battle, Field Marshal Gerd von Rundstedt, from his headquarters in a chateau outside Paris, wired Adolf Hitler a terse report: "No armed Englishman remains on the continent."

While the Führer was reading these tidings from von Rundstedt, first word that the Dieppe raid had been mounted was reaching the homefronts in Great Britain and the United States. After an almost unending series of defeats in the Pacific, the African desert, and elsewhere, the Western Allies were seen finally to be taking the offensive. The influential *New York Times* headline the next morning would blare: TANKS AND U.S. TROOPS SMASH AT FRANCE. Most American newspapers and radio stations heralded the involvement of their nation's armed forces in the blow against Hitler's Fortress Europe. (Actually, 50 U.S. Rangers played a limited role in the Dieppe raid.) Even the reserved *Times* of London got caught up in the euphoria. Its headline proclaimed: ALLIES INVADE FRANCE. But in London and in Washington, Eisenhower, Marshall, and other American military leaders were shocked by the Dieppe bloodletting. If the ill-fated raid was a ploy to dissuade the American "newcomers to war" from a major invasion of northwest France in 1942, it had succeeded all too well. The American and British homefronts were shocked a few days later when the truth of the Dieppe debacle emerged.

Josef Goebbels, meanwhile, reaped a propaganda bonanza that even he had not foreseen. German newspapers ran macabre pictures showing mounds of Canadian and British corpses, twisted wreckage of downed Royal Air Force planes, and blackened hulks of Allied tanks and landing craft stranded on the beaches of Dieppe.

The British prime minister received word of the Iron Coast disaster in Cairo, where he and General Brooke had flown after their meeting with Stalin. Churchill promptly wrote to his deputy prime minister, Clement Attlee, in London: "My general impression of Jubilee is that the results fully justified the heavy costs." He did not elaborate.

Field Marshall Brooke, who for months had been engaged in almost incessant wrangling with the American high command, snorted on hearing of the Dieppe debacle: "It is a lesson to the people who are clamoring for the invasion of France [in 1942]!" Those "people" were George Marshall, Dwight Eisenhower, and Secretary of War Henry Stimson.

In the wake of the bloodbath on the French coast, America's military leadership focused its full attention on Operation Torch. An attempted invasion of northern France in 1942 was now out of the question.

4

"Let's All Get *Equally* Confused!"

On August 21, two days after the Dieppe debacle, General George Patton returned to Washington from his ten-day fact-finding trip to London. He had only seven weeks in which to plan and organize the North African operation, since D-day was then set for October 7. Slowly the huge venture was taking shape, though London and Washington were revising the master plan almost daily. Patton would command the Western Task Force, one of the three—and the largest—in the complicated operation. It would sail directly from Hampton Roads, Virginia, near Norfolk, storm ashore either at Casablanca (as Patton wanted) or Oran (as Eisenhower proposed). Western Task Force would be all-American—navy lifting army.

Despite his customary bouyancy, George Patton entertained no illusions that his task would be easy. Never had a major invasion been mounted from 3,000 miles away. There were no textbooks, and no precedents. Patton's mission was to assemble an untested, partially trained force of some 38,000 men, move the force and its vehicles, weapons, ammunition, and supplies to another continent across an ocean infested with German U-boats, storm the defended shores of

North Africa, defeat whatever hostile force might be encountered, secure a large beachhead, and prepare to drive hundreds of miles eastward.

The United States Navy's task would also be one of monumental proportions. No navy had ever transported and protected such a large force over such distances and disembarked that force for an amphibious assault. Patton's fighting men would be carried in 36 transports, cargo vessels, and tankers, escorted by 88 warships ranging from the venerable battleship *Texas* to the tugboat *Cherokee*. Masterminding the Western Task Force naval operations was fifty-five-year-old Rear Admiral H. Kent Hewitt, who had earned the Navy Cross for gallantry in World War I. The gray-haired, low-key Hewitt was known in the navy for his insistence on giving credit to others, and for his tactful, conciliatory demeanor in dealing with his peers in other services.

Hewitt, described by fellow officers as massive in physical size and in character, would need all the tact—and forbearance—that he could muster. Hardly had an impatient George Patton arrived back in Washington from London than he promptly declared war on the United States Navy. At times it was a long-range conflict: Cavalryman Patton would shoot from the hip in the direction of Norfolk, Virginia, where Hewitt had his headquarters at the Nansemond Hotel in nearby Ocean View. Hewitt in turn would roll out his big guns and fire a verbal volley toward Washington where Patton had an office in a musty third-floor loft in the old Munitions Building on Constitution Avenue.

By nature Patton was inclined to underestimate the problems of those in other services, often dismissing their apprehensions as thinly veiled cowardice. Patton was dynamic, quick-triggered, and often given to snap judgments. Hewitt gave the impression of being deliberate, and he carefully weighed the pros and cons of any proposal. The stage was set for a violent explosion that was not long in coming.

On August 24, Admiral Hewitt and a group of his key officers flew to Washington for their first meeting with General Patton in the loft of the Munitions Building. The army leader took an immediate dislike to the admiral's apparent casual approach to the task and to his low-key demeanor. His irritation turned to hostility when Hewitt's staff often interjected what Patton construed to be "defeatist views." It was almost as though the navy were trying to sabotage Torch, he thought.

32

Finally, Patton exploded, raking the visitors with the most intense and profane verbal abuse. The navy delegation retreated in consternation, convinced that it would be impossible to work with someone of Patton's volatility. Kent Hewitt was thoroughly enraged. He went directly to his boss, Admiral Ernest King, who was himself noted for brusqueness and a hair-trigger temper. Unless the army removed the combustible Patton, Hewitt suggested, the navy should pull out of the Western Task Force, presumably leaving Patton's assault force marooned in the United States.

King immediately hurried to see Patton's superior, General George Marshall, and made a formal demand: dump Patton from command of the Western Task Force. The chief of staff, aware of Patton's explosive nature, wasn't about to dump the soldier he was convinced would be a superb leader. He outlined Patton's virtues, offered suggestions on how to handle the army's bad boy, and hoped that Admiral Hewitt and other navy leaders would overlook Patton's tantrums for the good of Torch. Despite Marshall's plea to his navy counterpart, it looked as though Patton would be out of a job—an outcast from the war before he ever got into it.

A leery Kent Hewitt finally agreed to continue to work with Patton, but the general himself was unrepentant. Shortly after the altercation in the Munitions Building, three British planning experts arrived in Washington at the request of General Marshall to share their expertise on amphibious operations with the Americans. Astonished that Patton's and Hewitt's headquarters were more than two hundred miles apart, the British experts suggested that all those involved with such intricate planning, where hour-to-hour coordination was often required, move under one roof. Patton roared: "Go anywhere near that bunch of rattlesnakes? Not me!"*

Hidden away in Washington's old Munitions Building was a secretive group of brigadier generals and colonels who would never make the headlines—or even get their names mentioned in the newspapers—but

---

* Hastings Ismay, *The Memoirs of General Lord Ismay.*

on whose shoulders rested the fate of Torch. They were logisticians, charged with the awesome task of getting the right men with the right equipment to the right place at the right time. Torch called for the biggest overseas landing force ever assembled up to that time. These Services of Supply (SOS) officers would have to provide 700,000 different items—including 38 million pounds of clothing and equipment and 22 million pounds of food. There would be 10 million gallons of gasoline to go ashore in five-gallon containers carried by individual soldiers or landed in bulk by tankers. The supply list for Torch included 580 ratcatchers, one hundred alarm clocks, and hundreds of stepladders, rubber stamps, steel safes, and cartons of prophylactic condoms. There were fumication bags (newly developed) for the soldiers' endless battles with lice. Men would have goggles especially made for Africa with two kinds of lenses, one for dust and one for the sun—both of which could be expected in quantity. Further complicating the enormous SOS function was the vital necessity of keeping everything secret. Hundreds of thousands of items would be delivered to ships in cartons marked XY, or Z2, or L-10, leaving GIs and enemy spies alike wondering what was in the containers.

In the knowledge that hostile eyes and ears were everywhere, the planners encouraged observers to believe that the feverish activity in the Munitions Building was for the purpose simply of moving more troops to the British Isles. "Britain" and "Ireland" were code words used for Algeria and Morocco. Some officers knew that a large movement was in the works; some knew the destination but not the size; others knew the size but not the destination. Transportation Corps officers, hunkered over desks in tiny rooms, never mentioned the words Oran, Algiers, or Casablanca. Even when only two of them were in a room, these traffic planners used code words for these ports, or else had hand signals for conveying to each other the names of the North African cities.

Hundreds of miles inland, engineer soldiers practiced feverishly—often against a stopwatch—to load everything from cans of peas to 30-ton tanks onto every type of freight car existing in the United States, without every being told why. Nothing was left to chance by the Torch planners. Even if saboteurs, secret Nazi weapons, or acts of God should destroy three-fourths of the bridges in the eastern United States, troops would be transported from the interior to ports of embarkation by preselected alternative routes.

The production and distribution of more than 1,000 different types of maps was carried out under the most intensely secret conditions. Officers and men taking part in these ultrasensitive matters were given no leaves and were, in fact, more or less under arrest. Maps were shipped to warehouses at ports of embarkation where, watched by armed guards, soldiers packed them into containers for distribution to the proper units at sailing time.

Safeguarding the secrecy of Torch on the American side was the Counter-Intelligence Corps (CIC), composed mainly of people who had worked in law enforcement as civilians. No one was above its scrutiny. Acting under the orders of unspecified higher authority, CIC agents informed the Torch supreme commander, General Eisenhower, that his own staff and aides were to be shadowed for weeks to determine if, through negligence or alcohol, anyone might be leaking Torch secrets. Only much later would Eisenhower learn that CIC agents, presumably acting under the orders of Chief of Staff Marshall, had been surveilling the supreme commander himself for nearly three weeks.

While these massive problems of supply, logistics, and security were being wrestled with daily on both sides of the ocean, in London on August 25 General Mark Clark was rousted out of bed at 3:00 A.M., in his apartment at the Dorchester Hotel, to read a copy of a cable sent by General Marshall to Eisenhower. Apparently Washington was still gripped by the jitters. Two days previously, D-day for Torch had been postponed to October 15, and it had been tentatively agreed that the three task forces would strike simultaneously at Casablanca, Oran, and Algiers. Now Marshall's cable said the American chiefs felt that Torch was on too large a scale and that Algiers should be dropped due to "the limited military forces available."

"The hazard is too great," Marshall wrote, "especially considering the extreme seriousness of the effect on the peoples of occupied Europe, India, and China if the United States should fail in its first major operation."

Eisenhower and Clark were shocked. This was the most depressing news yet. "The war's going to be over before we even get into it," the supreme commander said. Both men were still downcast when they arrived at 10 Downing Street that night to dine with Prime Minister Churchill. The British Bulldog spoke glowingly of Torch as "one of the great opportunities of the war," then abruptly asked the Americans what was on their minds. Clark, the chief planner, was fed up with the situation, and with the latest change in signals. He felt that the Anglo-American leadership had been floundering around for too long. While most young, ambitious two-star generals would have kept their counsel, Clark spoke out. "The greatest need is for someone with the necessary power to make some decisions," Clark declared in frustration. "We're in the middle of day-to-day changes. We must have had ten sets of plans. There have been so many changes we are dizzy. We'd like to get one definite plan so we can go to work on it."

An awkward hush fell over the dining room. Churchill stared at Clark and puffed on his cigar, but seemed to feel that the young general had hit the nail on the head. "I'll get in touch with President Roosevelt at once," he said.

Talk flourished and drinks flowed until 2:00 A.M. As General Clark was leaving, he told Churchill again, "The planners of Torch are tired of piddling around. Every minute counts. What we need is the green light." The prime minister nodded and promised immediate action.

Mark Clark, by pointedly criticizing the indecisiveness of the American and British hierarchies, had placed his promising career on the line. Either the high level strategists would cease "piddling around," or the two-star general would find himself transferred to a paper-shuffling post in the bowels of the War Department in Washington.

True to his word, Churchill contacted Roosevelt. After considerable wrangling between the Americans and British, the two Allies reached agreement. There would be three, not two, assaults—at Casablanca, Oran, and Algiers.

Nevertheless, signals continued to fly between London and Washington. There were yet more changes to Torch. On August 29, President Roosevelt injected a new proposal—the landings in North Africa should be all-American. The British, the president suggested, could go ashore in a follow-up role after the landings. This drastic new view was based on the known hostility of most French army and navy officers in North

Africa to anything British. In June 1940, after France had surrendered to Nazi Germany, the powerful French fleet had been based at Mers el Kebir in North Africa. Churchill, fearful that Hitler would take over these warships, had ordered Operation Catapult, an attack on the French fleet. On July 13, 1940, a British naval force of battleships and aircraft carriers opened fire on the French warships *Dunkerque*, *Jean Bart*, *Richelieu*, and *Strasbourg* at Mers el Kebir. Only the *Strasbourg* escaped; the others were sunk or badly damaged with a loss of 977 French sailors. The next day torpedo-bombers from the carrier *Ark Royal* sank another French warship, killing 151 members of the crew.

Roosevelt's proposal to exclude the British from the Torch assault stirred up another blizzard of counterproposals between London and Washington as the clock ticked on toward D-day. An exasperated Eisenhower privately called it the "Transatlantic Essay Competition."

On August 31, Mark Clark called together the 37 American and British officers in his planning staff at Norfolk House. "Some of you men are less confused than others about Torch," the general declared. "Let's all get equally confused." An officer asked if a firm D-day had been set. Clark replied, not to his knowledge, but that "they" had been talking about postponing it once again, to about October 30.

Finally, Churchill and his advisors gave in. The Torch assault *would* be made exclusively by American troops, although many would be carried in British vessels. The prime minister, always alert to innovative approaches, suggested that British troops participate in the initial assault dressed in American uniforms, a proposal he soon abandoned.

Meanwhile, Hitler was nearly a thousand miles from London, receiving a prominent Balkan diplomat. The German warlord had recently moved his battle headquarters eastward to Vinnitsa in the Russian Ukraine. Code-named Werwolf, this new center of operations for the final heave to take Russia out of the war was a collection of wooden huts and log cabins nestled in thick woods, out of sight of snooping Soviet aircraft.

Hitler was ebullient, as well he might be with Russia on the verge of collapse. The British had received a shattering reversal on the sands of Dieppe. He was little worried about the role of America in the war, convinced that the Third Reich would emerge triumphant no later than in 1943. The average American soldier, Hitler had opined to aides, was nothing more than "an effeminate ribbon clerk."*

Now Hitler told his visitor that Europe was safe from British invasion. Field Marshal von Rundstedt had 29 divisions there, including such crack outfits as the 2nd and 4th Panzer divisions, the 2nd Parachute Division, and the Hermann Göring Division. On the other hand, the British were unpredictable and might try anything, Hitler observed. "If only soldiers had the say in Britain, this operation they are peddling around as their 'Second Front' would not take place. But as lunatics like that drunkard Churchill, and numbskulls like that brilliantined dandy [Foreign Minister Anthony] Eden, are at the tiller, we have to be prepared for just about anything."†

---

* Only after the Battle of the Bulge, where the Americans fought with great gallantry and tenacity, would Hitler change his view.

† David Irving, *Hitler's War.*

5

Top Secret: Airfields A and B

Operation Torch was rife with chilling imponderables. Among the foremost of these unknown quantities was the supreme commander himself, Dwight D. Eisenhower. His rise in the army had been speedy in recent months. In less than a year he had come from obscurity as a staff colonel in Texas to command of his country's largest combined amphibious operation.

Known since childhood as Ike—a nickname that seemed to fit his homespun personality—he had never led even a platoon in battle. Since graduating from West Point in 1916, Eisenhower had held mostly a series of staff assignments, including a stint as an aide to General Douglas MacArthur in the Philippines in the mid-1930s. Now the affable one-time Kansas farmboy was facing the ultimate challenge—welding an allied coalition, with its jealousies and divergent national interests, into a successful effort on the battlefield. Eisenhower would have to prove that, despite historical precedents to the contrary, the allied concept could work.

All summer, well-meaning old army friends had been bombarding Eisenhower with tales of the failure of allied coalitions going back to the days of the Greeks, 500 years before Christ, and down through the centuries to the bitter disputes that raged between the French and the British in 1940 when Hitler was annexing most of Europe. They had warned Eisenhower that allied unity in the high command was unattainable. It was whispered in his ear that any general placed in Eisenhower's position was an ideal scapegoat should Torch meet with disaster. They were hectic days—and nights—for the supreme commander at bustling Grosvenor Square, which the Americans had labeled Eisenhowerplatz because so many military offices were crammed into the complex of buildings. Eisenhower customarily put in 18- to 20-hour days. Often he ate lunch, sometimes only raisins and crackers, at his desk. Much of his time was spent refereeing lower-level disputes and explaining to socialites why he could not attend parties.

A thousand intricacies had to be resolved. No problem was too large, or too small, to reach his desk. How much toilet tissue should be taken ashore the first week? Difficulties were endless. Grand strategy, specific objectives, tactics, procurement of landing craft (of which there was an acute shortage), allocation of warships, organization of air forces, establishment of assault and follow-up units, designation of weapons, identification of naval bombardment targets—all these matters had to be resolved rapidly and often simultaneously. Then there was Winston Churchill and his insatiable wish to be kept up to the minute on even minor details of Torch developments. For Dwight Eisenhower, each interminable delay was an ordeal.

Piled atop the mountain of military problems confronting Eisenhower and Mark Clark was what one exasperated American general had called "the goddamned French political mess." It involved bitter quarrels between French factions, French national pride, conflicting definitions of "honor" as conceived by different members of the French officer corps, and a lethal dispute over which of two French governments was the legally constituted one. Mixed up in it all were the towering egos of French leaders and would-be leaders, all jockeying for position.

When the Germans crushed France's army in only six weeks in mid-1940, the armistice agreement specified that Germany would occupy the northern half of France, while the French could establish their own government for the nation in unoccupied France, with its capital at Vichy. Hitler had no intention of allowing a potentially hostile, if defeated, France to govern itself, however. He installed a revered French hero of World War I, eighty-four-year-old Marshal Henri Pétain, as the puppet ruler of France. The bewildered Pétain was never in control of the French government and was helpless to halt the constant power struggles within his entourage.

When Hitler had overrun northern France, a relatively unknown French general named Charles de Gaulle had escaped to Great Britain, organized an army from among Frenchmen who had also chosen to continue the fight against the Nazis, and proclaimed himself head of the Free French government in exile. De Gaulle, six-foot-seven, ambitious, and with a large and zealous following among the civilians of France, was despised by officers in the French army headed by Marshal Pétain and his commander in chief of the armed forces, Admiral Jean-François Darlan (who had been described by King George of Great Britain as "shifty-eyed and devious"). At the time of France's surrender, professional officers in the army and navy had to reach anguishing individual decisions: Should they flee (if possible) to England and continue the fight, or give up armed struggle and accept orders from Pétain's Vichy government? From the point of view of those officers who decided Vichy was the legal government of France, de Gaulle was a deserter.

French armed forces in North Africa had been limited by the 1940 armistice to 120,000 men. Through clandestine contacts, Allied leaders in London had learned that there was considerable pro-American sentiment among French officers there. On the other hand, disturbing bits of information continued to trickle into 20 Grosvenor Square to the effect that the French in North Africa would resist an Allied invasion "with all the means at their disposal."

This complex situation presented one of the major imponderables of Operation Torch: Would the French army and navy strenuously resist invasion by another nation, or would the invaders be welcomed as liberators and comrades-in-arms against Germany? This dramatic uncertainty stalked Dwight Eisenhower's days and even the few hours of sleep he managed to steal at night. If the French chose to fight, the beaches of Northwest Africa would run red with American blood. The

120,000 French fighting men would outnumber the 112,000 American troops to take part in the initial assault (200,000 more American and British soldiers would follow). The 14 French divisions in North Africa were poorly equipped, but their officers were capable and many had been battle-tested during the 1940 fighting against the Wehrmacht. There were 250 French tanks, most obsolescent but serviceable. Between 155 and 170 French combat planes were based at Moroccan airfields, Allied intelligence indicated, and within two hours after the alarm some 165 to 210 additional warplanes could be hurried to the coast from inland. Almost half of the French aircraft were Dewoitine fighters, superior in maneuverability to carrier-borne fighters of the U.S. Navy. About the same number of French planes were thought to be twin-engine bombers. French combat pilots were keenly trained and capable.

Should the Luftwaffe rush fighters and bombers to northwest Africa (perhaps on being tipped off by U-boats in the Atlantic or spies in Spain at Gibraltar), and should the Luftwaffe base its aircraft in nearby Spanish Morocco, the 160 American carrier planes available to Torch could be quickly overwhelmed.

Allied invaders, especially General George Patton's Western Task Force sailing from the United States, would confront yet another menace—the French fleet. At Casablanca and farther south along the Atlantic coast were moored several French battleships, including the *Jean Bart* with modern radar and a battery of 15-inch guns, and the *Richelieu*. Each warship had a long cruising range and could be a serious threat to any approaching convoy. Several French submarines, moreover, were lurking in Casablanca harbor.

There was even more to worry about from the Spaniards. Sir Samuel Hoare, British Ambassador to Spain, was deeply concerned over Allied convoys having to squeeze through the 20-mile-wide Strait of Gibraltar to enter the Mediterranean Sea. On the north of the Strait was Spain, and along the southern shore was Spanish Morocco.

On September 2, Ambassador Hoare wrote General Eisenhower: "The temptation [for General Francisco Franco] to cut our lines of communication [at the Strait of Gilbraltar] will be very great. We shall appear to have our neck between two Spanish knives, and Spanish knives are traditionally treacherous. The Germans will be on Franco's back, dinning into his ears, 'Now is the time.' Let no one underrate the power of this temptation or think that because nine out of ten Spaniards do not want war, General Franco might not risk it for the big stakes that it might offer."

While these high-level concerns were being aired, on the night of September 6 General Mark Clark summoned his airborne advisor, thirty-year-old Major William P. Yarborough, to his headquarters at Norfolk House. Yarborough had been one of the handful of American officers who had pioneered the nation's effort to organize a paratrooper force in 1940. Innovative and energetic, the officer from New York City had designed the American paratrooper's most prized possessions—the parachute wings and jump boots.

Yarborough had come to the British Isles the previous July, at the express wish of General Clark, to be airborne advisor for Torch. Arriving at Norfolk House, the major was greeted warmly by Clark, who then got right down to business. Pointing at a gigantic wall map of North Africa, Clark asked, "Bill, what would you say if I wanted to drop paratroopers right there—within a few weeks?"

Yarborough looked at the spot to which Clark was pointing and was startled. The site of the proposed drop by the 509th Parachute Infantry Battalion, which had arrived in Great Britain only a few weeks before, was not just across the Channel in Normandy where he had expected it, but in Algeria, North Africa—more than 1,600 miles from England.

Yarborough hoped he was concealing his astonishment. Sixteen hundred miles by air, and then a mass bailout by a green battalion of paratroopers onto a pinpoint target! Even the Wehrmacht, when it startled the world in 1940 and 1941 with mass airborne operations to seize Holland, Belgium, and the Mediterranean island of Crete, had flown no further than 200 miles en route. And Germany had been training troops in airborne operations since 1929.

General Clark's pointer had touched two major airports—La Sénia and Tafaraoui—located a few miles south of the major port of Oran, which was to be seized by seaborne troops of the Center Task Force. It was at these two facilities that Clark wanted to drop the 509th Parachute Infantry Battalion before H-hour on D-day for Torch. Yarborough understood why. Tafaraoui was the only hard-surfaced airfield from Oran to the Atlantic seaboard, hundreds of miles to the west. Opposition fighters and bombers taking off from these two airports could create havoc for the invasion fleet and for the troops storming ashore near Oran. La Sénia was ten miles south of Oran, and Tafaraoui was five miles farther inland. As Major Yarborough turned all this over in his mind, General Clark inquired evenly: "Well, Bill, can it be done?"

"That's difficult to answer on the spot," Yarborough replied. "With extra fuel tanks, our C-47s [troop-carrier aircraft] can fly that distance —but barely. These planes carrying our paratroopers would be unarmed, of course, are slow, and would be unescorted and highly vulnerable to attack from Luftwaffe fighters. But if I mull it over and come up with a plan, may I present it to you in the morning, sir?"

"Of course," the lanky general replied. "*Early* in the morning." Then the proposed parachute assault grew even more complicated as Clark put international politics into the picture. He did not want merely one plan, he wanted two of them. The French army and air force, still feeling humiliated after being defeated by the Wehrmacht in only six weeks in 1940, had maintained a "neutral stance" in North Africa. The French, thought to be sympathetic to Americans, *might* allow United States forces to land without a fight. Then again, honor might require the French to resist with all the means at their disposal.

"We're going to try to convince the French that they should come out on our side," General Clark observed. "But if they do not, we'll fight them as we would any other enemy."

Yarborough saluted and said, "See you in the morning, sir." There would be no sleep for the airborne advisor that night.

Hurrying through the blacked-out streets of London to his own office, Major Yarborough felt a good deal of excitement over the pending paratroop operation. Himself a veteran of 44 parachute jumps, Yarborough knew that not a single American paratrooper had ever bailed out into battle, and that the fledgling airborne branch still had to prove itself. There were influential American generals, schooled in the static trench warfare of World War I, who looked on paratrooper forces as a gimmick.

Seated at his desk as the clock approached midnight, Bill Yarborough quickly wrote down the pluses and minuses of the proposed parachute operation. Eager as he was to have the 509th Parachute Infantry make America's first mass combat jump, he was alarmed by the minus factors. Previous drops into combat by German paratroopers had been made after flights of only about one-eighth the distance of the Torch operation. After an exhausting ten-hour flight from England in cramped C-47 cabins in bucket seats, weighted down with combat gear, would even the keenly conditioned Americans be physically and psychologically capable of fighting once they landed in North Africa?

There were more negative factors: Engine exhausts of the C-47s had no flame-dampers to conceal the aircraft from Luftwaffe night fighters. The navigational lights on the aircraft, which would have to be illuminated in flight to keep the planes from crashing into each other, could be seen from the ground, where the sky armada could presumably be spotted by German agents. In effect, the attacking sky train would paint a lighted trail in the sky because most of the flight would be at night. There were too few qualified celestial navigators to go around, so how could all of the pilots, none of whom had flown such lengthy missions, be expected to reach a tiny target after a night flight of 1,600 miles? The final leg of the flight would be over a vast stretch of the Mediterranean sea; would the C-47s run out of fuel over water?

Finally, the Luftwaffe had skilled and experienced pilots based at several points not far from the flight route. If the lumbering, unescorted C-47s were detected, German pilots could have one of their biggest turkey shoots of the war.

Every instinct told Major Yarborough, "Reject this idiotic 'suicide mission.'" But, bleary-eyed from lack of sleep, he began listing the plus factors. For one thing, the 1,600-mile flight and all the negative factors Yarborough had just listed made it likely that the Germans would be caught off guard. Probably the Germans would not even have considered that such a daring and unprecedented airborne mission might be undertaken by the Americans. Surprise, one of the most crucial ingredients to success on the battlefield, might be in the Americans' favor.*

---

* The German high command was fully aware that the 509th Parachute Infantry Battalion was in England. Within hours of their arrival at their British base at Chilton Foliat in Berkshire several weeks previously, the paratroopers were

For Yarborough, there was something else at stake. If American paratroop leaders were ever to prove the enormous potential of airborne operations, then the mass drop in North Africa to capture two key airfields would dramatize it. If Yarborough were to say to General Clark in a few hours, "Sorry, but this is all a little too much for us," when would American planners ever call on parachute formations in a combat operation?

Shortly after daybreak, Yarborough shaved hurriedly, put on a fresh uniform, and dashed off to Norfolk House. With him he carried two proposals: "Plan Peace," in which the C-47s loaded with paratroopers would land unopposed at La Sénia airfield if negotiations with the French were successful, and "Plan War," in which the French were expected to fight. Plan War would have the 509th Parachute Infantry Battalion bail out near both La Sénia and Tafaraoui airports, seize both facilities, and destroy all French airplanes at the two bases.

For over an hour, Yarborough briefed Clark on the two airborne plans. Clark was delighted. "Okay," he said. "Let 'er go."*

Lieutenant Colonel Edson Raff, the peppery leader of the 509th Parachute Infantry Battalion, was summoned to Norfolk House from Chilton Foliat. Since his unit's arrival in July, Raff had been itching for a good fight, so on learning of the parachute mission, he felt a surge of excitement. "If the air corps will get our people to the right place, I assure you we'll grab those two airfields," Raff told General Clark—adding quickly, "with or without French cooperation."

The thirty-year-old Raff, who had been a star on the West Point swim team, rushed back to Chilton Foliat and plunged his paratroopers into the most intensive combat training. Spurring him on was the exhilarating thought that he would lead his country's first combat parachute

---

greeted by the Nazi broadcaster, Lord Haw Haw, over Radio Berlin: "Welcome to England, men of the 509th Parachute Infantry. Please enjoy yourselves while you can before your lives are needlessly tossed away in Churchill's war."

* After the war, William Yarborough rose to three-star rank. In the early 1960s he commanded the Green Berets.

mission—and Raff intended to be the first man to bail out over North Africa.

Colonel Raff's war room took on a new aura of significance—and secrecy. An armed guard was posted at the door around the clock with orders to let no one in without a signed authorization from Raff. Inside the war room, illuminated by powerful overhead lights, were meticulously created scale models of two airfields, labeled A and B.

The identities of A and B were closely guarded secrets, which led to intense speculation among the troopers. Company and platoon leaders and small groups of their men were allowed in the war room at specified times to be briefed in detail on the impending assault on airfields A and B. Rumors were soon rampant in the Nissen huts and training grounds of the 509th Parachute Infantry Battalion. "Those two goddamned airfields have got to be across the English Channel in France," a trooper declared to comrades. "Like hell they are," countered another. "They're in Belgium." And the wildest rumor of all: "We're going to jump on two airfields in Berlin and kidnap Adolf Hitler." Only hours before takeoff would the curious men of the 509th Parachute Infantry be told of the locale of airfields A and B.

On September 8, two days after General Clark had summoned Major Yarborough to Norfolk House, the American paratroop mission to secure La Sénia and Tafaraoui airfields was in danger of being scrubbed. The airborne operation was under fire from the British.

Ordered to report to General Eisenhower's office on Grosvenor Square on the September 8 were Lieutenant Colonel Raff, Major Yarborough, and Colonel William C. Bentley, whose 60th Carrier Group would lift the 509th Parachute Infantry Battalion to the targets. When the three Americans arrived, they were confronted by British Air Vice Marshal William Welsh, who was head of air operations for Torch.

There was electricity in the room as the eager Americans listened to a recitation by Marshal Welsh on why the paratroop mission should be canceled. Some transport planes might be "lost" en route, troopers and crews captured, resulting in the danger that the enemy might be tipped off to the invasion. What's more, the air marshal said, it would be better to hold back the three squadrons of the 60th Carrier Group for the rapid movement of conventional forces eastward into Tunisia, where the Wehrmacht was expected to rush strong ground and air reinforcements from Europe once the Allies had landed in Algeria and Morocco.

The tense conference adjourned with the question of including American paratroopers in Torch still hanging in the air. Only later, through the vocal insistence of General Clark, was the airborne mission approved.

6

A Mystery Man
Visits Eisenhower

During these hectic days, Eisenhower and his staff at Grosvenor Square and Clark with his planners at Norfolk House were beset by a monumental problem that threatened to disrupt Torch—even to the extent of its being canceled. Supplies—mountains of them—were mysteriously failing to arrive in the United Kingdom. German U-boats were sinking supply ships daily, but entire shiploads of guns, ammunition, spare parts, and other crucial matériel were simply disappearing, lost in a logistical maze in the United States or sidetracked by parties unknown.

One cargo of combat equipment for the 1st Infantry Division (posted in the British Isles and scheduled to assault Oran) started out from New York on three occasions and each time was lost or otherwise diverted. On September 12, Mark Clark learned that the 1st Division—the Big Red One—had not as yet received its weapons. Clark investigated and learned that the 1st Division weapons had not even been shipped from New York.

General Clark, under enormous pressures as D-day drew closer, contacted Colonel Everett Hughes of the Services of Supply (SOS) and applied some pressure of his own. "You must make it vividly clear to

Washington," the angry Clark declared, "that if those weapons aren't here by September 26 our boys in the Big Red One will have to [storm the beaches] virtually with their bare hands!"

While General Clark and Torch planners were coping with these problems of supply, on September 14 U.S. Marine Corps Lieutenant Colonel William A. Eddy flew into London from his post as naval attaché at Tangier, French Morocco. Actually, Eddy was an American spy and saboteur; the attaché assignment was his cover. For months the marine had been establishing contacts with locals, with French military men, and with resistance groups in North Africa, and had been ferreting out valuable enemy secrets. Now Colonel Eddy rushed to London to conduct a series of espionage conferences with British cloak-and-dagger agencies—and to present Mark Clark with a startling proposal:

> I recommend that on D-Day, when the landing operations actually begin, I be authorized to arrange for the assassination of the members of the German Armistice Commission at Casablanca* and for any members of the German Commission who may then be in Oran. About twenty of the German army and navy officers live in a hotel in Casablanca and the assignments have already been made for this job to men who have the demolition materials already in their hands. I might add that our principal agent in Casablanca is the father of a boy who was shot as a hostage [by the Germans] in Paris recently, and the father is impatiently awaiting permission to carry out this assignment.

Clark read the proposal and wrote on the margin, "O.K. Looks good to me." But when it reached higher American levels, it was squashed. Even though commission members were Wehrmacht officers, General Clark was advised, measures such as these simply were unacceptable. At a time when the most brutal, no-holds-barred violence was raging in Europe, the Americans were still trying to conduct their part in the conflict by Marquis of Queensberry rules.

---

* This German commission was working hand-in-glove with the Vichy French.

Two days later, a top-secret conference of high-level American and British government officials convened in London to discuss political aspects of Torch. Along with generals Eisenhower and Clark were U.S. ambassador to England John G. Winant and President Roosevelt's troubleshooter, W. Averell Harriman. They were shocked to read the draft of a letter that Roosevelt intended to send immediately to General Charles de Gaulle and the Free French faction. "We're coming into North Africa at an early date," the president had written.

Those in the room realized that the Free French organization was, as one conferee put it, "leaky as a sieve," and that the contents of the Roosevelt letter would soon be in the hands of Hitler and the Oberkommando der Wehrmacht. The American president went on to compound the problem by suggesting in his draft to the politically ambitious de Gaulle that one of de Gaulle's rivals for control of the French army, General Henri-Honoré Giraud, should be made commander in chief of all Allied troops in North Africa, including the Americans and British. Giraud, taken prisoner in 1940, had escaped from confinement in Germany and was then living in unoccupied France.

A discreetly worded signal, explaining the potential hazards involved if the letter were sent, was transmitted to the White House. Roosevelt's letter to "*Mon Cher Generale* de Gaulle" was never dispatched.

During these hectic days, Supreme Commander Eisenhower often did not know what event might suddenly surface to claim his attention. On the afternoon of September 14 Kay Summersby, an attractive, willowy divorcée in her early thirties, was idling away the time in General Eisenhower's suite at 20 Grosvenor Square. A former fashion model and a native of Ireland, Mrs. Summersby had been the supreme commander's driver since the previous June. Not only had Eisenhower been impressed with her ability to guide his olive drab Buick sedan through London's maze of narrow, winding streets in blackouts, but her vivacious personality had given the overburdened general's morale an occasional boost.

Suddenly Summersby was shaken from her reverie by a shout, "Kay, the Big Boss wants you pronto!" Eisenhower told the civilian driver to get his sedan ready, that he had to rush to Telegraph Cottage, his pastoral hideaway setting 30 minutes outside London. Speeding through rural Kensington, Eisenhower seemed preoccupied and, uncharacteristically, said virtually nothing. Only once did Summersby hear him mumble something about "big doings for a colonel . . ."

Summersby also rode in silence, for she had long made it a policy never to ask questions or interrupt Eisenhower during periods of meditation. But in the back seat of her Buick she had heard more top-secret talk about Operation Torch than most Allied generals knew. So she presumed that this unexplained dash to Telegraph Cottage had something to do with the invasion.

Reaching the cottage, mysteriously named decades before by its elderly owner and now being rented for $32.50 per week, General Eisenhower strode briskly to the garden where he shook hands with a tall, slightly stoop-shouldered American officer wearing an ill-fitting uniform. The visitor would later be introduced as Lieutenant Colonel McGowan.

Inside the cozy dwelling, Summersby and three members of the household staff, sergeants Mickey McKeogh, John Hunt, and Walter Moaney, were excruciatingly curious about this episode. They took turns tiptoeing into the kitchen to look out into the garden where Eisenhower and McGowan spent the afternoon whispering to each other as though Abwehr spies were on all sides.

With the arrival of darkness, the two whisperers moved inside by the crackling fireplace. Within minutes, one after the other, high-level Allied military officers arrived at Telegraph Cottage. At 6:00 P.M., amid the clinking of wine glasses, thick clouds of cigar smoke, and intensified whispering, the group had dinner. At 7:30 P.M. Ambassador John Winant, W. Averell Harriman, and H. Freeman Matthews trooped into the cottage.

Mrs. Summersby and the three GIs sat anxiously in the kitchen, trying to solve the unexplained mystery of the clandestine gathering. Were the Germans about to launch some fearsome new enterprise? Why were these high-level leaders paying such attention to a lieutenant colonel with an unmilitary bearing? Only much later would they learn the real identity of Lieutenant Colonel McGowan. He was civilian

Robert D. Murphy, the American underground chief in French Northwest Africa. Among other complex factors, the lengthy, hush-hush conference dealt with a now crucial question: Would the French fight when the Allies started pouring ashore in Algeria and French Morocco? The unencouraging consensus: They might or they might not.*

At a small airport on the outskirts of London just before dusk on September 15, an aircraft touched down and rolled to a halt at one end of the field. Two figures in unkempt clothing deplaned and glanced around nervously. Two men hustled them to a little-used hangar, where the group was joined by two young Americans—operatives in Colonel "Wild Bill" Donovan's OSS.

The two arriving passengers were known by fictitious names and carried false identity papers furnished by the OSS. Their real names were Carl Victor Klopet and Jules Malavergne, and they represented the fledgling American agency's biggest coup to date. They had been smuggled out of French Morocco by the OSS to play crucial roles in Operation Torch.

Carl Klopet had lived in Casablanca for many years, and his work in the marine salvage business had given him intimate knowledge of ports, beaches, and coastal defenses along the entire French Moroccan shoreline. Jules Malavergne had been a ship's pilot on the Sebou River at Port Lyautey for 20 years and knew every shallow, sandbar, and twist in the river channel. One of General Patton's sub–task forces would assault Port Lyautey, 60 miles northeast of Casablanca, and plans called for sending a destroyer charging up the Sebou in an effort to capture a key island airdrome.

Not only did Klopet and Malavergne represent an intelligence bonanza in navigational matters about which Allied knowledge was almost nonexistent, but the Frenchmen, through their extensive connections,

---

* Kay Summersby would remain Eisenhower's close confidante and aide throughout the war. Even though she was a native of Ireland, Eisenhower later would cut through red tape and neatly skirt United States Army tradition to obtain a commission for Summersby. She attained the rank of captain.

would be able to identify pro-Nazi and pro-Allied sentiments among French military and government leaders in Northwest Africa.

On the afternoon of September 19, more security leaks were discovered. An aide had slipped into the supreme commander's office and advised General Eisenhower that a French officer outside was demanding an immediate audience. The visitor said that he had a highly important message from General Charles de Gaulle.

Eisenhower winced but said that the French officer should be shown in. The visitor entered, saluted smartly, and was greeted warmly by the supreme commander. He turned out to be de Gaulle's chief of staff. Offered a chair, the Frenchman declined and, speaking formally in fluent English, told Eisenhower and a staff officer who was with him, "Sir, I am directed by General de Gaulle to inform General Eisenhower that General de Gaulle understands that the British and Americans are planning to invade French North Africa. General de Gaulle wishes to say that in such a case he expects to be designated as commander in chief. Any invasion of French territory that is not under French command is bound to fail."

There was a long silence. Then Eisenhower, with no change of expression, said, "Thank you." The Frenchman saluted and left, whereupon the worried supreme commander turned to his staff officer. "Do you suppose there has been a breach of security somewhere?"

Since the beginning, the Combined Chiefs of Staff had ordered that the politically ambitious de Gaulle and his Free French be kept in the dark concerning all aspects of Torch, including the very fact of its existence. This latest episode added to the worries burdening Eisenhower.

Operation Torch was beginning to shape up, and on September 20 the final piece of the massive, highly complicated plan was put in place— D-day would be Sunday, November 8. Complex factors of moon, tide, and logistics dictated the final selection of D-day, but there had been another key consideration: The Western Allies had taken a leaf from the Japanese, who had attacked Pearl Harbor on a Sunday morning when many American servicemen could be expected to be off duty or nursing hangovers.

Five days later, on September 25, a Catalina flying boat carrying Royal Navy Lieutenant J. H. Turner was winging southward from London, bound for Gibraltar. Turner, a courier, was clutching a special container with a self-destroying bomb in the event the Catalina crashed. Inside the sturdy container was a top-secret letter from General Mark Clark to General Mason-McFarlane, the governor general of Gibraltar. Clark was giving Mason-McFarlane information on Torch: D-day, targeted areas, troop and sea strength—the works.

Suddenly those aboard the lumbering, unarmed Catalina saw Luftwaffe fighter planes diving on them out of the sun. There were bursts of machine-gun fire, and moments later the hulking aircraft plunged crazily and hit the water. Some hours later, Lieutenant Turner's body washed ashore near Cadiz and was discovered by two Spanish fishermen. Police rushed to the scene, searched the body, and discovered the container strapped to the victim's chest. The document-destroying bomb had failed to explode.

Two days later, Spanish authorities delivered the courier's corpse to the British at Gibraltar—with the top-secret letter sealed inside the container. But had the container been opened during the 48 hours, the compromising letter photographed, and the receptacle resealed? Abwehr agents were known to be operating in the locale where the corpse washed ashore, and "neutral" Spanish officials had been working closely with the Nazis.

The episode triggered a tremendous flap in London. Grim conferences were called to assess the situation. Over these deliberations hovered the frightening possibility that Adolf Hitler was at that moment reading the secrets of Torch. This risk would haunt the high command until the first American set foot on North African soil, but the invasion was ordered to proceed as planned.

7

Lethal Duel of Wits

In late September, German intelligence agencies were beginning to get wind of a massive Allied amphibious operation in the making. Determining the accuracy of the evidence was largely the job of the Fremde Heere West (Foreign Armies West), an agency set up the previous year by Adolf Hitler to guard against deceptions by the Western Allies and to determine the enemy order of battle. The FHW was perplexed. Despite rumblings of invasion picked up from secret sources, FHW agents in Paris, Lisbon, Madrid, Ankara, Cairo, London, and as far away as Rio de Janeiro had been sending in a steady flow of reports which together indicated that the Anglo-Americans had neither the manpower nor the equipment to launch a major operation.

Fremde Heere West chiefs reported to the Führer that the rumors of an impending major Allied operation were the result of falsehoods planted worldwide by British secret agencies. Churchill, the FHW reported, was bogged down with a rebellion in India and threats to the security of British oil fields in Iraq and Persia, so could give no thought to offensive action. The Anglo-American high command was dormant, still in shock over the Dieppe disaster, the FHW analyses declared. At

El Alamein, in the North African desert, the British plan was clearly to dig in and hold on, to keep Field Marshal Rommel from smashing through to Cairo and to the vital Suez Canal. Anticipated reinforcements of tanks and troops had not arrived, so an offensive at El Alamein by Lieutenant General Bernard Montgomery appeared out of the question for the foreseeable future. (Actually, new tanks and infantry formations had been pouring into Montgomery's Eighth Army for many weeks.)

At his battle headquarters Wolfsschanze (Wolf's Lair), tucked away in a pine forest near Rastenburg in East Prussia, Adolf Hitler was relieved to receive this Fremde Heere West report on the impotence of the Americans and British. Now he could focus his attention on the Wehrmacht's huge offensive to capture the Caucasian oil fields and put the Red Army out of the war.

Hitler's encouraging intelligence report from the FHW was a triumph for a supersecret British agency known as the XX-Committee ("Double-Cross Committee"). It had been organized in January 1941 under the strictest security, with the task of hoodwinking Adolf Hitler and the Oberkommando der Wehrmacht about Allied intentions and capabilities. In the shadow war of wits, the XX-Committee and the Fremde Heere West would emerge as clandestine archenemies.

A division of MI-5, the British counterintelligence agency, the XX-Committee for many weeks had been conducting a clandestine campaign to mask Operation Torch by convincing the Germans, through a worldwide program of stratagems, that the Western Allies did not have the potential for a large offensive. Then, as D-day for Torch neared and it became impossible to "hide" hundreds of Allied ships, the British would seek to confuse the Germans as to the convoys' destination.

As speculation grew that the Anglo-Americans were preparing for a massive blow—speculation often innocently abetted by the American and British press—British agents throughout the world began to spread rumors in a "sibs" campaign masterminded from London.*These rumors were whispered confidentially in embassies known to be sympa-

---

* *Sibs* was taken from the Latin *sibilare,* meaning to hiss.

thetic to the Nazi cause; in the Vatican, where German emissaries came in daily contact with Roman Catholic functionaries; and in bars and hotels from Rio de Janeiro to Tangier to Madrid to Lisbon to Ankara. There was a single theme: The Americans were not ready for war, and the British military machine had been disabled by three years of almost constant defeats.

A major component of this campaign was the use of "turned" Nazi spies apprehended by the XX-Committee in England. Scores of agents in the pay of the FHW or the Abwehr were unmasked and given a choice between being shot and switching their allegiance to the British to supply their former German masters with disinformation furnished by the XX-Committee. Few chose the firing squad.

To account for the increased activity in the British Isles and adjacent sea lanes, Allied agencies enlisted as a cover Operation Jupiter, a proposed attack in modest strength against Norway. Early in 1942, Winston Churchill had conceived and promoted Jupiter, adding background authenticity to the operation, but he had later quietly abandoned it in favor of Torch. Americans in the know at all levels now took delight in joining the duel of wits. Lieutenant Commander Harry Butcher, Eisenhower's aide and confidant, placed a pair of arctic boots and a heavily lined parka in a corner of his office. The cold-weather gear was quickly spotted, as Butcher knew it would be, by enterprising reporters alert for some clue to Allied plans. Within days, articles began appearing in American newspapers speculating that the Anglo-Americans might strike the Wehrmacht in an arctic locale. This could mean only Norway. .

These were hectic, tension-filled days and nights in a large Victorian stone mansion 40 miles north of London outside the little town of Bletchley Park, hard by the tracks of the London Midland and Scottish Railway. At this top-secret center, coded radio messages between Adolf Hitler and his generals were intercepted and deciphered, as were countless Wehrmacht commands. Even some U-boats in the Atlantic were receiving instructions that had been copied and understood by the British listeners. This fund of special intelligence was code-named

Ultra. Its existence would be the most successfully guarded Allied secret of the war.*

Ultra had its origin in 1939, just before the outbreak of war. British intelligence agents, together with the Polish secret service, had stolen a precise copy of the highly secret and complex German coding machine named Enigma. So sophisticated was Enigma that Hitler and the Wehrmacht considered its code unbreakable.

A team of Great Britain's leading cryptanalysts and mathematicians, working for months under the most intense secrecy, had solved the "unbreakable" Enigma code with the aid of another highly complex British machine—Ultra. From that point, German secret signals were intercepted by the British, decoded, and made available to a handful of top military and governmental officials. Often the British leaders were reading the secret German messages before the signals arrived at the desks of their intended German recipients.

Now, in the nerve-wracking period of early October 1942, the Bletchley Park nerve center was on guard for any indication, among hundreds of intercepted signals, that the Germans were aware of preparations for a strike at French Northwest Africa. Ultra ears were particularly searching the incoming messages for clues that the Abwehr or Fremde Heere West had been provided with copies of the entire Operation Torch plan after the British courier's body had been washed ashore in Spain.

As the days passed, there was relief in the Anglo-American high command: So far, the German assessment remained that the Western Allies were incapable of major offensive action. Ultra, however, remained vigilant; the situation could change at any moment.

Across the English Channel, the B-Dienst,† the German counterpart

---

* Not until 25 years after the end of World War II would Great Britain permit the world to learn of Ultra's existence. In the event of war with Russia during that period, Ultra would have been used again for decoding Russian wireless signals.

† For Beobachtungsdienst or observation service.

of Ultra, had been trying to uncover Anglo-American intentions through the intercept of Allied wireless signals. But having no system equivalent to Ultra, the Germans could not produce conclusive evidence of a looming Allied offensive. Unknown to the German high command, the XX-Committee was feeding B-Dienst with misleading information in a code which the British knew the Germans had cracked.

Only Winston Churchill and two or three senior people in his intelligence services were aware of a startling factor that helped befuddle the Führer and the Oberkommando. Admiral William Canaris, the spymaster of Abwehr, was secretly in league with the British. The fifty-five-year-old Canaris had been a highly successful spy in World War I, ferreting out secret Allied information for the Kaiser. Hawk-nosed, slightly stooped, keen of wit, the Abwehr chief was a conspirator in an ultrasecret group known as the Schwarze Kapelle (Black Orchestra), whose members were active and retired German generals and prominent civilian leaders dedicated to the overthrow (violent if need be) of Adolf Hitler.

Now Field Marshal Wilhelm Keitel, Hitler's austere advisor, was demanding that the Abwehr produce convincing evidence of Allied intentions. Can't do it, Canaris responded. All Abwehr sources seemed to have dried up.*

While German intelligence agencies labored feverishly to unlock the secret of Allied intentions, D-day for Torch drew closer and British and American security leaks began to multiply. The looming North African invasion was being discussed all but openly in London and Washington. At Claridge's in the British capital, an American naval officer with a few too many drinks under his belt complained loudly that he was being

---

* Over the decades, the British have steadfastly denied any clandestine connection with Admiral Canaris—even though Hitler had Canaris hanged as a traitor toward the end of the war for conspiring with the British to overthrow him. But curiously, years after the war, a high British official stood up in Parliament to recite a eulogy to Admiral Canaris—still never once acknowledging wartime collusion.

overworked in the name of an impending amphibious assault. General Eisenhower, learning of the incident, was furious. He called the offender to his office, read him out, and angrily instructed aides, "Send the son of a bitch home—on a slow boat!"

Another alarming incident occurred right in 20 Grosvenor Square on September 7. Page 117 from the daily diary kept for General Eisenhower by his naval aide, Lieutenant Commander Harry Butcher, came up missing. It had simply vanished. This page carried a top-secret directive from the Combined Chiefs of Staff outlining objectives for Torch. A frantic search by all ranks, from the supreme commander on down, failed to turn up missing page 117. Investigators concluded that it had become lost while an entire month's sheets were being sent to be microfilmed. Or had it? And why was only that one particularly revealing sheet missing?*

Another security flap erupted on September 19, when the London bureau manager of the United Press sent a message to his New York office alerting it that the invasion would take place in Casablanca and elsewhere in French Morocco. Investigators could not confront the UP man; to do so would have confirmed that his prediction had been accurate. Worse, it could not be determined whether the dangerous message had been sent by cable or by radio. A cable would have been reasonably secure, while there was an excellent chance that German monitors across the Channel would have picked up a radio message. It was one more worry for Torch commanders and planners.

A confidential secretary in a London military office broke regulations and took home a top-secret memorandum from Churchill to his chiefs of staff suggesting that a *fourth* landing be made, this one at Bône, 210 miles east of Algiers. While boarding a bus to go home, the memo, one of several he had carried with him, fell out of his pocket. A housemaid found the secret document, looked at it curiously, and took it home, where she turned it over to a soldier who was billeted there. Seeing the words MOST SECRET stamped on the memorandum, he took it directly

---

* As far as is known, the missing page was never located.

to the Air Ministry and turned it over to the chief of staff. Had this critical document been seen—or photographed—by hostile parties? Intelligence officers had no way of knowing.

As with Torch planners in the United States, keeping secret the printing and distribution to units of thousands of military maps was a monumental task for the British. They had their maps printed in a small shop in a country town at a distance from London, away from the prying eyes of Abwehr agents. But while one large batch of maps was being trucked to various military commands, the covering on one container flew open and maps of Algeria and French Morocco were scattered for hundreds of yards along the road. Gusts of wind blew countless copies into the fields. The driver kept going, unaware that he was leaving a stream of top-secret maps in his wake. A short time later, two local policemen on routine patrol discovered and examined the maps. Noting locales in French Northwest Africa, they gathered up as many maps as they could find and took them to their station. From there they telephoned the headquarters of de Gaulle's Free French in London: "Are you folks missing a large bunch of maps of Algeria and French Morocco?"

From a security point of view, it would have been difficult to pick a worse place to phone—short of the Oberkommando der Wehrmacht in Berlin. The Americans and British had continued to keep General de Gaulle in the dark on Torch, fearing leaks. Miraculously, the de Gaulle officer on the line showed no interest in the find.

Even Winston Churchill himself unwittingly contributed to the danger that the secret of Torch might fall into German hands. Churchill loved talking on the telephone, and often on impulse would call President Roosevelt, using the private line in his underground bunker in London.

Churchill considered his overseas link with Roosevelt to be secure from eavesdroppers because a sophisticated "scrambler" mixed up his words as they were spoken, then unscrambled them when his words passed through Roosevelt's private phone. The prime minister used code words whenever possible, but did not know that the Germans *were* listening in. Despite the scrambler and the code words, they may have ferreted out considerable useful information. German intelligence had learned of the scrambler on the private Churchill-Roosevelt connection and developed means for unscrambling at least parts of the high-level conversations. The Wehrmacht eavesdropping was done from a highly technical facility built on the English Channel coast in the Netherlands.*

The Anglo-American high command and those charged with the security of Torch were still worried that the third major ally, Russia, might tip off the Germans on the impending assault against French Northwest Africa, hoping to draw the British and Americans deeper into the bloodletting. Churchill had told Stalin the previous August of Anglo-American plans for Torch. Only the timing of D-day, which had not yet been selected, was withheld from the Soviets.

Now, in early October, a bombshell dropped on the Western Allied leaders in London. The Russian ambassador to England, Ivan Maisky, leaked the outline of Torch to two reporters in London. General Eisenhower, Churchill, and British security authorities were dumbfounded. Maisky, an experienced, intelligent diplomat, must have realized the extreme danger of leaking such crucial secrets. Had he acted on instructions from Stalin? There was nothing the Anglo-Americans could do about it; after all, Ambassador Maisky *was* an "ally."

Meanwhile, at Fremde Heere West in Zossen, near Berlin, reports were arriving from French Northwest Africa that large numbers of American spies were pouring into the region under the guise of embassy clerks, consuls, and legation guards. Fanning out, the Americans had begun reconnoitering harbors at Casablanca, Oran, Algiers, and elsewhere—under the eyes of experienced German agents.

So transparent had been the infiltration of these novice American spies, and so obvious were their espionage efforts, that the Fremde Heere West considered the entire cloak-and-dagger operation an elaborate *ruse de guerre* to deceive the Germans into believing that an invasion

---

* Anthony Cave Brown, the foremost authority on clandestine operations in World War II and author of the 1975 book *Bodyguard of Lies,* said that high German intelligence chiefs said after the war that the Germans continued to listen to the Churchill-Roosevelt telephone conversations to at least the spring of 1944.

of French Northwest Africa was being prepared. What the FHW did not know was that this was the first major mission for the fledgling U.S. Office of Strategic Services (OSS), formed and led by a prominent Wall Street banker turned master spy, Colonel William J. "Wild Bill" Donovan. The OSS had been hastily thrown together when President Roosevelt and other leaders recognized that the nation had been plunged into global war "blind"—without any centralized intelligence and espionage service. Now, only a few months after its inception, the OSS was being asked to match wits with a Germany steeped in centuries of clandestine operations on an international scale.

On a warm afternoon in early October, Donald Q. Coster, a young vice consul at the American embassy in Casablanca, was seated alone in a dingy waterfront café there. The soft-spoken New Yorker had been a Madison Avenue advertising executive, but had dropped that career in favor of the challenge of an overseas assignment with the State Department. Two young men passed Coster's table, and since the café was crowded the vice consul invited them to join him. The newcomers said they were Austrians who had been in France when the Wehrmacht struck in 1940; they had been interned by the Vichy French and had later escaped to Casablanca. The one who said his name was Walter was talkative and told of "running on to Teddy Auer" on a Casablanca street.

The name rang a bell with Coster—then a chill shot up the American vice consul's spine. Teddy Auer was Major General Theodore Auer, the sinister chief of the German Armistice Commission, whose function was to "assist" the French in governing Algeria and French Morocco. Auer's spy system in Northwest Africa was efficient and ruthless.

"I knew him [General Auer] in Paris before the war," Walter was saying. "We made a deal with him. We supply him with secret information and he keeps us out of jail." Walter quickly assured Coster that "we're both very anti-Nazi, of course, and we want Hitler's ass."

Don Coster's mind was in a whirl. Here, by accident, was the pipeline he had been seeking to the sinister General Auer. For Coster was a spy —albeit a new one—for Wild Bill Donovan's OSS. A few weeks before, Donovan had called Coster into his office to tell him he was being sent to Casablanca, "the most important place in the world at this moment."

The World War I legend and holder of the Congressional Medal of Honor added that French Northwest Africa would be invaded "one of these days." (If Coster did not know the date of D-day, Gestapo torturers could not extract it from him.) The former ad exec's mission was to try to make General Auer and the German Armistice Commission believe that, "if and when we invade," the attack will be at Dakar. How Coster accomplished that goal, the heavily burdened Donovan had said, would be up to him.

Dakar, some two thousand miles south of Casablanca, was a plausible point for an Allied invasion. It was directly across from Brazil, which had declared war on Nazi Germany in August, becoming the first South American country to do so. Brazil was a logical springboard for an invasion of Africa.

Young Coster, an instant spy, swallowed hard. He wondered why he had left the advertising business, where the worst hazards were irate clients. He knew little more about spying than what he had seen in Hollywood movies. OSS had pounded into his head that General Auer was cunning, ruthless, and knew all the tricks. Had these two friendly Austrians been planted to draw him out? Or did they really hate Nazis? With visions of himself sprawled dead in a dark Casablanca alley, Coster decided to risk it. He would pose as a loudmouthed rich playboy, who drank too much and talked too much. While drunk he would "spill the beans" that the Western Allies were planning on invading Dakar.

The "vice consul's" judgment of his two new friends proved accurate. A few days later Walter and his friend told General Auer of the drunken State Department official's revelation that Dakar was the Allied target. General Auer was delighted. He broke open a bottle of champagne and shared it with his two crack Austrian agents.

Meanwhile, back in the United States, on the night of October 10, the hastily trained, partially equipped men of Major General Ernest N. Harmon's 2nd Armored Division were conducting a final practice amphibious landing before departing for the beaches near Casablanca. A "dry run," the GIs called such an exercise. In the darkness, 2nd Armored troops slithered down rope ladders on ships in Maryland's Chesapeake Bay, scrambled into small assault boats, and headed for designated points on shore. The boat coxswains were sailors of Rear Admiral Lyal

A. Davidson's task force, which would carry Harmon and his soldiers to North Africa. The beam of a lighthouse on shore helped guide these novice navigators to their targets. Even so, the dry run was a fiasco. Only one boat, carrying General Harmon, reached its target. The remainder of the assault boats were scattered for miles up and down Maryland's coastline, and it took until noon the following day to round up all the stray lambs.

Privately, Ernie Harmon, a scrappy, salty-tongued fighting man who had been decorated in World War I, was brought to near-despair by the disastrous dress rehearsal. "If they can't find an objective in peaceful Chesapeake Bay, with a lighthouse beacon to help," he complained to an aide, "how are they going to find an objective in darkness on a foreign shore and under conditions of war?"

Harmon, known to his colleagues as "Old Gravel Voice," was not the only American combat commander alarmed and depressed at the prospect of taking a poorly trained and ill-equipped force into battle. In Washington, General Patton was using terms like "gloom" in his personal diary. To Eisenhower, however, he wrote, "You can rest assured that when we start for the beach we shall stay there, whether dead or alive, and if alive, we will not surrender." Paradoxically, he ended his note by saying, "I shall have complete confidence in the operation [Torch]."

Whatever his real thoughts, outwardly General Patton was characteristically buoyant. But on October 20—three days before his Western Task Force would shove off for Africa—Patton wrote a letter to his wife Beatrice with instructions that it was to be opened "only when and if I am definitely reported dead." To his brother-in-law, friend, and confidant Frederick Ayer, Patton poured out his true feelings in a note:

> *The job I am going on is about as desperate a venture as has ever been undertaken by any force in the world's history.*

The general asked Ayer to take care of his wife and children "should anything happen to me."

Yet later that day, Patton and his former sparring partner in the bureaucracy, Admiral Kent Hewitt (their relationship was now one of mutual respect, even friendship), made a farewell call on President Roosevelt at the White House in Washington. Patton was at his fire-eating best, and the fact that he was talking with the President of the United States only slightly inhibited his exuberant profanity. Taking his leave, the general reassured Roosevelt: "Sir, all I want to tell you is this—I will leave the goddamned beaches either a conqueror or a corpse."

In the meantime, a harassed and overburdened General Eisenhower had dug himself out from under a mountain of work in London to travel to Inverary in western Scotland. Ike was to witness a night amphibious landing by the 1st Infantry Division, regarded as one of the army's best trained. The supreme commander was appalled by what he saw.

The men of the Big Red One were to storm ashore in the darkness along a stretch of beach on a huge loch, capture several "enemy" coastal batteries, then plunge inland to seize a "German" airport. On the run into the beach, some assault craft got lost. Once the troops, who looked physically fit and were in high spirits, reached the shore, they milled about—not knowing what to do next. Eisenhower was disconsolate. He was especially concerned over the inexperience of the lieutenants, captains, and majors. He strode up to a captain who was holding a bazooka. "Do you know how that bazooka is to be used in combat?" he asked.

"No, sir," was the frank reply. "We just got one a couple of days ago. All I know about it is hearsay."

The supreme commander winced.

Back at his desk at 20 Grosvenor Square two days later, Eisenhower buzzed his naval aide, Lieutenant Commander Butcher. The general had told the former Columbia Broadcasting System vice president several weeks before, "Butch, why I want you around is because I have to have someone I can let my hair down to occasionally without it being blabbed all over hell's half-acre." Now the downcast supreme commander was letting his hair down. Crowning his monumental pile of problems was the poor showing made by the Big Red One in the Scotland exercise. Eisenhower told Butcher that he was in a "state of the jitters" and could not concentrate. His frame of mind was a reflection of the enormous burden that had been suffocating him night and day for several months.

8

A Cloak-and-Dagger Mission

At 9:55 A.M. on Sunday, October 18, General Mark Clark strode into his office at Norfolk House and was greeted by his chief of staff, Brigadier General Al Gruenther. The forty-two-year-old Gruenther, who had a photographic memory, a keen intellect, and was an expert at bridge, was clearly excited.

"I've got a message for you," Gruenther declared. "And it's red hot."

Clark's curiosity was piqued. He had received messages marked TOP SECRET and EYES ONLY, but could not recall receiving a signal described as "red hot." It was a message to Eisenhower from General George Marshall in Washington. Clark had just started to read it when the red telephone, a direct scrambled line between Norfolk House and 20 Grosvenor Square, jangled impatiently. Clark snatched up the instrument.

"Come up," Eisenhower said crisply. "Come right away!" The Allied commander replaced the phone without awaiting a reply.

Mark Clark rushed the two miles to Grosvenor Square. Walking into Eisenhower's office, he said, "When do I go?"

"Probably right away," Eisenhower replied.

The "red hot" cable from General Marshall was the text of an urgent signal from Robert Murphy (code name: Colonel McGowan), then in Algiers, who had the impressive title Consul of Embassy on Special Mission to French North Africa. With his numerous contacts with high-level French military and political figures in North Africa, Murphy was actually a shrewd upper-grade espionage agent for the United States. Murphy said that he had been in close touch with General Charles Emmanuel Mast, French commander in chief in Algiers, and that Mast had asked urgently that an American delegation slip into North Africa to confer with him and French officers on Allied plans for Torch.

An isolated house along the Mediterranean coast had been selected for the rendezvous site, Murphy wrote. Mast's startling signal indicated that it could be arranged for the French army to cooperate with the Allies instead of fighting them. It implied that if General Henri-Honoré Giraud, then in Vichy France under close surveillance by Hitler's secret police, could be spirited out of his homeland to take part in the covert conference, conditions would be improved for gaining the cooperation of the French armed forces in North Africa.

Giraud, it will be recalled, was the celebrated French military figure who had been captured by the Germans in 1940, been held prisoner in Germany, and had slipped back into France after a daring escape. Giraud was considered to be the most desirable candidate to take over French leadership in North Africa once the Allies had invaded.

General Mast's signal specified that the American delegation should come into Algeria by submarine, and that it should be headed by a "senior general officer." Mark Clark was itching to be that senior general; Eisenhower already had Clark in mind for the job.

There was elation in Eisenhower's office. Here was a plan that might turn the entire Torch operation into a quick success—perhaps even allowing American troops to come ashore without a shot being fired. The secret mission to Algeria might fail, but what was there to lose, except the lives of the promising young American major general and those he chose to accompany him? Clark, excited as a schoolboy, understood the peril involved and shrugged it off.

General Mast had stipulated as the rendezvous date the night of October 21, only four days away. Eisenhower, Clark, and their staff officers quickly selected the men who would take part in the covert mission: Brigadier General Lyman L. Lemnitzer, chief of the Allied Force Plans Section, who was intimately conversant with Torch details; Colonel A. L. Hamblen, a shipping and supply expert; U.S. Navy Captain Jerauld Wright; and Colonel Julius C. Holmes, a former State Department official whose role would be that of political expert. Holmes spoke French fluently.

On into the afternoon, 20 Grosvenor Square bustled with activity. The party would fly to Gibraltar in two four-engine Flying Fortresses. Highly dangerous, warned air corps experts. No B-17 had ever landed in the small Gibraltar airfield, and there was doubt it could even be done. Clark would be in one aircraft and General Lemnitzer in the other, so that if Clark's plane was lost or shot down, Lemnitzer could continue with the mission. A British submarine would carry the delegation from Gibraltar to the Algerian coast.

At a specified time, longitude, and latitude, the submarine was to surface offshore, and the Americans were to look for a white light shone from a window, indicating that the meeting area was not under surveillance.

There was substantial risk of an ambush. Germans with French passports were reported to be infiltrating into North Africa. Intelligence services declared that some 500 Germans had already been given French passports. This host of Nazi agents, together with untold numbers of Algerians in the pay of the Führer, would greatly increase chances of the Oberkommando der Wehrmacht's learning of Torch. And if General Charles Mast in Algiers had learned of impending plans for an Allied invasion, how many other French officers—whether pro-Allied or pro-German—were aware that North Africa would soon be assaulted? Five? Ten? A hundred? Five hundred?

Other alarming pieces of intelligence began to dovetail that afternoon in Dwight Eisenhower's office. Recently Robert Murphy in Algiers had been asked to a secret meeting with the chief of Vichy French intelligence, a session conducted in a lonely farm area to avoid detection by the Abwehr. Murphy was shocked by what he had learned. The French intelligence head told him that he had been advised by both the Germans and the Japanese that North Africa was about to be invaded by the Allies. Hitler, the Frenchman told Murphy, was vigorously "urging" French leaders to resist the invaders to the utmost. Otherwise, Hitler's spokesmen had hinted, the Wehrmacht might be rushed in and take over French territories in northwest Africa. Worse, Hitler had arranged with Spain for the Wehrmacht to use the Spanish mainland and Spanish Morocco as bases for striking against an Allied invasion of northwest Africa. General Francisco Franco, who had maintained an officially neutral stance, was known to lean toward Adolf Hitler and Germany. Because of all these factors, it was vital that the invasion come "in a matter of days," the French intelligence chief had warned.

It was almost dark on October 18, a day after "Colonel McGowan's" report reached the American high command, by the time General Clark and his party arrived at an Eighth Air Force base at Polbrook, 75 miles northwest of London. Clark had replaced the two stars on his uniform with the silver leaves of a lieutenant colonel. Should he fall into hostile hands, he might have a better chance at escaping if his captors did not immediately know that they had bagged a top general.*

Stormy weather delayed their takeoff. Not a good omen, the American delegation agreed. Clark hopped onto a small cot in a tiny barracks room, but sleep wouldn't come. His mind was awhirl. If the party was late in arriving at the house on this forlorn sector of Algerian coast, it might affront the French delegation. If the Americans were unable to reach the site at all, the French might question the good faith of the United States leadership.

Clark was also concerned for the safety of his party. The summons could be a trick, perhaps orchestrated by the German Abwehr to capture him and obtain the invasion plans. Before leaving London, the general had left a note to be delivered to Mrs. Clark in Washington in the event he did not return.

He had finally fallen into fitful sleep when he was shaken awake. It was 6:30 A.M. Time to depart. German fighter planes were reported to

---

* Mark Clark had put on the lieutenant colonel's insignia before leaving London. A few officers had seen Clark wearing the silver leaves and there was wild conjecture as to whether he had "screwed up royally" and been "busted" three ranks.

be active along the English coast that morning. Clark then learned that his two B-17s would fly unescorted.

Climbing aboard the Flying Fortress, the *Red Gremlin,* piloted by Major Paul Tibbets, Clark issued an order that under no circumstances was either aircraft to land in Spain or Portugal.* It was not reassuring to anyone on board to note that all the secret documents were being carried in a tube heavily weighted to sink at sea.

At Gibraltar, Lemnitzer's plane touched down safely—the first B-17 ever to do so on the short strip of blacktop. The *Red Gremlin* followed, and several British soldiers rushed toward the parked planes gesturing for everyone to stay inside. An officer explained to Clark that Nazi agents had the Gibraltar airstrip under surveillance, that the strip was only 300 yards from Spanish territory, and that the curiosity of the enemy spies aroused by the appearance of the first Flying Fortresses ever to land there ought not to be rewarded by having a delegation of high officers get out of the aircraft. "We're sitting here in a goldfish bowl," the British officer explained.

It was suggested that General Clark and the others remove their coats and hats. This done, a large automobile with drawn blinds pulled up next to the B-17 doors. The Americans leaped in and were whisked off to the house of Gibraltar's governor, Lieutenant General F. N. Mason-McFarlane.

Clark quickly entered into solemn discussion with several British admirals and the Royal Navy's commander of submarines in the Mediterranean, Captain Barney Fawkes. The American, though customarily resolute, was inwardly doubtful about the success of the enterprise. There were too many unknown factors; the mission had been mounted with too much haste. Clark badly needed encouraging words that he failed to receive.

The British navy officers, Clark gathered, seemed to believe that this whole thing was a crazy adventure dreamed up by inexperienced Yanks. They talked of the shoreline in Algeria being infested by hostile patrols, of spotting planes making systematic flights over the Mediterranean,

---

* In 1945, as a colonel, Tibbets would pilot the *Enola Gay,* a B-29, which dropped the atom bomb on Hiroshima.

and of a French army and navy alert for intruders. Finally Clark told them, "Gentlemen, we're going, come hell or high water."

Depressed by it all, General Clark had a visitor, Royal Navy Lieutenant Norman Ambury Auchileck Jewell, the handsome young skipper of the submarine HMS *Seraph*. Jewell made an immediately favorable impression. Unlike the others, he was brimming with confidence.

Clark inquired, "Lieutenant, do you know what this is all about?"

"All they told me, sir, was that I was to take some Americans some place and land them at night on the African coast, then bring them out again."

Clark explained the mission, searching Jewell's face for indications of pessimism. The navy officer said reassuringly: "I'm sure we can get you in there and get you out again."

There was no time to lose. After dark, the American party scrambled aboard the *Seraph*, and minutes later the submarine cast off. Already on board were British Commando Captain Godfrey B. "Jumbo" Courtney and a few of his men, who would go ashore with the delegation.

Clark had never been on a submarine before and quickly found that the craft was not constructed for six-foot-three-inch men. He had to move around stooped over at all times, and when going to the head had to crawl there on all fours. But he was impressed with the efficiency and cheerfulness of the British crew, most of them youngsters. "Do you know what your sub is up to?" Clark asked a two-headed youth.

"Oh, yes, sir," was the prompt reply. "We were told we're taking some Americans on some crazy mission."

That night the *Seraph* ran on the surface. After daybreak, Clark and Lieutenant Jewell agreed that they could not possibly reach the rendezvous point on time inching along at two or three knots under water. They would continue on the surface in daylight—and take their chances.

That night Clark and his fellow landlubbers managed to get some sleep. But the Americans awoke with a start at 6:30 A.M.—the dive klaxons were sounding. Lieutenant Jewell assured the army officers that they were not under attack, but that with the sub now so close to the North African coast it would be foolish to continue running on the surface.

Shortly before dawn on October 21, Lieutenant Jewell surfaced *Seraph* off the rendezvous point. The sea was calm, the wind still; it was ghostlike. On the submarine's bridge, the only sound was the gentle lapping of the water against the hull. On shore a white light was spotted, but it was too near daybreak to risk landing.

Jewell took the boat down again, and his frustrated passengers prepared for another day in the cramped space. When it was daylight, a periscope was run up for a few seconds and the house on shore reconnoitered. Yes, that's the one, it was agreed. Two hours after dawn, two fishing boats dropped their anchors directly between the rendezvous house and the submarine. A trap? Lieutenant Jewell edged the *Seraph* back out to sea.

Then the sub's radio crackled. It was "Colonel McGowan" calling from a clandestine location in Algiers, 60 miles away. Before shoving off, Mark Clark had made arrangements for Robert Murphy as McGowan to contact the French conspirators and set a new date for the rendezvous if Clark's party could not arrive in time.

Murphy's coded signal alarmed the landing party. The first word decoded was *police*. With relief, it was discovered that the sub's radiomen were using the wrong code book.

When the message was finally decoded correctly, it said that the rendezvous had been reset for the night of October 21–22, and that if no contact was made at that time the "interested parties" would expect Clark the following night, October 22–23. That meant one, possibly two more days lying underwater off the Algerian coast. Clark's concerns were not allayed by the knowledge that General Patton's force for Torch had already sailed from the United States.

A quick conference decided that in the event Lieutenant Jewell on *Seraph* heard nothing after the delegation had gone ashore, the boat was to loiter submerged five miles offshore for 24 hours; then, if still no signal was heard from the shore party, *Seraph* was to return to Gibraltar without them.

Shortly after dark the submarine surfaced. At midnight the Americans on deck spotted a white light at the house, beaming out to sea. Jewell edged the vessel closer to shore, then stopped. Silently the Americans began scrambling into tiny folbots, frail and tipsy craft, for the long paddle to the beach.

The shoreline, covered by a fine haze, was approached in a V formation. In the lead folbot was Colonel Julius Holmes and Captain R. B. Livingstone. Clark's boat and the others remained 200 yards offshore until a coded flashlight signal from the beach indicated that Holmes and Livingstone had landed and that all was clear.

Reaching shore, the Americans glanced around. The beach seemed deserted. A few hundred yards ahead, looking very black and ominous, was a high cliff. Carrying their boats, Clark and the others made a dash for the cover of the wooded elevation. Just as the Americans started up the incline they heard an alarming rustling noise ahead. Several people were picking their way down the bluff. Clark and the others pulled out their pistols and froze.

Suddenly the shadowy shapes of a few men emerged into a clearing and moved directly toward the stone-still Americans. No one showed a light. A low American voice from the unknown group called out softly, "Welcome to North Africa!" It was Robert Murphy, the underground chief. The men with him were French officers.

The newly landed delegation heaved sighs of relief. They had not fallen into a Nazi trap. For several days, Clark had been honing a short speech which he intended to deliver in French, but in his excitement and exertion, carrying a folbot and other gear, Clark forgot about his prepared oration. Instead he pumped Murphy's arm and said seriously, "I'm damned glad we made it."*

Quickly the two groups climbed up the steep path to the rendezvous house, a red-roofed French colonial villa of white stone enclosing a courtyard. Only 100 feet away was the main highway to Algiers. The villa's wealthy owner, Monsieur Tessier, had sent five Arab servants away for several days to protect the secrecy of the conference.

---

* Mark Clark must have indeed been at an emotional peak to have used the word *damned*. Seldom did he employ even mild profanity. Instead, when thoroughly riled on occasion, Clark would explode with "Ybsob!" Only the initiated knew that stood for "yellow-bellied son of a bitch."

"Where's General Mast?" Clark asked.

"General Mast is driving from Algiers," a French officer replied. "He will be here about five A.M." Algiers was 60 miles away.

Almost at the predicted time, General Mast arrived. He spoke little English, but his first words were: "Welcome to my country."

Eating a breakfast of coffee, bread, jam, and sardines on a small table in the living room, Clark, Mast, and Robert Murphy discussed military strategy in North Africa. Clark could talk only in generalities. This still might be a ruse to extract Allied intentions from the American officers. He conveyed the impression to General Mast that the Allies were in the early planning stages for an operation "somewhere in the Mediterranean." The American was on guard against revealing to the French commander in Algeria the fact that large Torch elements were already at sea.

Although Mast's true allegiances were unknown, Clark became increasingly impressed with the courtly, soldierly man's sincerity. It was an uncomfortable moment when the French general asked: "How large will the American effort be?"

"Half a million Allied troops could come in," Clark improvised, "and we could put about two thousand aircraft and hundreds of navy ships." General Mast was impressed by so massive a potential for invasion.* Clark gained the impression—rightly—that Mast in fact knew the Allies had something big in the works.

At noon, General Mast had to return to duties in Algiers. Nazi agents had been shadowing him, and he did not want to arouse suspicions by a longer absence. All that afternoon, General Mast's officers produced voluminous written information: locations and strengths of French army and naval units; sites where gasoline, ammunition, and supplies were stored; details about which airports would be heavily defended and others on which paratroopers could land with less opposition.

It was about 4:00 P.M. when the telephone jangled impatiently. Tessier answered, then whirled around and shouted: "Get out! The police will be here in a few minutes!"

---

* Actually, 112,000 Americans and British would go ashore in the first Torch landings, supported by only some 160 warplanes.

French officers dashed in every direction, some leaping through windows. Others changed quickly into civilian clothes, then bolted for the doors. Some scrambled for the cover of the brush along the beach; others jumped into cars and sped off toward Algiers. Can't blame them, Clark thought. The Frenchmen's lives would be in jeopardy if they were caught conspiring with the enemy.

Clark raced up the stairs and called to the sleeping British commandos. "Where shall we go?" they replied. "Take to the woods on the beach," Clark shouted, "and get the folbots out of here—fast!" But time had run out. Only one commando, carrying a walkie-talkie radio, reached the beach to warn the waiting submarine of the raid. Tessier just managed to lock up the room in which the boats had been stashed when a police car pulled up in a swirl of dust.

Tessier motioned the Americans through a trap door from the patio into a wine cellar. Clutching musette bags loaded with incriminating French documents, the Americans hustled into the cellar.

Tessier, Robert Murphy, and Murphy's assistant, Ridgeway Knight, sat calmly in the living room as the police banged on the front door, then Tessier let them in. The three conspirators put on a superb display. They greeted the policemen warmly, offered them drinks, and clanked bottles around. In the pitch-dark cellar, the Americans crouched tensely, hardly daring to breathe. They could hear every word being spoken above them.

Murphy, a touch of indignation in his voice, identified himself as the American consul in Algiers. Then, retreating a little into embarrassment, he explained that there were women in the upstairs rooms and he would appreciate it if the police did not compound his difficulties by poking into the love chambers. Still suspicious, the police moved about the downstairs, obviously searching for something. Clark and the others in the cellar presently heard the footsteps near the trap door.

Clark knelt at the foot of the steps, holding a carbine. If the police came down the stairs, he intended for his group to shoot their way out if need be. He hoped it would not happen that way. A shoot-out would certainly attract attention, and it might be many hours before the Americans could reach the submarine.

The police footsteps halted. Were they suspicious of the trap door and what might be underneath? At that moment, one of those crouching down below, British Commando Captain Jumbo Courtney, was seized with a coughing fit. Sputtering and gagging in the blackness, he finally whispered to Clark, "General, I'm afraid I'll choke."

The irritated Clark whispered back: "And I'm afraid you won't."

For a full hour the police moved around. Finally they told Tessier that they would have to drive back to town to check with their chief for further instructions. But, the stern-faced policemen assured Tessier, they were convinced that something suspicious was afoot.*

Only much later would Clark and the others learn what had caused the police raid: Tessier's Arab servants had become suspicious at being sent away. After spotting footprints on the beach, they had gone to the police in Cherchel, a small town a short distance away.

After the police had driven off, those in the cellar heard the trap door being opened. "This is Bob," Murphy called down. "They've gone, but they'll be back."

"How soon?" Clark asked as he climbed out of the wine cellar, blinking.

"Pretty damned soon," Murphy said. "You'd better get the hell out of here."

The folbots were lugged from Tessier's house to the beach, where the conspirators hid in nearby woods until darkness. Captain Livingstone had notified the *Seraph* offshore that the landing party was in trouble and would try to make it to the submarine at once. The waves were up now, but Clark was determined to get out to the *Seraph*. Knowing that he would get soaked, Clark took off his trousers and stripped to his shorts and OD shirt. He put his moneybelt, containing a few hundred dollars in gold he had brought along to buy the landing party out of trouble, into his rolled-up trousers, leaped into a folbot, and began paddling.†

---

* General Mark Clark recognized that Tessier was a true French patriot for risking his life by letting the meeting be held at his home. Later Clark obtained a commission in the French army for Tessier and had him assigned to Clark's headquarters, where he served for the remainder of the war.

† Later, when the clandestine adventure was made public, United States media tried to outdo each other in specifying the amount of money in gold General

It was bitterly cold in the water. When a wave overturned Clark's folbot, he had to swim back to shore and he could not locate his trousers. The capsizing convinced the party that launching was impossible with the sea as rough as it was. They slipped back into the woods.

A Frenchman was sent into Cherchel with a pocket full of gold to try to buy or rent a boat, but the impoverished fishermen there, suspicious of a stranger waving gold, would not take the risk. Stealing an automobile and driving west to Spanish Morocco was discussed and rejected; the nominally neutral Spaniards could scarcely be trusted.

It was now near midnight—dark and foreboding. Huddling in the woods, Clark and his team were chilled, wet, exhausted and hungry. The general, with no trousers, was the coldest of all. Clark decided to climb the bluff to Tessier's house to get some food and warm clothing, hoping that the police were not back yet. Tessier, urging Clark to leave promptly, gave the general bread and wine, two sweaters—and a crucially needed pair of pants. At that moment, headlights split the darkness; the police were already back.

"For God's sake, get the hell out of here," Tessier said.

Clark needed no urging. Barefoot, his soles already sliced up by jagged rocks during the upward climb, he leaped over a cement wall and dropped ten feet to a jarring landing on the path to the beach. Limping painfully, the general arrived back at the shoreline woods. It was 1:30 A.M.

At 4:00 A.M., with daylight approaching, police searching the area, and the *Seraph* only three-quarters of a mile out and in danger of detection, Clark decided another try would have to be made. The party scrambled back into their folbots, whereupon several overturned, soaking secret French papers in the musette bags and briefcases.

Clark felt he had been paddling for hours. Finally a black shape emerged ahead—he and his companion had nearly paddled into the *Seraph*. The other boats, righted after overturning, arrived shortly afterward. The last was Colonel Holmes's boat. A big wave smashed it into the submarine, breaking its fragile wooden supports. Holmes barely scrambled up onto the Seraph before the little boat, carrying Holmes's

---

Clark had been carrying. The speculative figure eventually reached several million dollars instead of the actual few hundred.

briefcase stuffed with French documents, disappeared under the water.

Clark knew that a folbot had an air pocket at each end which might refloat it. If it were washed up onto the beaches and the secret documents fell into hostile hands, Robert Murphy, Tessier, General Mast, and other conspirators on shore would be cashiered. But there was no time to search for the briefcase. The sky was already lightening and Lieutenant Jewell said he would have to submerge.

As the *Seraph* headed for home, the shivering landing party put a considerable dent in one of His Majesty's rum kegs, which Royal Navy submarines carried for emergencies. But not before General Clark affixed his signature to a formal document declaring that this situation was, indeed, an "emergency."

On October 24, one week after Clark's departure from London, a Gibraltar-based flying boat assigned to the mission by Prime Minister Churchill landed next to the surfaced *Seraph* in mid-Mediterranean. Clark, concerned that he would not arrive in time for his documents to assist Torch, had radioed for the Catalina to pick up his delegation.

Standing on the deck of the submarine, Lieutenant Jewell and his crew cheered as the Catalina, with Clark and the others aboard, raced along over the water past the *Seraph* and lifted off. Gazing out a window, Mark Clark saluted the British sailors. "Gallant men," he said to his seatmate. It seemed to the general that he had spent half of his life under water.

The French resented the 1940 British attack on the French fleet at Oran. In the foreground is the Provence. *Behind it to the right is the battleship* Strasbourg, *which reached the safety of the open sea. Burning fiercely is the* Bretagne. (National Archives)

This cargo vessel, being torpedoed, was one of four or five a day being sunk by German submarines off America's eastern seaboard by mid-1942. (National Archives)

A U.S. Navy blimp, on the lookout for U-boats, hovers over a convoy off the eastern seaboard of the United States. (U.S. Navy)

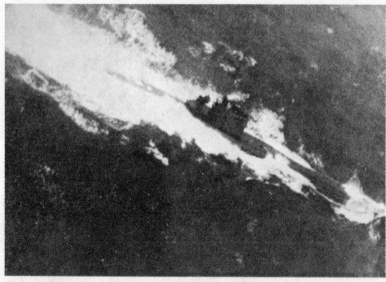

German submarine U-402 sinking after being struck by a 500-pound bomb from a U.S. Navy patrol plane off the east coast of the United States. (U.S. Navy)

Despite Allied warships, a U-boat torpedoes a ship in a convoy bound for England. Such bold action threatened the mounting of Operation Torch. (U.S. Coast Guard)

Disabled by depth charges from U.S. Coast Guard cutter Spencer, *this U-boat was riddled by gunfire and sank a few moments later.* (U.S. Coast Guard)

A member of a sunken U-boat's crew pleads for rescue from the Atlantic waters. A U.S. vessel picked him up. (U.S. Coast Guard)

U.S. Coast Guardsmen watch from the deck of a cutter in an Atlantic convoy as a depth charge explodes. The attack forced a U-boat to the surface. (U.S. Coast Guard)

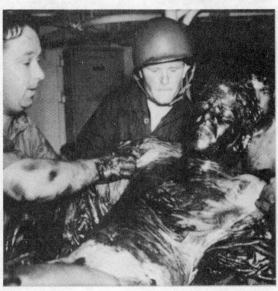

A badly injured seaman, covered with oil, moments after being pulled from the water. His ship was torpedoed during the run across the Atlantic. (U.S. Coast Guard)

Marshal Henri Pétain shakes hands with German Führer Adolf Hitler. (U.S. Army)

W. Averell Harriman, Roosevelt's troubleshooter. (National Archives)

Harry Hopkins, President Roosevelt's trusted civilian advisor. (National Archives)

Admiral Ernest J. King wanted a primary effort made in the Pacific. (U.S. Navy)

Robert D. Murphy, American master spy. (U.S. Army)

General Dwight D. Eisenhower. (U.S. Army)

Brigadier General James H.
Doolittle. (U.S. Army)

Admiral Karl Dönitz. (U.S. Army)

Lieutenant General George S. Patton. (U.S.
Army)

The Big Three: Prime Minister Winston Churchill, President Franklin Roosevelt, Premier Josef Stalin. (National Archives)

Field Marshal John Dill ("The Americans are thoroughly organized for peace"). (National Archives)

General Alan Brooke, General George Marshall's sparring partner, opposed a cross-Channel attack in 1942. (National Archives)

German Enigma. *Its code was unbreakable, Hitler thought.* (National Archives)

U.S. Secretary of War Henry L. Stimson. (U.S. Army)

Rear Admiral H. Kent Hewitt. (U.S. Navy)

Operation Torch headquarters were deep inside the Rock of Gibraltar. (Author's collection)

Marshal Henri Pétain's huge photo was prominently displayed in most large buildings in French Northwest Africa, where he was highly regarded as a hero and patriot. (U.S. Army)

Major General Mark W. Clark (saluting), Eisenhower's deputy and chief planner for Torch, and Major William P. Yarborough, who planned and participated in America's first paratroop operation. (Author's collection)

Bleak coast of North Africa where General Mark Clark landed by submarine on a secret mission just before Torch. (Mark W. Clark)

House atop bluff where General Clark met with pro-Allied French officers. (Mark W. Clark)

Basement where General Clark and his party hid from French police officers. (Mark W. Clark)

9

"The Entire U-boat Pack is Lying in Wait!"

Storm demons were loose over southwestern Scotland on the morning of October 21. It was cold, miserable, and sheets of rain pelted the broad expanse of the Clyde River on the Atlantic Ocean near Glasgow. Many miles to the south, at the bustling English port of Liverpool, the weather was just as bad.

At both locales, day and night for 48 hours, British trains loaded with American troops, bone-tired after long journeys in unheated compartments, rolled onto dockside tracks. Burdened with steel helmets, rifles, full field packs, and heavy overcoats, the grim-faced GIs struggled up gangways and, one after the other, disappeared into gray transport ships.

The novice American soldiers took a weird assortment of "extras" with them on their way to battle. One man carried a violin case, another a banjo, and a third a bugle or trumpet. A tall youth went up the gangway leading a large black dog of uncertain ancestry. Several GIs hid puppies in their overcoats. Others went aboard lugging colorfully wrapped boxes tied neatly with bright red ribbons—gifts from back home. All that day, supplies and the soldiers' belongings were hoisted aboard transport vessels—bedrolls, barracks bags, thousands of them. Not all would find their owners.

Officers and a contingent of female nurses from Roosevelt Hospital in New York City were assigned small but relatively comfortable cabins on the upper decks. The infantrymen were jammed in the stifling holds below. A few GIs were philosophical. "Look at it this way," one called out to comrades jostling for a modicum of space, "at least we'll come out of this knowing what sardines in a can feel like." The men in the holds, two levels of which were below the water line, learned that the British vessel was a converted refrigerator ship. "That figures!" an American exclaimed. "In peacetime this tub carried slabs of beef. Now it's lugging GI meat."

Shortly after daylight on October 22, 46 Allied cargo vessels with 18 escorting warships slipped out of the Firth of Clyde and set a southward course. Astern of this convoy was another flotilla of 39 transports of the Eastern Assault Force (target: Algiers), and the Center Task Force, which would go ashore at Oran.

Operation Torch, which General George Patton had labeled "as desperate a venture as history has known," had been launched. It would be the mightiest amphibious assault seen up to that time and America's first major offensive since the Meuse-Argonne bloodbath in World War I.

Decked out in foul-weather gear, Admiral Harold Burrough, a resolute British seafarer, surveyed the gigantic convoy from the bridge of his flagship, *Bulolo*. A few weeks before, he had told General Clark that he would consider his task successful if he got half of his convoy to Algiers and Oran through the expected gauntlet of Luftwaffe dive bombers and U-boat wolfpacks in the Mediterranean.

As Admiral Burrough's armada steamed south, instructions for "battle stations" in case of attack were issued. Army officers were to remain in their cabins; men down below were to stay in the holds. Troops in the bottom decks observed that this would assure them the "honor" of being the first to drown.

A clutch of American war correspondents were on one crowded transport. They included Will Lang, of *Time* and *Life* magazines; Red Mueller, of *Newsweek;* Joe Liebling, of *The New Yorker* magazine; Ollie

Stewart, of the Baltimore *Afro-American;* Gault MacGowan, of the *New York Sun;* Robert Neville, of the U.S. Army publications *Stars and Stripes* and *Yank;* and a wiry little man with a balding head and a fringe of almost white hair which made him look considerably older than his 40 years. His name was Ernie Pyle and he would emerge as the most famous American war reporter of them all, the champion of the down-trodden infantryman.*

Only hours before sailing, these correspondents, under pain of the most excruciating penalties should they breathe a word, were told the expedition's objectives. Only a handful of top officers in Admiral Burrough's armada were "in the know" as to the targets.

Each day for the next two weeks, new rumors raced through the vessels bound for French Northwest Africa. Many were believed, though only until new and more incredible stories replaced them. The convoy was heading for Gibraltar and would be there in 12 hours, or two days, or a week; several American aircraft carriers had joined the flotilla during the night (though nobody had sighted one); the convoy was bound for southern France or Egypt or the Bahamas; the entire operation was an enormous smokescreen to confuse the Germans.

As the blacked-out convoy neared Gibraltar, the bottleneck between the Atlantic Ocean and the Mediterranean Sea, a talented collection of entertainers aboard the transport carrying the war correspondents put on what was billed as a variety show. These players had been professionals in civilian life, and their show rivaled the raunchiest burlesque, with a hairy corporal (announced as Gypsy Rose Lee) doing a striptease that got down to the barest essentials.

Troops clad in life preservers rocked the wardroom with cheers for the entertainers. But everyone's joy was tempered by radio reports received that afternoon. A U-boat pack was lying in wait near the Strait. There was not a man aboard who did not expect a torpedo attack at any moment—every moment—on that warm moonlit night.

A day after the Algiers and Oran assault forces had edged out of the Firth of Clyde in Scotland, some 3,000 miles to the west, just before

---

* An enduring World War II legend, Ernie Pyle was killed by a sniper's bullet on a remote Pacific island only a few days before the war ended.

8:00 A.M. on October 23, the first ships of Admiral Kent Hewitt's Western Task Force stood out of Hampton Roads, near Norfolk, Virginia. The convoy crossing 3,000 miles of rough Atlantic Ocean would be commanded by Hewitt from his flagship, the specially equipped cruiser *Augusta*. With Hewitt was General George Patton, who stood before a mirror in his tiny cabin and practiced a fierce scowl that he called his "battle face."

On the second day at sea, General Ernie Harmon, the scrappy leader of the 2nd Armored Division, was standing on the bridge of a troop transport, taking in the spectacle of the more than 100 ships. Suddenly Harmon saw something unsettling. In the distance was the transport *Calvert*, crammed with the light tanks he had to have for his assault on the port of Safi (south of Casablanca), being towed back toward Hampton Roads by a tug.

Harmon made hurried inquiries and learned that the *Calvert*'s boilers were considered unsafe and that tanks, soldiers and crew would have to be reloaded onto another vessel which would try to rejoin the convoy at sea. (Five days later General Harmon would be relieved to see the *Titania* join the armada with the *Calvert*'s tanks and men.)

The American soldiers were still being trained while sailing to battle. Just prior to shoving off from Hampton Roads, shipments of late-model weapons were received, still in crates and cartons. The assault troops were fascinated by the bazooka, a long tube that fired a rocket and was supposed to knock out enemy tanks. No one on board had ever seen a bazooka before, much less fired one. The Americans could only hope that, when the shooting erupted, the bazookas would work.

On his crowded transport, General Harmon was keeping his concerns to himself. Just before sailing, he had been summoned by Admiral Lyal Davidson, commander of the Safi task force, to the flagship *Philadelphia*. Harmon had climbed up the rope ladder clutching a secret book of instructions put together by naval planners. The book was as thick as the New York City telephone directory. He was met by Admiral Davidson, who was carrying a copy of the same heavy book.

"Harmon," the admiral asked, "have you read this book and do you understand it?"

"No, sir," the candid Harmon replied. "I haven't read it and I doubt

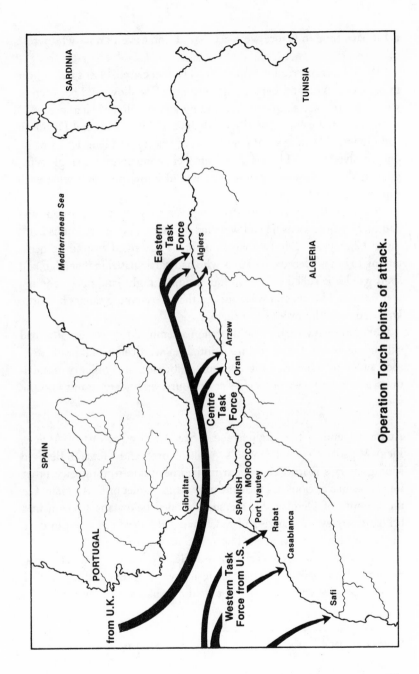

Operation Torch points of attack.

if I'll have time to before we reach Safi. I don't even know who wrote it."

"Well, I haven't read it either," Davidson declared. "Let's talk it over in my cabin. You and I are going to run the Safi show, and between us we must arrive at a simple understanding which will make it a success."*

There in the cabin, virtually on the eve of battle, Admiral Davidson and General Harmon went over a host of vexing problems and, one by one, resolved them. These agreements were condensed to a single type-written sheet. Now army and navy would know precisely what each expected in the Safi assault.

Despite arriving at these basic agreements, Ernie Harmon was haunted by the fiascos he had watched in the practice amphibious land-ing at Chesapeake Bay two weeks before. He walked around on deck, talking to boyish-faced coxswains who had participated in that affair and soon would be called on to conduct a similar night landing—only in a war setting. The general was shocked that these young sailors had little knowledge of the task facing them.

Obtaining navy permission, Harmon assembled these coxswains, had silhouettes of the Safi coastline painted on wardroom bulkheads, told each sailor to memorize the contours, estuaries, and military installa-tions, and in essence conducted a crash course on how to assault a hostile shore.

At the far end of the Mediterranean Sea, 1,200 miles east of Algiers, Field Marshal Erwin Rommel's Afrika Korps and General Bernard Montgomery's British Eighth Army had been confronting each other for weeks in a curious lull near the ugly Arab hamlet of El Alamein. On the evening of October 23, the sun dropped below the horizon in a brilliant display of orange and red, leaving the desert cloaked in deep shades of blue and lavender. The night air was tranquil.

At a wooden table concealed in a defile, Lieutenant General Georg Stumme, Rommel's temporary stand-in, was relaxing and enjoying a leisurely supper with his staff. The field marshal was at Semmering, in

---

* Major General Ernest N. Harmon, *Combat Commander*.

the Austrian Alps, convalescing from an illness. Here on the desert, Stumme's mind was relatively at ease.

If the British were to attack, Stumme and his 100,000-man German-Italian Afrika Korps would be in peril. Field Marshal Rommel had been furious at the Führer for several weeks over promised shipments of ammunition, fuel, tanks, guns, and troops that had never arrived. But the 750,000-man British force was still licking its wounds from the shellacking it had received at Tobruk. Moreover, the Afrika Korps had been advised by Fremde Heere West (as the result of a deception by the XX-Committee) that Montgomery's anticipated guns and new tanks had not arrived.

Suddenly, at 9:40 P.M., an enormous roar and brilliant flashes lighted the sky to Stumme's east. Hundreds of Montgomery's big guns, scrupulously camouflaged until now, had begun the heaviest artillery bombardment of the war. Operation Lightfoot, designed to drive the outnumbered Afrika Korps back hundreds of miles into Tunisia, had been launched.

Without waiting for the smoke to clear, Montgomery sent hundreds of his new tanks into Afrika Korps lines. Within hours, General Stumme fell dead from a heart attack, leaving the Afrika Korps without a leader.

Erwin Rommel climbed out of his sickbed and rushed back to the El Alamein front, but there was little he could do. From Montgomery's opening shot the Afrika Korps was doomed. It faced a far larger, better equipped, and heavier-gunned British force, its supply lines from Italy and Germany had been all but severed, it lacked accurate intelligence, and was nearly out of fuel.

While the ailing Rommel was fighting "blind," Bernard Montgomery was holding an unbeatable card: He knew of each planned Rommel move in advance. Ultra was intercepting the field marshal's orders to his troop commanders, rapidly deciphering the radioed signals, and putting them on Montgomery's desk—often before the messages were relayed to their intended German recipients.

Erwin Rommel, customarily resolute, was near despair. By radio he pleaded to Hitler for fuel and ammunition to help stave off disaster. Bernard Montgomery read that signal before the Führer received it.

Hitler's response, likewise furnished by Ultra to Montgomery before Rommel got it, was unyielding:

> In the situation you find yourself in there can be no other thought but to stand fast and throw every gun and every man into the battle. . . . As to your troops, you can show them no other road than that to victory or death.

Rommel obeyed the order of his commander in chief. There would be no retreat. His men would stand fast *and* die. In anguish, Rommel wrote a letter to his wife, Lucie Maria, at their home near Ulm in southern Germany: "At night I lie open-eyed, racking my brains for a way out of this plight for my poor troops. We are facing very difficult days, perhaps the most difficult a man can face. The dead are lucky. It's all over for them."

In London, General Eisenhower was watching the bitter fight at El Alamein with intense interest. Its outcome would have a direct bearing on Torch. Ike, who had been a boxer at West Point, said of the situation: "We're going to give Hitler the old one-two." Montgomery's "one" would strike with such impact that Rommel would be pushed westward all the way to Tunisia. Then, with the Desert Fox hanging on the ropes, Eisenhower would unload "two"—the knockout punch—from behind after Torch forces had landed west of Tunisia.

Far from the El Alamein battleground on the afternoon of October 24, the sun was warming the broad avenues, carefully manicured terraces, and stuccoed houses of Lisbon, Portugal. In a comfortable frame house just outside the city, Ludovico von Karsthoff, a tall, heavyset man with black hair and a friendly disposition, was playing host to a visitor and longtime friend, thirty-one-year-old Dusko Popov, a Yugoslavian businessman who had just arrived by clipper plane from the United States.

Though the atmosphere was friendly—von Karsthoff was always a gracious host—and the cocktails were relaxing, the two men were soon in a serious discussion. The subject was espionage. Von Karsthoff, an Austrian by birth, was chief of the Abwehr in Lisbon. His real name was Major von Auenrode. His guest was one of the Abwehr's crack spies who, during the past two years, had funneled many vital Allied secrets to Berlin from his post in London. Popov had been given the code name Ivan by the Abwehr.

Dusko Popov was a member of a wealthy Belgrade family. He held a law degree from the university there, and had gone to Germany to enroll at Freiburg University for his doctorate. There Popov had been approached by the Abwehr and asked to spy for the Third Reich. Why not? It sounded exciting. And, he told his Abwehr contact, he had long been a staunch admirer of Adolf Hitler and his ideals.

Actually, Popov despised the regime that had brutally subjugated Yugoslavia. He had gone immediately to the British embassy in Belgrade, told his story, and become a double agent. MI-6, the British intelligence agency, gave Popov its own code name: Tricycle.

For the past two years, Popov had led a perilous double life. Under the direction of MI-6, he had passed a steady stream of Allied "secrets" from England, where the Abwehr had sent him. Then, in late 1941, the Germans had sent Popov to the United States to obtain industrial secrets. But MI-6 had given Tricycle a more crucial assignment: to return to Portugal on some pretext and help deceive the Germans on Torch. Now, in Lisbon, to boost Abwehr confidence in him he was relating to von Karsthoff figures on airplanes delivered from the United States to England—figures furnished by the XX-Committee and partially accurate. The Lisbon spymaster rubbed his hands together. Ivan always produced.

Then, as instructed by British intelligence, Popov went on to relate a story to the attentive von Karsthoff, a tale designed to account for the hundreds of Allied vessels now bearing down on Gibraltar. "I have learned from extremely reliable informants—they're at such high levels that I can't reveal identities even to you—that Malta is in a disastrous position and its population is close to starvation. The British, with American help, are soon going to come to Malta's rescue."

There was something else he had heard in New York and Washington: rumors of a combined American, Canadian, and British operation against Norway. Popov knew that the Abwehr had already heard this report. MI-6 had arranged for a pair of double agents in England, code named Gelatine and Balloon, to send the rumor to Berlin.

At Buckingham Palace on October 29, generals Eisenhower and Clark were received by King George. Introduced to the shy, friendly monarch, Clark was greeted with: "I know all about you. You're the one who took that fabulous trip. Didn't you, by the way, get stranded on the beach without your pants?" The missing-pants episode refused to die. The next day Clark received a message from Robert Murphy in Algiers saying that "our French friends" had found Clark's pants, which had washed up onto the beach, and that they were having the garment cleaned and pressed, and hoped to return it personally on his next visit.*

On October 30, the day after Eisenhower and Clark dined with the king of England, agents of MI-6 at Gibraltar were in a state of excitement. They had learned that Admiral Wilhelm Canaris, the slight, astute Abwehr boss, was in Algeciras, a small town virtually overlooking Gibraltar where the Abwehr had a secret headquarters. The MI-6 Gibraltar agents quickly hatched a plan for a coup that would rock the world: They would slip into Algeciras under cover of night, kidnap Canaris, and fly him to London as a prisoner of war.

Intelligence chiefs in London—who had no doubt hastily consulted Churchill—fired off a signal to Gibraltar: Cancel proposed coup. Admiral Canaris was far more valuable to the Allied war effort in Berlin at Adolf Hitler's elbow than he would be as a guest of His Majesty's government in London.†

As D-day for Torch drew closer, Allied officers in London responsible for the security of the operation confronted a major problem. For many months General Eisenhower had been highly visible as he dashed about London and the British Isles. Now that he was about to depart for Gibraltar to take direct command of the Torch assault, how could his sudden absence be covered? Observers were sure to note his disappear-

---

* Mark Clark did get his pants back—shrunken by the salt water. Several years ago the celebrated trousers were placed on permanent display in the Smithsonian Institution in Washington, D.C.

† Anthony Cave Brown in *Bodyguard of Lies,* quoting London journalist Ian Colvin, who had studied Canaris's loyalties.

ance, and the Germans would suspect that a major Allied operation was imminent.

Word was leaked to two reporters that Eisenhower was secretly returning to Washington "for consultation." The next morning, the *Washington Post* carried a front-page story of the supreme commander's recall to the States. That afternoon, reporters questioned President Roosevelt about the report at a news conference. The chief executive replied that for him to "mention the movement of army officers would only aid the enemy." Some 50 reporters left the White House duly convinced that Eisenhower was in Washington and, as intended, they published their conclusions. The success of the ruse left Eisenhower himself with a bothersome reaction: What would wife Mamie think when she read that her husband was in Washington and that he had not even phoned her? There was no help for it.

On the night before General Eisenhower was to depart for Gibraltar, he and a few friends were watching a private screening of a Bob Hope comedy (appropriately named *Road to Morocco*) in a room on Wardour Street, London's film district. Unexpectedly, a message from General George Marshall arrived at Eisenhower's office. Because General "Beetle" Smith, the supreme commander's chief of staff, had left for dinner without leaving word where Eisenhower could be reached, the night duty officer knew only that the Big Boss was somewhere in London viewing a movie. But the duty officer was resourceful. General Eisenhower, who was supposed to be in Washington for conferences, was soon being paged in every public theater in London.

10

The Führer
Is Hoodwinked

On the night of November 3 Covering Force H, commanded by British Vice Admiral Neville Syfret on his flagship *Duke of York*, began slipping through the Strait of Gibraltar, a narrow body of water about 32 miles long and from 8 to 23 miles wide. Syfret's force included two other battleships, *Renown* and *Rodney*, the aircraft carriers *Formidable* and *Victorious*, three cruisers, and seventeen destroyers.

Covering Force H had the crucial mission of defending Torch landing operations against the Kriegsmarine, the Italian navy, and the Vichy French fleets. British submarines already in the Mediterranean took up patrolling stations off Messina (northeast Sicily), off the northwestern corner of Sicily, and off Toulon in southern France. Aircraft from Gibraltar, Malta, and Great Britain began reconnaissance flights over the sea between Spain and Sardinia, between Sardinia and Sicily, and over ports in southern France.

Hardly had the first ship in Admiral Syfret's covering force edged its bow into the Strait than Abwehr watchers in Spain and a few miles away in Spanish Morocco reported these naval movements to Berlin.

On the morning of November 4, a major at the Oberkommando der Wehrmacht (OKW) penned in the official war diary: "The concentration of such an important [Allied] naval force in the western Mediterranean seems to indicate an imminent operation, perhaps another convoy to Malta."

The efforts of the double agent Dusko Popov (Tricycle), along with countless supporting operations by the XX-Committee, had apparently paid off. Even the Oberkommando der Kriegsmarine, the naval high command which seldom agreed with its German army rival on anything, concluded that Malta was indeed the destination of a relief convoy bringing food for the starving population of that small island.

But Grand Admiral Erich Raeder, commander in chief of the Kriegsmarine, was covering all bets. He told Hitler that other Allied convoy destinations could be Tripoli or Benghazi behind the beleaguered Field Marshal Rommel in order to trap the teetering Afrika Korps; Sicily, Sardinia, the Italian mainland—or even French Northwest Africa.

In the welter of conflicting intelligence, Hitler decided that the Allies intended to storm ashore at Tripoli or Benghazi with four or five divisions in order to destroy the Afrika Korps by attacking it from the rear. The Führer yearned for another massive slaughter of Allied ships like the one inflicted on Admiral Burrough's Malta relief convoy the previous August, when only five vessels had made it into port.

Hitler sent a signal to Field Marshal Albert Kesselring, known to the Americans as "Smiling Al," the *Oberbefehlshaber Süd* (commander in chief South) in Italy. Kesselring, regarded by the Western Allies as one of the most capable Wehrmacht commanders, was ordered to concentrate his Luftwaffe units in the eastern Mediterranean in order to pounce on the Allied convoys as they headed for Tripoli, Benghazi, or perhaps Malta. The Führer ordered street barricades erected in Tripoli and Benghazi in anticipation of house-to-house fighting. He personally radioed his submarines in the Mediterranean—bypassing the navy high command, as was his wont—saying, "Army's survival in Africa depends on destruction of British naval forces. I expect determined, victorious attack."

There was a flaw in the Führer's exhortation to his U-boat command-

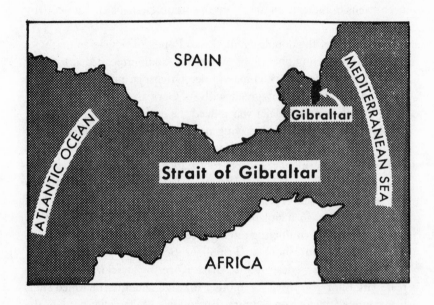

SPAIN

ATLANTIC OCEAN

Gibraltar

MEDITERRANEAN SEA

Strait of Gibraltar

AFRICA

ers: The Kriegsmarine had stationed most of its submarines in the central and eastern Mediterranean, far to the east of where the British and Americans intended to storm ashore.

But the Axis did not entirely denude its strike forces in the vicinity of Gibraltar, where Allied convoys would have to enter the Mediterranean. Nine German and 26 Italian submarines and 76 Luftwaffe fighter planes were patrolling the sea lanes around the Rock of Gibraltar, and *Schnellboot* squadrons (motor torpedo boats) in the region had been alerted for action.

As more than 1,400 Allied vessels of all types converged on Gibraltar, a German wolfpack there suddenly sped southward and 24 hours later was engaged in a running duel with British convoy SL125. Commanded by Rear Admiral C. N. Reyne, the SL125 consisted primarily of empty cargo vessels and a warship escort, bound for England from Sierra Leone along the Atlantic seaboard of Africa. The battle between the

U-boats and the Phantom Convoy went on for more than six days, and 13 of Admiral Reyne's vessels were sunk, most of them empty cargo ships.

It was a curious action by the U-boat wolfpack, and had left the "gate" at Gibraltar wide open. Why had the wolfpack suddenly sprinted to the south to intercept a convoy of empty vessels? And why had the U-boats dogged the Phantom Convoy for several days? Had the XX-Committee convinced the Kriegsmarine that convoy SL125 was carrying a wealth of valuable equipment and supplies? Had the XX-Committee even arranged for Reyne's convoy of empty vessels to come along at that time, a sacrificial victim to Torch? Years after the war, Admiral Reyne said only, "It was the only time I had ever been congratulated for losing ships."

The destruction of the Phantom Convoy permitted Admiral Burrough's huge flotilla carrying the Eastern and Central Task Forces, bound for Algiers and Oran, to slip up to the Strait of Gibraltar undetected.

Now the B-Dienst, which relied almost exclusively on wireless monitoring, became aware that the Allies were involved in massive naval movements. Two weeks previously, B-Dienst had reported to Hitler that the number of ships in Scotland's Firth of Clyde—this was Admiral Burrough's armada—had risen from 8 to 43. It had also deduced that the British in recent days had been trying to hoodwink B-Dienst with a series of fake radio signals from the English Channel indicating that the Allies were preparing to launch another Dieppe-type assault against northern France.

B-Dienst personnel were masters of their trade and hard to fool. Monitoring posts had been set up in Spain long before, to check on British naval traffic in the Mediterranean—as Franco looked the other way. But B-Dienst, possibly taken in by XX-Committee machinations and swayed by the prevailing view in the OKW, concluded that the huge Allied convoys were bound for Egypt to help in Montgomery's assault on Rommel's teetering Afrika Korps. Amid a blizzard of conflicting reports on Allied intentions, all German intelligence agencies agreed on one point: The harbor and airfield at Gibraltar were rapidly filling up.

On the evening of November 5, Lieutenant Karl Redl, an Abwehr agent, was peering through a powerful telescope from a villa at Algeciras, Spain, from where he had a panoramic view three miles across the Bay of Algeciras to Gibraltar. Since October 2, Redl and two other Abwehr men had been conducting around-the-clock observation of the harbor and airstrip. Their boss, Admiral Wilhelm Canaris himself, had been gazing through this same telescope only a week before, unaware that British MI-6 agents at Gibraltar were planning on kidnapping him.

Periodically for three weeks, there had been flurries of activity at the Rock with warships and aircraft coming and going. Redl and his two assistants had even viewed a practice amphibious landing by a small British detachment. But November 5 had been quiet, and Gibraltar was socked in with heavy rains and low clouds. Not a ship had budged in the harbor all day long. At 6:00 P.M. Lieutenant Redl reported to higher headquarters: "Nothing to report."

Suddenly, at about 8:00 P.M., there was movement in the harbor. One by one, a few vessels began slipping into the Mediterranean; an hour later two battleships moved out, and then other warships departed. At 10:00 P.M. Redl and his men could make out the silhouettes of a blacked-out convoy—Admiral Burrough's armada—sailing eastward through the Strait of Gibraltar at 15 knots.

Alerted by Redl, Luftwaffe reconnaissance planes were out in force after dawn. Soon pilots began making reports as conflicting as those received from agents on the ground. The Mediterranean convoy was heading northeast, southeast, or due east, according to separate sightings. Confusion was compounded when the German ambassador in Madrid signaled that the Spaniards thought the convoy would hit Italy. At the same time the German military attaché in Madrid contradicted the ambassador and reported that the Allied flotilla was headed for Rommel's rear. Sources in Vichy France told the Abwehr that the convoy would strike at French Northwest Africa, but this was discounted in Berlin.

Far to the east of Gibraltar on the morning of November 5, the Afrika Korps, now a vestige of its former might, was in full retreat from El Alamein.

Despite the enormous advantages General Montgomery held—including his reading of Rommel's orders in advance through Ultra—the Desert Fox had somehow managed to hold against British onslaughts for nearly 12 days. Trudging along on foot for the 60 miles back to a new defensive position at Fuka were thousands of weary, dust-covered German and Italian soldiers. Rommel's gasoline supply had nearly gone. He had once commanded more than 500 armored vehicles—now he had 12. The debacle about which he had repeatedly warned Hitler was becoming a reality.

As the bedraggled Afrika Korps was struggling back through the desert on the morning of November 5, hundreds of miles away a heavy rain was pounding an airport near Bournemouth, England. Gusts rocked six Flying Fortresses that squatted, like huge ducks on a pond, with engines running and ready for takeoff. These big aircraft would carry Eisenhower, Clark, and other high-level officers to the Torch command post at Gibraltar. The Allied brass were distributed in different aircraft, in case one or more were shot down.

Major Paul Tibbets, pilot of the *Red Gremlin* and commander of the six-Fortress flight, approached Eisenhower, who was to ride in his plane. Tibbets gave his professional assessment, which was against taking off in the foul weather, but he left it up to the supreme commander to make the crucial decision. Eisenhower had no choice—he *had* to reach Gibraltar with his key personnel, or Torch, already developing, could fall apart. "Go!" Eisenhower ordered, strapping on his seat belt.

At 8:20 A.M., with its windshield wipers in a losing battle with the rain, the *Red Gremlin* sped down the runway and lifted off. Seconds later came the *Boomerang*, carrying General Mark Clark and others, followed by a Fortress with Brigadier General James H. "Jimmy" Doolittle, commander of American air forces for Torch, among the passengers. Shortly afterward, Doolittle's aircraft developed a malfunction and had to return to its base.

The five Flying Fortresses wave-hopped all the way to Gibraltar, seldom getting more than a hundred feet above the water. There was rain, fog, and virtually zero visibility. A sudden downdraft could have dropped the aircraft into the ocean. Finally, the majestic Rock of Gibraltar loomed out of the haze, and Major Tibbets began gaining altitude. He stuck his head out of the pilots' compartment and called back to General Eisenhower: "This is the first time I have ever had to *climb* to get into landing traffic at the end of a long trip."

Now a new hazard emerged. Three fighter planes were racing directly toward the *Red Gremlin*. All on board held their breaths as the B-17 gunners manned weapons, but the fighters wagged their wings and sped away. A yellow alert had been sounded on Gibraltar with the approach of the five Flying Fortresses, and the three Spitfires had been scrambled to look over the newcomers. General Eisenhower's plane touched down at 4:22 P.M. on the jammed Gibraltar airstrip, where aircraft were parked wingtip to wingtip.

Unknown to the supreme commander, concern for his safety was growing by the minute back at headquarters in Grosvenor Square. Due to a series of communications mishaps, Eisenhower's *Red Gremlin* was unreported for nearly two hours after word had been received of the safe arrival of General Clark's *Boomerang* and the other three Flying Fortresses. Winston Churchill, in his bunker at Story's Gate in London, telephoned American headquarters at 20 Grosvenor Square every ten minutes after being told that Eisenhower's plane was overdue. So anxious was Churchill over the missing Fortress carrying the supreme commander that when a signal arrived that Eisenhower had landed safely at Gibraltar, General Beetle Smith, Ike's chief of staff and alter ego, and General Pug Ismay, Churchill's military advisor, carried the good tidings personally to Story's Gate. When they walked into Churchill's office, the ashen-faced prime minister exclaimed: "Don't tell me he's drowned!" Assured that Eisenhower was safe, Churchill said, "I never had the slightest idea that it would be otherwise."

General Eisenhower's battle headquarters on Gibraltar, though safe from even the heaviest bombings, were cold, damp, and dismal. Cut out of solid stone in recent months, the supreme commander's office was a half mile inside the Rock and was reached by tunnels whose forbidding blackness was relieved only at intervals by the glare of naked light bulbs.

Almost immediately the supreme commander set up a conference of key personnel. The subject: dignified, sixty-three-year-old Henri Giraud, the French four-star general on whom the Western Allies were depending so heavily to halt bloodshed when the invasion struck. Just before departing England, Eisenhower had received an urgent message from Robert Murphy, who had been doing more clandestine work in Algiers: "Unless Kingpin [Giraud's code name] lends his name to the invasion, the French may resist desperately."

Giraud seemed the ideal candidate to rally the French army, navy, and air force in northwest Africa to the Allied cause. The name of the tall, lean general had been associated with neither of the two warring French factions, nor with their leaders, Marshal Pétain of the Vichy government and General de Gaulle of the French government in exile. And Giraud was thought to be greatly admired by French officers for his distinguished war record.

All this was moot, however, if General Giraud could not be spirited out of France. He had been under constant surveillance by the Gestapo at his home in Lyons.

Fog and haze blanketed the coast of southern France that night of November 5. Hardly more than a half mile off the rocky shoreline, a submarine rose out of the waters of the Mediterranean, shut off her diesel engines, and remained motionless on the surface for long minutes. Several men scrambled out of the hatch and peered toward the shore, trying intently to part the darkness. There! A blinking blue light on the beach. It flashed several more times.

"Okay, that's it," a man on deck said in a stage whisper. "Get the folbot in the water." The submarine was the *Seraph,* the same British boat that had taken General Clark and his group to the parlay in North Africa two weeks before. Giving the muted orders on the deck was the same self-assured young skipper, Lieutenant Norman Jewell. Technically, however, he was not in command of the *Seraph* on this mission, which was to pick up General Giraud and whisk him off to Gibraltar. The French General had specified that he was to be picked up by an American submarine; Giraud held such strong feelings against the British since the shelling of the French fleet in 1940 that he refused to ride in a British warship. The Americans had no submarines in the Mediterranean, so to assuage General Giraud's honor an American officer,

Navy Captain Jerauld Wright (who had been with Clark on the secret mission), was placed in technical command of the *Seraph*. Captain Wright had a significant handicap: he knew virtually nothing about commanding a submarine. So Lieutenant Jewell quietly ran the show.*

As three British sailors paddled the folbot quietly toward the dark beach, the muted blue light flashed once more with the prearranged code. The boat scraped onto the sand and four shadowy figures approached—General Giraud (who had evaded the Gestapo by slipping out a rear door of his Lyons home), Captain André Beaufre, Lieutenant Hubert Viret, and Aspirant (officer candidate) Bernard Giraud, the general's son.

Reaching the *Seraph* on the return trip, Giraud was the last Frenchman to climb out of the folbot and up the slippery side of the submarine. He lost his balance, fell into the water, and nearly drowned. A British sailor grabbed the general by his coat collar just before he went under and hauled him onto the deck.

As the *Seraph* set a course for Gibraltar, an alarming signal was received at the Rock from Captain Wright, "skipper" of the submarine: "Task gone. Radio failing."

The news raced through the Rock's underground offices. What did Wright mean by "task gone"? Was "task" Giraud, on whom so much counted? Where had the French general "gone"? Was he dead?

General Eisenhower and other key Allied leaders on Gibraltar had no way of knowing that the *Seraph*'s radio, for some unaccountable reason, had garbled the signal, which should have read: "Task done."

The anxiety at Torch battle headquarters was short-lived. An hour later a Catalina flying boat radioed that it had picked up Giraud from the submarine and was bringing him to Gibraltar.

Meanwhile, in England, the malfunction had been repaired on General Jimmy Doolittle's Flying Fortress, and on the morning of November 6 it was winging alone toward Gibraltar. The forty-five-year-old Doolittle was the weatherbeaten, diminutive officer who had electrified the

---

* Years after the war, Vice Admiral Jerauld Wright became Atlantic Commander of NATO.

United States the previous spring by leading a bombing raid on Tokyo. Now a national hero, he had a long list of aviation "firsts." He had been the first to span the American continent in a single day, the first army pilot to execute the hazardous outside loop, and was now in command of Eisenhower's air force in America's first major offensive of World War II. Suddenly a shout rang out in Doolittle's plane: "Bandits at nine o'clock!"

Moments later bullets began ripping through the Flying Fortress, as four Luftwaffe fighters bore in for the kill. One of the enemy slugs tore into the arm of the copilot; others hissed past the head of General Doolittle and the other passengers. A terrific racket erupted inside the heavy bomber as the GI gunners, most in combat for the first time, returned the fire. "I got one! I got one!" a boyish-faced machine-gunner shouted excitedly. No one saw an enemy plane go down.

The four Luftwaffe fighters, apparently at the limit of their range, turned and headed for home after two or three passes. Doolittle calmly returned his attention to maps of Morocco and Algeria.

Inside the Rock of Gibraltar on the afternoon of November 6, British Admiral Andrew B. "ABC" Cunningham, chief of the Torch naval forces, bustled into General Eisenhower's eight-by-eight foot office with a piece of paper. The admiral was grinning, even though the message seemed a gloomy one. It was a frantic SOS to all Allied ships —uncoded due to the urgency—from the destroyer *Janine,* stating that she had been bombed and was sinking. The latitude and longitude given placed her in the eastern Mediterranean.

Actually, the *Janine* was steaming normally, hundreds of miles west of the phony longitude and latitude she had signaled. This was Admiral Cunningham's scheme to reinforce Hitler's view that the convoys assembling around Gibraltar were bound for Malta, Tripoli, or Benghazi. Cunningham's stratagem was to provide the Oran and Algiers convoys with another hour or two before they were detected by the Luftwaffe.

At the same time, General Eisenhower was handed an alarming report from his chief meteorological officer: The weather was deteriorating badly in the path of General Patton's Western Task Force, and big waves were lashing the coast in the Casablanca region where Patton was

to land. This information was radioed to Patton who responded in a signal: "Don't worry. If need be, I'll land in Spain." It was Patton at his best, saying that if he could not fight at Casablanca he would just as soon fight General Franco, the Spanish dictator, who had been working closely with the Nazis. Patton's signal boosted spirits in the gloomy caves of Gibraltar.

The myriad deception plans of the XX-Committee had proven effective in the case of some experienced Allied press correspondents, who prided themselves on being in the know. Four war reporters accredited to the headquarters, including Wes Gallagher of the Associated Press, Chris Cunningham of United Press International, and George Ure of the *Times* of London and Reuter's, shoehorned into General Eisenhower's tiny cubicle for a briefing. Each had fallen victim to the Norway-invasion stratagem and had lugged along heavy Arctic clothing and other winter gear.

Shortly after dawn on November 7—D-day minus 1—depressing news was received on Gibraltar. Luftwaffe planes had hit the transport *Thomas Stone*, carrying elements of the U.S. 39th Infantry Regiment, when its convoy was 150 miles northwest of Algiers, bound for the beaches east of that city. More than 800 men were lost when the transport sunk, the signal stated.

The signal, however, had been inaccurate. A Luftwaffe bomb had broken off the *Thomas Stone*'s screw and rudder, leaving it dead in the water, while its convoy continued onward. With the small corvette *Spey* standing by, the damaged vessel awaited the arrival of a tug—which could take days. But Major Walter M. Oakes, commander of the 2nd Battalion of the 39th Regiment, whose troops were on board, had no intention of sitting out the Torch assault.

Major Oakes calculated that by using the small assault craft on the *Thomas Stone*, most of his battalion could reach the beaches in time to participate in the capture of Algiers, 150 miles away. The infantry officer persuaded the vessel's American skipper, Captain Olten R. Bennehof, to accept the risk of remaining for a few hours after dark without the protection of the *Spey* until the arrival of two British destroyers known to be on the way to the stricken transport.

At dusk, Major Oakes and over 700 men in 24 assault boats began a perilous journey of 150 miles with the *Spey* as an escort. Oakes and his men could only hope that the unpredictable Mediterranean would remain placid; even moderately heavy waves could swamp the tiny craft. Soon the motors of the small boats, built for about a ten-mile run into a beach, began breaking down, one by one. The long night was an ordeal of pauses for repair.

During one pause, nervous, seasick, and exhausted soldiers in several craft opened a withering burst of small-arms fire. Soon shouts rang out: "Cease firing! Cease firing!" Silence returned. The anxious GIs had been blazing away at the dim silhouette of one of their own landing craft, mistaken in the darkness by jittery men for a submarine.

At daybreak, an easterly breeze further impeded the 24 boats, and a dejected Major Oakes was forced to concede that he and his 700 men would never reach Algiers in time to help assault the port. Reluctantly, he gave the order for his men to crowd aboard the *Spey* and scuttle the assault boats. With soldiers packed onto every inch of her decks and other spaces, the *Spey* began arduously inching toward Algiers.*

On Gibraltar at midafternoon that day, November 7, four-star General Henri Giraud was shown into Eisenhower's office. He was dressed in rumpled civilian clothes and had a dark growth of beard on his face, yet he maintained a precise military bearing. Inwardly, the supreme commander was elated that this celebrated French figure had arrived safely. This was the one man who might assure a peaceful entry into French Northwest Africa.

Almost at once the scenario went wrong. Although Giraud was thought to understand English, he insisted that a French interpreter be used. Eisenhower outlined the Allied invasion plans—H-hour at some beaches was less than ten hours away. It was explained that what was wanted was General Giraud's signature on a letter stating that the United States, anticipating Hitler's intention of seizing French Northwest Africa, was beating the Germans to the punch and was calling on all French fighting men to rally to the Americans. Giraud's role, the

---

* The *Spey* arrived at Algiers after dark. Tugs towed the wounded *Thomas Stone* into Algiers harbor four days later.

letter concluded, was that he would "resume my place in combat among you."

Giraud's reaction was a prolonged, icy silence. "Now," he finally said, stiffly, "let's get it clear as to my part. As I understand it, I am to assume command of all Allied forces and become the supreme commander in North Africa."

Eisenhower and Mark Clark were stupefied. It was as though a bomb had been set off. Finally Eisenhower said, "There must be some misunderstanding."

Giraud, it developed, had other faulty impressions. He thought that the Western Allies, who were barely able to muster the resources for Torch, were going to launch a simultaneous massive invasion of southern France to keep Hitler from overrunning the unoccupied half of Giraud's homeland.

General Eisenhower, finding it difficult to keep his temper under control, argued with the French general for an hour. He promised Giraud the governorship of North Africa, plus ample finances to build an army. The Frenchman was unimpressed. None of these would do. He had been promised the role of supreme commander over *all* Allied forces. Speaking through the interpreter, he declared: "General Giraud cannot accept a subordinate position in this command. His countrymen would not understand and his honor as a soldier would be tarnished."

As Eisenhower became exhausted by the contest, General Mark Clark, who had a sharp tongue when riled, took over the persuasion effort. Always in the backs of Eisenhower's and Clark's minds was the knowledge that Giraud could save immense American—and French— bloodshed if he would only sign this letter to be widely distributed in Morocco and Algeria. Always it was the same: "I am General Giraud! My prestige! My family!"

For three hours the wrangle went on. Clark was growing increasingly hot under the collar, aware that the first Americans would be storming ashore in North Africa in only six hours. Eisenhower and Clark now were convinced that Giraud was stalling: He would sit on the fence for 48 hours to see how the Allied invasion was going. Finally Clark blurted: "We would like for the honorable general to know that the time for his usefulness to the Americans is *now*. After tonight we have no need for the honorable general." The Americans and British could not give him the supreme commander's role, Clark explained, but they would make him commander of all French forces he could rally to his side.

"Then I shall return to France," Giraud said stiffly.

"How are you going back?" Clark snapped.

"By the same route I got here."

"Like hell, you will. That was a one-way submarine you were on."

Giraud said nothing. In a tone of disgust, Clark said to Colonel Julius Holmes, the interpreter: "Tell him this—if you don't go along, general, you're going to be out in the snow on your ass."

The Frenchman made no reply. As all were pretty well exhausted, it was decided to break up the session and get a few hours of sleep in preparation for D-day, now only two hours away.

On his departure from Eisenhower's tiny cubicle, the French general turned and said, still through his interpreter, "Giraud will be a spectator at this affair."

Minutes later the communications center at Gibraltar sent a coded signal in French, signed "Giraud," to General Raymond Mast at Casablanca. Mast had met clandestinely with General Mark Clark in North Africa two weeks before and was one of the principal pro-Allied conspirators there. The signal indicated that Giraud was working closely with the Allies and that he intended to arrive in Algiers or Casablanca shortly after the D-day invasion.

Aides noted something curious about the signal sent out over Giraud's signature: The hand printing on the original looked suspiciously like that of General Eisenhower.

At the precise time that Allied commanders were arguing with their recalcitrant French general, Adolf Hitler's private train was speeding through the night on its way from the *Führerhauptquartier* at Wolfsschanze in East Prussia to Munich. The train had departed Hitler's battle headquarters that afternoon at 1:40 for the annual speech he gave in Munich observing the anniversary of the 1923 putsch which had launched the World War I army corporal on his rise to dictatorship over 90 million Germans and most of Europe.

Colonel General Alfred Jodl, Hitler's closest military advisor, opened a 7:00 P.M. war conference on the blacked-out train by relating the current position of the Allied fleet in the Mediterranean. The convoy, latest reports indicated, was heading due east and would probably pass Sicily soon while heading for Malta, Benghazi, or Tripoli. (In fact, the Allied armada had suddenly shifted its course southward and was steering for Algiers and Oran.) Twirling his horn-rimmed spectacles, Hitler thought out loud: "If these reports are true, this is the greatest fleet in the history of the world."

11

A French Military Coup Fails

As hundreds of Allied vessels were slipping into position off Casablanca and Safi and Algiers and Oran, operators of some 25 clandestine radio stations along the coast were listening intently to the British Broadcasting Corporation in London. The French-speaking announcer began reading off a litany of phrases, most of which had no meaning: Crickets are chirping in the grass; *Allo Robert—Franklin arrive.* Robert was Robert Murphy and Franklin was President Roosevelt.

The operators bent to their sets. There it was again! *Allo, Robert—Franklin arrive.* It was the phrase the undercover radio operators had been waiting weeks for—the Allied invasion of Algeria and French Morocco was about to strike. Like a brush fire, word of the imminent landing was flashed to key agents and sympathetic French officers. Resistance groups sprang into action. Within hours, working in the darkness, they seized power stations, communications centers, police stations, and rail and road centers.

At the American consulate in Algiers, the peripatetic Robert Murphy, who had been working undercover for a year with resistance groups, pro-Allied French officers, and government officials, got into his dusty little sedan and raced to the hillside villa of General Alphonse Juin in suburban Lambiridi. Juin, whose arm had been badly mangled in previous fighting, was the senior French army officer in North Africa. His ultimate loyalty was unknown. For this reason, despite his rank, Juin had been given no advance information on Allied invasion plans.

It was known that Juin despised the German Nazis and the Italian Fascists. But like many French officers he had been required to take a pledge not to fight against the Axis as a condition for his release as a prisoner of war after the fall of France in 1940. To the Allies, Alphonse Juin was a bad risk.

At 12:30 A.M. the platoon of Senegalese guards protecting Juin's Villa des Oliviers permitted the American consul to pass through the courtyard gate. Murphy banged loudly on the front door, and a sleepy General Juin, in striped pajamas, slowly opened the portal. Without preamble, Murphy informed Juin that an enormous American armada was at that moment poised off French Northwest Africa, and that in less than an hour American troops would be storming ashore. Murphy was careful not to mention British participation.

Juin, who had graduated from St. Cyr Military Academy at the top of a class that included General Charles de Gaulle, was enraged on learning what was taking place without his knowledge. Murphy tried to calm him down, but the fifty-four-year-old Juin refused to be placated, even when the consul assured him that America was invading French territory at the specific request of General Henri Giraud.

"Where *is* Giraud?" Juin demanded to know.

Murphy had to admit that he didn't know. But at that moment Giraud was fast asleep on Gibraltar, pledged to be "a spectator at this affair."

In less than an hour, General Juin recovered from his shock, anger, and embarrassment. Realizing the momentous events that were unfolding, he pledged his loyalty to the Allied cause. After all, a pledge made to the Nazis under duress was invalid. Now Robert Murphy was in for a shock: Juin would not officially make this decision until he had checked with Admiral Jean-François Darlan, commander in chief of all French armed forces and number-two man in the Vichy hierarchy. Darlan, Juin added, happened to be visiting in Algiers.

Darlan in Algiers at that moment! Murphy could hardly believe his ears. With American troops slated to storm ashore at Algiers as he and Juin were talking, there was a good chance that Admiral Darlan might be captured. Murphy recalled the pungent words of Prime Minister Churchill: "If you have to kiss Darlan's ass, do so—but *get* that French fleet." Providence was apparently intervening on the side of the Allies. Darlan, who was held in high regard by French military officers, was in fact in Algiers by chance, at the bedside of his young son Alain who had been stricken with polio.* Darlan was *the* French leader who could prevent bloodshed.

Juin promptly telephoned the residence in Algiers where Admiral Darlan was staying and advised the number-two Vichy officer that the American consul was at his villa with startling news. Speeding through the dark streets of Algiers, Darlan arrived within 20 minutes. Hardly had he seated himself in the living room than the news of unfolding events made him furious. "I have known for a long time that the British are stupid," bellowed Darlan, "but I'd have believed the Americans were more intelligent. Apparently you have the same genius as the British for making massive blunders."

Pacing the floor, the diminutive French admiral continued with his diatribe. If the stupid Americans had only waited a few weeks, they could have received "full cooperation" from within France and in Africa. He was extremely worried about Adolf Hitler's reaction to Torch. What would the Führer do about unoccupied France when he learned that the Americans and British had invaded a vast territory just across the Mediterranean Sea?

Darlan's tirade was actually comforting to Murphy. Unless the admiral was a consummate actor, it suggested to the American that Darlan was indeed in Algiers by chance and that the secret of Torch had not leaked into the Vichy government and thereby to the Oberkommando der Wehrmacht.

Murphy inquired if the admiral would cooperate with the invaders if

---

* Some Allied historians would later declare that Admiral Darlan was not in Algiers to see his critically ill son, but because he had secretly learned of the Torch invasion and wanted to join the Allies. This view fails to take into account the fact that a casket had already been purchased for the son's funeral.

Marshal Pétain approved. Of course he would, Darlan replied. The admiral called in an aide and dictated a message to Pétain in Vichy. But when Murphy, his vice consul Kenneth Pendar, Darlan, and a naval subordinate left the house to go to the French admiralty to send the message to Vichy, they discovered that General Juin's Senegalese guards had been replaced by 40 French *aspirants* (officer candidates) who had been alerted by Murphy after the consul had heard the BBC message *Franklin arrive*.

Darlan erupted in a new fit. Murphy had deliberately committed treachery, he sputtered, placing these Allied-loyal *aspirants* around the Villa des Oliviers in order to make him a prisoner. Darlan's suspicions were reinforced when the *aspirant* leader declared that he had orders not to allow anyone out of the villa but Murphy and his assistant Pendar.

While awaiting the historic developments along a thousand miles of African coastline, Murphy, Darlan, and General Juin talked over the complicated French political situation. At one point Murphy got up to look out the front door and now it was his turn to be shocked: The *aspirants* were gone, and in their place were members of the national police, whose allegiance was to Juin. The tables had been turned again. Robert Murphy was now the prisoner. The American knew that he could be summarily shot as a Nazi agent.*

All across French Northwest Africa, the intricate coup which pro-Allied French officers had been developing was in motion. Its purpose: to establish General Giraud as undisputed leader of French forces in Africa and to assure that the Americans would be greeted as liberators. Robert Murphy, who was known to most of these French officers by his *nom de guerre*, had for months been coordinating details of the coup.

---

* Alphonse Pierre Juin would prove to be one of the ablest generals in Mark Clark's army. He and his men distinguished themselves in vicious fighting against Rommel's Afrika Korps and later in the mountains of Italy. It was Juin and his French fighters who, in mid-1944, finally broke the prolonged and bloody stalemate at Cassino in Italy—a feat for which Juin never received the full credit due him and his men, except from General Mark Clark.

Now, unbeknownst to his French associates, Colonel McGowan was a prisoner at Villa des Oliviers in Algiers.

Each French general in the Allied conspiracy was risking his life; if the invasion should fail, the "traitors" (as viewed by Vichy) would be executed. The coup began at 1:00 A.M., just before the first American soldier splashed ashore. Major General Émile Béthouart, commander of the French Casablanca Division and a confederate of General Henri Giraud, hopped into a jeep at Casablanca and raced 50 miles to Rabat, headquarters of the French army in Morocco. Béthouart was protected by a battalion of Colonial Moroccan Infantry, young men who had fled France to continue the fight against the Nazis.

Béthouart confronted Major General General Georges Lascroux, in charge of the Moroccan army headquarters, demanding that he cooperate with the invading Americans "in the name of General Henri Giraud." The bewildered Lascroux balked, so Béthouart had him arrested and hauled away. Béthouart then took over Lascroux's position.

Next Béthouart buttonholed the commander of French air forces in Morocco, Major General Louis Lahouelle. Confused by the sudden turn of events, Lahouelle agreed not to resist the invaders if the French navy also refrained from opposition. Lahouelle promptly telephoned Vice Admiral François Michelier, naval commander in Morocco, who not only indignantly refused to cooperate with the invaders but got General Lahouelle to change his mind and fight the Americans. General Béthouart responded by having his Colonial Moroccan bodyguards arrest Lahouelle.

In Casablanca, Admiral Michelier, a die-hard Vichyite, knew that a military coup by some French officers was unfolding. Minutes before he had received General Lahouelle's telephone call, he had been presented with what amounted to an ultimatum by Lieutenant Colonel Eugène Mollé, General Béthouart's chief of staff. It said, in effect, to cooperate with the American landings . . . or else.

Michelier had been furious on receiving Béthouart's ultimatum. He bellowed at Mollé that Béthouart was stupid and a naive victim of an elaborate Allied hoax. There was no American armada lying offshore, the admiral declared—bad weather, a high surf, and failure of his coastal air or submarine patrols to spot hostile vessels before darkness proved that the Americans could not land that night.

Still, Michelier was taking no chances; maybe an Allied fleet had slipped in unnoticed. He telephoned the assistant commander of Béthouart's first-rate but ill-equipped Casablanca Division, Brigadier General Raymond Desré, and directed him to cancel Béthouart's orders for the division to remain in barracks. Instead, the division was to be rushed to its prescribed coastal defenses and "resist any invaders with every means at your disposal." Michelier was acting in his role as Casablanca sector commander.

Just after 3:00 A.M., members of the American consulate in dimmed-out Casablanca peered out from behind drawn blinds to see a long stream of French trucks with heavily armed soldiers, Citroën automobiles, motorcycles, and other vehicles hastening through the dark streets toward the coastal batteries and other positions. The noise of grinding gears and revved motors echoed ominously in the night air.

At his headquarters in Rabat, five-star General Auguste Paul Noguès, resident general of Morocco, was anguishing over his course of action—or inaction. Just prior to 2:30 A.M. Noguès had received a hand-delivered letter from General Émile Béthouart stating that General Henri Giraud, backed by American troops, planes, and warships, was taking command of all French forces in North Africa. Giraud, the document declared, had appointed Béthouart to command all French troops in Morocco.

Béthouart's letter also informed the befuddled Noguès that orders were being issued to French forces in northwest Africa not to oppose the American landings. The letter requested that Noguès issue confirming orders for Morocco. Or, if the resident general preferred, he could simply disappear until the invasion had been accomplished, then resurface to be appointed to a responsible post.

Auguste Noguès had been an enigma to Robert Murphy and to other pro-Allied officers in North Africa. After the French debacle of 1940, General Noguès had been zealous in his desire to resume fighting the Nazi war machine. At great personal risk he had concealed from the 300-member German Armistice Commission both troops and an amount of war matériel well in excess of the amount permitted. Somehow, though, over the interminable months, Murphy had noted a distinct change in Noguès's attitude. Almost imperceptibly the once anti-Nazi zealot had become dispirited, and by late October 1942 Noguès apparently intended to fight any Allied invaders.

General Noguès's view on this D-day morning might have been altered had he read a letter that lay unopened and unnoticed in a stack of mail on his desk. It had been delivered to him by an American vice consul at 12:55 A.M. Had the harassed Noguès gotten around to opening the envelope, he would have found a letter with the heading, THE WHITE HOUSE, WASHINGTON, D.C. Signed by President Roosevelt, it was a plea for America's "traditional friends" to join in helping to throw Adolf Hitler's Wehrmacht out of North Africa and ultimately to bring Nazi Germany to its knees.

General Noguès, lacking this datum, appraised the situation as he saw it. There was no evidence that a large Allied fleet was offshore. Admiral Michelier had issued orders to resist, and a telephone check with the commanders of the Meknes and Marrakech garrisons confirmed that they were remaining under Noguès's orders, not going over to General Giraud. Noguès acted. He ordered a general alert throughout Morocco, then contacted General Béthouart and directed him to dismiss his battalion of eager young Moroccan Colonials. Béthouart, who now realized that the coup in Morocco had failed and that the name Giraud had not sparked the magic that had been anticipated, was arrested by General Noguès and sent to Meknes to stand trial for treason.

By 1:00 A.M. on D-day, the entire coastline of northwest Africa for hundreds of miles had taken on a martial air. An Allied radio station aboard a ship in the Mediterranean, using the wavelength of the Rabat transmitter, was constantly calling out, "*Hallo, Maroc!* [Hello, Morocco!]" and playing "The Marseillaise" and "The Star Spangled Banner."

At 1:20 A.M. a voice came over the airwaves, speaking in fluent French, identifying itself as that of Dwight D. Eisenhower, supreme commander of *American* forces. (Actually, the radio-recording voice was that of Colonel Julius Holmes, one of Eisenhower's staff officers; the supreme commander's French was fractured at best.) Eisenhower assured the French military and citizens that the Americans were coming in as friends and liberators, and gave instructions on how to assist in the operation.

Three o'clock. Late radio listeners in northern Africa and southern Europe heard another American voice, speaking in near-perfect French with a tinge of Ivy League accent. *"Mes amis* [my friends]," the voice began, "this is President Franklin Roosevelt of the United States." The voice was firm and resolute, hopefully with just the right touch of friendly persuasion. "Have faith in our words. Help us where you are able." The president's concise broadcast asked all loyal Frenchmen, "all men who hate tyranny, to join with the liberators who at this moment are about to land on your shores." The plea concluded with a Rooseveltian flourish: *"Vive la France éternelle!* [May France live forever!]"

Overhead in the nighttime Mediterranean sky, from Safi and Casablanca a thousand miles eastward to Algiers, the throb of airplane engines permeated the night. Four-engine bombers had taken off from Malta and Gibraltar, but they did not drop explosives. Rather, they loosed a blizzard of folksy leaflets bearing the signature of Dwight D. Eisenhower. He called for cooperation with the liberators and declared that the Americans were coming as friends.

Part 2

A Mighty Armada Strikes

12

America's First
Paratroop Mission

It was chilly and damp at a bleak locale known as Land's End, a cape in Cornwall, in the westernmost point of countryside in England. Land's End is beautiful but forbidding, with granite cliffs up to 100 feet high that have been carved into dramatic contours by the Atlantic Ocean. Off in the distance, about a mile from shore, the blinking Longships Lighthouse marked dangerous reefs.

A short distance inland at two Royal Air Force fields, members of the 509th Parachute Infantry Battalion were gathered in small groups, conjecturing about why they were in this "godforsaken hellhole." They were proud of the fact that they would be the first paratroopers in American history to participate in an airborne operation, an elation tempered by the knowledge that the moment of truth—face-to-face confrontation with an enemy—was nearly at hand. It was November 7, 1942—D-day minus 1.*

---

* During the war this parachute outfit had three different numerical designations. When activated it was the 504th Parachute Battalion and at the time of Operation Torch it was the 2nd Battalion, 503rd Parachute Infantry. Later

Two days before, the crack battalion had been hustled aboard a train at Chilton Foliat and taken to Land's End. A platoon of troopers, mainly recent replacements, had remained at Chilton Foliat conducting exceptionally loud training exercises so that anyone watching would gain the impression that it was business as usual for the battalion.

At 11:00 A.M. on this November 7, Lieutenant Colonel Edson Raff briefed his officers. For the first time, lower ranks learned the true identities of airfields A and B, the objectives they had been training for weeks to seize. Most of the initiates were shocked—they had been convinced the airborne assault would be made just across the English Channel.

"Enormous stakes are involved," Raff declared. "Not only will we spearhead the invasion, but the future of the paratroops is on the line. If we do well, the airborne will be greatly expanded. If we fail our paratroop units may be disbanded."

Under the wings of squat C-47s, excited parachute officers briefed their men. Told of the two plans that had been drawn up by Major William Yarborough—Plan War and Plan Peace—many paratroopers were confused. They had been trained to fight, not to analyze complicated international politics. Growled Sergeant Ray Cagle to a comrade: "Are we supposed to go over there and fight or kiss our opponents?"

If the cloak-and-dagger discussions between high Allied officials and French leaders in North Africa were successful, Plan Peace would be in effect. In this case, the 509th would lift off after dark that night—D-day minus 1—so as to land in the C-47s at La Sénia airfield the next morning in daylight. If Plan War was executed, meaning that the French forces were expected to fight, the 39 C-47s would take off four hours sooner, in daylight, in order for the paratroopers to make a midnight drop over Tafaraoui airfield.

Late on the afternoon of November 7, with Raff's parachutists and air corps crew standing tensely by their C-47s on five-minute alert, word came through on the radio: Plan Peace.

One of those awaiting the takeoff was Lieutenant Archie Birkner.

---

it became the 509th Parachute Infantry Battalion, the designation by which it is most widely known.

Only a short time previously, the young officer had removed his regular uniform and, like the other paratroopers, had pulled on full-length woolen underwear (longjohns to the American GIs). The nights in North Africa would be cold. After pulling his lightweight jump suit over the heavy underwear, Birkner taped the legs so that the baggy pants and bulging pockets full of hand grenades would not catch in the doorway if he had to bail out. Finally, he checked the small American flag, of the kind each trooper had sewn to the sleeve of his jump jacket. He was ready to go.

Nearby, Captain Carlos C. "Doc" Alden, along with Captain William Moir, the battalion surgeon, was seated under the wing of a C-47. As the gray day began to fade into darkness, Alden scribbled in his small pocket diary a plea to his creator: "Dear God, in Thy wisdom help me to come back. But if I do not, then help me to do my duty as an American and as a man."*

Among the 556 paratroopers preparing to scramble aboard the carrier aircraft was Major Yarborough, General Clark's airborne advisor, who had conceived and planned the parachute operation. If America's first airborne attack met with disaster—and the odds were heavy that it might—it would be Yarborough's neck on the chopping block. At his own insistence, he was going along as a combat paratrooper, taking his chances along with the others.

Suddenly, across the blacked-out Predannack and St. Eval airfields, shouts rang out. "Okay, load 'em up! Next stop—North Africa!"

Scrappy Colonel Ed Raff raced by jeep from plane to plane, shaking his fist and shouting to the troopers: "Men, you know what to do. If the bastards open fire, give 'em hell."

The raucous revving of powerful engines echoed across the dark, damp countryside, and at 9:05 P.M. the first C-47 sped down the runway and lifted off. One by one, the others followed, and the sky train set a course for Oran, Algeria, 1,600 miles away.

Climbing steadily, the troop carrier planes leveled off at 10,000 feet. Soon loud curses rang out in the dark, crowded C-47s as frigid outside

---

* Captain Alden would become one of America's most decorated paratroopers by the war's end.

air seeped in. Blankets were hurriedly passed around, and the troopers bundled up. All were thoroughly miserable due to the arctic air and orders that required the men to wear their parachutes, as well as their cumbersome inflatable lifebelts, called Mae Wests after the busty Hollywood movie star, at all times during the ten-hour flight.

For several hours, the flight to Algiers was right on course and in precise formation. But over the Bay of Biscay strong easterly winds, heavy rains, darkness, and inexperience of air corps navigators all conspired to scatter the sky train. The C-47s winged on alone or in tiny clusters, the paratroopers unaware of this alarming development.

A second significant factor, likewise unknown to the 556 paratroopers and air crews, entered the picture. Shortly after the flight had lifted off from Land's End, senile Marshal Henri Pétain, the French World War I hero, had again issued orders for his forces in Northwest Africa to "resist the invaders with every means at your disposal." Sympathetic to their historic friend, the United States, yet torn by loyalty to the government of France, many French officers prepared to fight. Colonel Raff and his paratroopers, who thought they would land unopposed at La Sénia airfield shortly after dawn, would have a rude awakening.

Meanwhile, at his headquarters on Gibraltar, General Eisenhower received word, originating from Robert Murphy in Algiers, that the French armed forces in North Africa were preparing to fight. Eisenhower scrapped Plan Peace and ordered the paratrooper flight to be notified that Plan War was in effect. Eisenhower still hoped, however, that local French commanders would not obey the order from Hitler's puppets in Vichy; he ordered American soldiers not to fire on the French unless the French fired first. "France is not our enemy, Nazi Germany is," the Allied commander had often remarked. Offshore from Oran, a British warship, HMS *Alynbank*, was frantically seeking to get a radio signal to the oncoming 509th Parachute Infantry Battalion flight. "Play ball! Play ball!" was repeated ceaselessly. That was the code signal that Plan War was now in effect, and for the paratroopers to be prepared to fight if fired on.

Paratroop and air corps officers in the sky train were becoming increasingly tense. They had monitored their assigned radio frequency but had not received a single message since leaving England. Only much

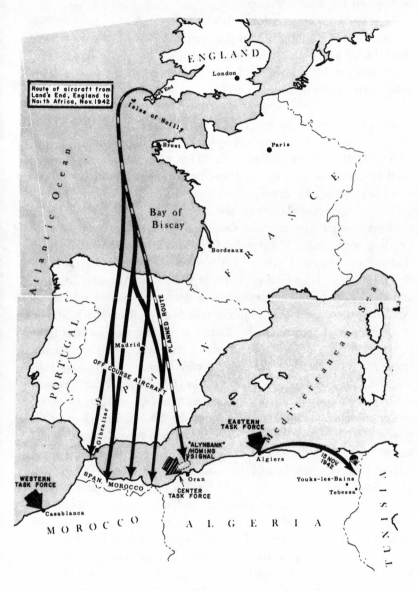

Map labels:

Route of aircraft from Land's End, England to North Africa, Nov. 1942

ENGLAND
London
Land's End
Isles of Scilly
Brest
Paris
FRANCE
Bay of Biscay
Bordeaux
Atlantic Ocean
PORTUGAL
Madrid
SPAIN
OFF COURSE AIRCRAFT
PLANNED ROUTE
ROUTE
Gibraltar
Mediterranean Sea
EASTERN TASK FORCE
"ALYNBANK" HOMING SIGNAL
Algiers
15 NOV 1942
SPAN. MOROCCO
Oran
CENTER TASK FORCE
Youks-les-Bains
Tebessa
WESTERN TASK FORCE
Casablanca
MOROCCO
ALGERIA
TUNISIA

Route of paratroop task force (Phillips Publications)

later would those in the flight learn that the *Alynbank* radio operator had been given the wrong frequency.

At Gibraltar, it appeared that America's first airborne operation was flying toward disaster. Perhaps the unarmed C-47s had already been detected by Luftwaffe night fighters and had been shot down. That could account for the flight's failure to respond to the frantic "Play ball!" signal from the *Alynbank*.

As the paratrooper flight progressed through the rainy night, the Oran battle convoy—British vessels carrying American assault troops—had edged silently into position some six to ten miles offshore. Homing in on the muted blue-light signals of five British submarines that had been lying just offshore for five days surveying the landing beaches through periscopes, the vessels hove to at about 10:45 P.M. Hazily outlined were the sleek configuration of cruisers and destroyers, and of command ships bristling with a maze of antennae. Crammed into the bowels of squat transports were men of General Terry Allen's 1st Infantry Division (the Big Red One), Major General Orlando Ward's 1st Armored Division, and the 1st Ranger Battalion led by a thirty-year-old, barrel-chested Arkansan, Lieutenant Colonel William O. Darby, affectionately known to his men as El Darbo. To the American fighting men on board, the names of their transports seemed quaint and steeped in British tradition—*Royal Ulsterman, Monarch of Bermuda, Warwick Castle, Clan Mac-Taggart, Glengyle, Duchess of Bedford, Llangibby Castle, Royal Scotsman.*

Oran, with a population of 200,000, was to be captured by a sweeping pincer movement. One combat team of the 1st Infantry Division (Z Force), which included Bill Darby's commando-type Rangers, would storm ashore 25 miles east of Oran, in and around the small port of Arzew. Y Force would be led by the assistant commander of the Big Red One, diminutive, fifty-five-year-old Brigadier General Theodore Roosevelt, Jr., son of a former president of the United States. They would come ashore at Les Andalouses ("Lots of Louses" to the GIs), 13 miles west of Oran. Z Force and Y Force would then attack Oran from east and west. Once the infantry had carved out beachheads, elements of Ward's 1st Armored Division were to land, plunge inland, and drive into Oran from the south. A flying column of the 1st Armored was to thrust on southward and, if need be, assist Colonel Ed Raff's paratroopers in seizing La Sénia and Tafaraoui airports.

Farther out to sea, cloaked by the blackness of night, lay a powerful British naval force commanded by Commodore Thomas Troubridge: the venerable old battleship *Rodney* with 16-inch guns capable of hurling a 700-pound shell 20 miles, the cruisers *Jamaica* and *Aurora,* the aircraft carrier *Furious,* and 31 other warships, including several destroyers. On board the *Furious* were 57 fighter-bombers.

Oran's harbor facilities were essential to future campaigns, so a daring plan, code-named Operation Reservist, had been designed to knock out covering French forts and capture the docks before they could be sabotaged. At 3:00 A.M.—two hours after H-hour—the HMS *Walney* and *Hartland,* former United States Coast Guard cutters transferred to the Royal Navy in 1941 and now crammed with specially trained assault troops, were to dash boldly into Oran harbor and carry out the mission. Commanding both vessels was Royal Navy Captain Frederick T. Peters, who had been chiefly responsible for planning Reservist and would be in charge of the daring operation. *Walney* and *Hartland* were not only relics but were unarmored and carried only one 5-inch gun apiece.

Captain Peters, a retired officer who had volunteered for this crucial mission, was optimistic about its chances. He not only contemplated seizing the big French guns above the city, but looked forward to receiving the surrender of Oran itself. Peters himself would be aboard the *Walney,* which would be the first vessel into the harbor.

The bulk of the assault force on the two cutters would be the 17 officers and 376 men of the 3rd Battalion, 6th Armored Infantry, of Ward's 1st Armored Division. The battalion was led by Lieutenant Colonel George F. Marshall, who had had to endure endless ribbing over the fact that his first name and surname were identical to those of the U.S. Army Chief of Staff. Also on board would be 4 officers and 22 sailors of the U.S. Navy, 6 American Marines, and 52 British navy officers and ratings. Counting the Royal Navy ship's crews, about 700 men would be involved in the venture.

Surprise would be crucial. The plan was for the *Walney,* cloaked by darkness, to ram through the floating boom forming the Oran harbor gate. With 200 American troops aboard, *Walney* was to dash the entire length of the harbor, lay alongside the Môle Centre (Middle Pier) and discharge its soldiers, who were to capture Fort Lamoune, which covered the head of the harbor.

Hartland was to follow the *Walney* through the broken boom, tie up to the first pier, the Môle du Ravin Blanc, and the remainder of Colonel Marshall's troops on board would claw their way up the steep cliff directly behind the pier to knock out the Ravin Blanc gun battery that looked down on the entire harbor. In the meantime, naval detachments in *Walney* and *Hartland* were to race onto other French ships to prevent their being scuttled and to protect the docks from demolition.

This charge into Oran harbor was called a "suicide mission" by the American fighting men involved. Its only chance for success lay in achieving total surprise. But with fighting taking place on both sides of Oran for two hours, and the inevitable noise of *Walney*'s bow crashing into the boom, what were the chances that French gunners looking down from Ravin Blanc battery and elsewhere in the harbor would be less than fully alert?

Those chances were slim to nonexistent in the mind of U.S. Rear Admiral Andrew C. Bennett, who would command the port on its capture. Bennett had vigorously protested the "Charge of the 700," but was overruled by higher authorities, who told him simply, "We've got to get that harbor intact if we are going to drive on eastward into Tunisia to hit Field Marshal Rommel in the rear."

As a result of Bennett's protest, one concession had been made: The *Walney* and *Hartland* would be allowed to withdraw if the essential element of surprise was lost. But once inside the harbor, would the two old cutters even be able to escape?

The entire Oran assault along 38 miles of beach could be a difficult and bloody task. Allied intelligence had reported that sea approaches to Oran and nearby Arzew were covered by 13 batteries of big coastal guns, most of which could be turned inland to fire on invading troops. Major General Robert Boissau's Oran Division had 10,000 men defending the coast, but he could pull in 12,500 more within five days.

Commanders in the Center Task Force had another concern. Only the day before, Gibraltar had received an urgent signal from Marine

Lieutenant Colonel William Eddy, the American naval attaché at Tangier, Spanish Morocco—a hotbed of spies. Eddy had warned that General Boissau in Oran had been tipped off to the invasion and that his troops would be on full alert.

Oran had known violence over the centuries. Roman legions wrested it from Carthaginians and in turn lost it to Arab conquerors. Spain took it over for a while, then lost it to the Turks. Around 1830, the French seized the port, which largely ended the violence for nearly 110 years. Then, in 1940, the British fleet, under the orders of a Winston Churchill fearful that the French naval force at nearby Mers el Kebir might fall into Hitler's hands, shelled Vichy's warships, an act in which hundreds of French casualties were inflicted. Now, only two and a half years later, a hailstorm of steel and explosives was again about to strike Oran.

As H-hour neared, General Terry Allen was circling the dark decks of his 1st Infantry Division command ship, the *Reina del Pacifico*, an old tub which for a generation had carried wealthy passengers between South America and California. The flamboyant Allen had taken the raw division, its ranks of civilian soldiers laced with professional officers, molded it, and now on the eve of battle could only hope that his efforts would produce results.

Allen paced through the blackness with two correspondents; no one spoke. They knew that other ships were lying all around them, but they could only sense their presence. Farther down the deck a light flickered for a split-second; someone had lighted a cigarette. "Put out that light, you stupid son of a bitch!" a voice hissed. All through the transport it seemed as though no one was speaking. Men walked softly, even though the hostile shore was some eight miles away.

Far off on the horizon toward Oran, there was a muted white glow. One of the civilian reporters touched Allen on the arm. "What are those lights?" he whispered.

"The shore," Allen replied nonchalantly.

But why the lights on the enemy shore? Or was it an enemy? Would the Frenchmen fight an invader? Were the lights on in Oran because the French were going to welcome the Americans as liberators? Or was it a trap of some sort? Whatever it was, the glow made the Americans aboard the dark transports nervous.*

Every effort had been made to assure the French that America was coming as a friend and liberator—including one project the GIs called a Rube Goldberg brainstorm. Despite many vigorous protests, assault leaders had been ordered to take ashore four mortar-type weapons, each heavy and bulky. They would shoot a pyrotechnic some 200 feet into the sky where it would burst into a magnificent display of the American flag, some 100 feet long, in red, white, and blue. "Billy Rose would go ape over that!" one GI said, referring to the Hollywood and Broadway producer noted for his colorful extravaganzas.

At 11:30 P.M. nautical noises poured over the dark seascape off Oran and Arzew. Windlasses whirled as booms on two score of blacked-out transports swung out landing craft and lowered them into the placid water. Muted loudspeakers squawked an occasional message.

Below in the cramped, dimly lit, dingy holds, American fighting men, most nervous and tense on the threshold of their first combat, wondered what cards fate would deal them. Each in his own way was steeling himself for the unknowable ordeal that lay just over the horizon. Some men read pocket Bibles. Here and there a soldier was dozing—or pretending to doze. Talk was subdued. On some transports the men listened blankly to a play-by-play broadcast of the Army–Notre Dame football game being broadcast from New York City by shortwave radio and piped over intercom systems. It was almost midnight when calls rang out on the transports: "Assault troops to your boarding stations!" It was the order no one wanted to hear and everyone knew was coming.

Burdened with combat gear weighing anywhere from 40 to 70 pounds, the men pulled their way up steel ladders and onto the decks. Shuffling along in the blackness, they took assigned positions along the railing just above their assault boats, which could be heard below scraping gently against the side of the transport.

Here and there friends clasped hands and solemnly wished each other

---

* Deliberately casual about the unexpected development at the time, General Allen admitted many years later that the lights in Oran had made him nervous also.

well. "See you on the beach!" many whispered. Stomachs felt queasy. Foreheads and palms perspired despite the chill.

Soon the loudspeakers blared: "Board your landing craft!" With a rustling of equipment, the assault troops climbed over railings and began the descent down the slippery rope ladders. Muffled curses rang out as men lost their footing or were struck in the face by the rifle barrels of comrades alongside. As each assault boat was filled, it circled its mother ship until all the landing craft in the first wave were crammed with soldiers and their weapons—including the newly issued bazookas.

A final order echoed over the seascape: "Away all boats!" With a raucous revving of motors that the nervous troops felt would "wake up the dead in Oran," the first wave headed for the dark beaches eight miles distant.

America's first major amphibious operation was underway.

13

Slaughter in Oran Harbor

Scores of tiny assault boats carrying Lieutenant Colonel Bill Darby's
Rangers were edging through the night toward Arzew, 25 miles east of
Oran. Motors were throttled back to half-speed. No sound came from
shore. It was eerie. Had the French been alerted? Would they fight? As
the shore drew closer, the Rangers gripped rifles and tommy guns and
braced for the first hostile shot that would signal the opening of the
struggle for French Northwest Africa. Orders had been specific: Don't
shoot until the other side fires.

Twelve fifty-five A.M. A thousand yards from the target of half of
Darby's force, the Arzew docks, throttles were opened wide, and with
a roar all landing craft surged forward. Moments later a stream of tracer
bullets from shore zipped across the seascape and splattered against the
front of the approaching assault boats.

As the Rangers prepared to spring from craft, a curious sight greeted
their eyes: The powerful beacon light at Arzew was shining brightly.
What did this odd occurrence mean? Was it some sort of signal to
French defenders along the Golfe d'Arzew that American troops were
racing toward the shore?

Half of the Ranger battalion, trained to strike stealthily but also hearing hostile shots for the first time, scrambled onto the Arzew docks, overpowered several French sentries after an exchange of gunfire, dashed through the black town for two blocks, and broke into a French army barracks. Despite the shooting on the docks, the entire French garrison was asleep in their bunks. Awakened by Ranger shouts and the prods of tommy-gun and rifle muzzles, sleepy-eyed French soldiers were taken prisoner.

Led by Colonel Darby, the remainder of the 1st Ranger Battalion stormed ashore nearby and began scrambling up the cliffs. The mission of the American commandos was to seize Fort du Nord and its battery of four 105-millimeter guns which covered the Golfe d'Arzew. Reaching the top after an arduous climb, Darby and his men slipped through the night to a ravine a mile inland. Darby motioned his men forward and they began inching along the ravine, which led to the rear of the battery. Scouts were sent forward, and as they began cutting heavy barbed-wire strands that protected Fort du Nord, a torrent of small-arms and automatic weapons fire erupted from the bastion.

Colonel Darby ordered his mortars to plaster the fort, and on the heels of the barrage he and his men charged forward, swept over the barbed wire and dashed into the enclosure. French defenders, not even knowing whom they had been fighting, surrendered after a flurry of gunfire. At 3:55 A.M. Bill Darby fired a green flare to signal watchers that Fort du Nord and its battery of guns had been captured.

Those watchers were several combat teams of United States Marines and sailors and Royal Navy seamen who had been hovering just outside the port entrance to Arzew. Spotting the green flare, the naval assault teams dashed into the harbor and, while sporadic gunfire echoed throughout Arzew, boarded and seized control of four French ships moored at the docks.*

Meanwhile the 18th Regimental Combat Team of the 1st Infantry Division—7,092 strong under Colonel Frank U. Greer—was heading

---

* William Orlando Darby would become an American legend. He was killed in action at age thirty-four only a few days before the war in Europe ended and was promoted posthumously to brigadier general.

for the beaches just southeast of Arzew. Loudspeakers with specially trained crews were placed in several of the leading assault craft in anticipation of a friendly response from French defenders. When close enough to shore to be heard, the crews were to blare out in deliberately designed "Americanized" French: *"Ne tirez pas! Ne tirez pas!* [Don't shoot!]"

Now, on nearing the dark shore, the loudspeakers went into action: *"Ne tirez pas! Ne tirez—"* The appeal was interrupted by heavy bursts of machine gun fire. Again: *"Ne tirez pas! Ne—"* More bullets. The operators ducked for cover. On their own initiative the psychological warfare scheme was hastily abandoned as gunfire from the beach drowned out the American message of friendship.

In the blackness, inexperienced young navigators on the assault craft became disoriented, and the first boats were 20 minutes late in reaching shore. For the next 15 minutes stragglers kept arriving at scattered points, resulting in Colonel Greer's combat teams being intermingled and in fragments. Confusion had the upper hand.

Inside adjacent Arzew where Darby's Rangers had landed, the sound of heavy gunfire echoed through the night as Colonel Greer tried desperately to bring order out of near chaos. As the harassed combat team leader was talking on a walkie-talkie, he was approached by a sergeant who wanted to know if it was time to fire the Rube Goldberg mortar. Preoccupied with the scrambled condition of his units, Greer snapped, "Okay, but take the damned thing somewhere away from here before you shoot it!"

With two companions, the sergeant lugged the heavy device only 50 yards away. Moments later there was a loud boom, followed by a brilliant pyrotechnic display in red, white, and blue in the sky over Colonel Greer's command post, which was out in the open. The flaming American flag was a beautiful sight to behold, dangling majestically 200 feet in the air.

All hell broke loose. French defenders had not known where the invaders had come ashore and had not found a specific target at which to shoot. Now machine gun tracers streamed past Colonel Greer and his command group, and mortars pounded the CP. For a long time Greer and his staff were stretched out with noses pressed into the sand.

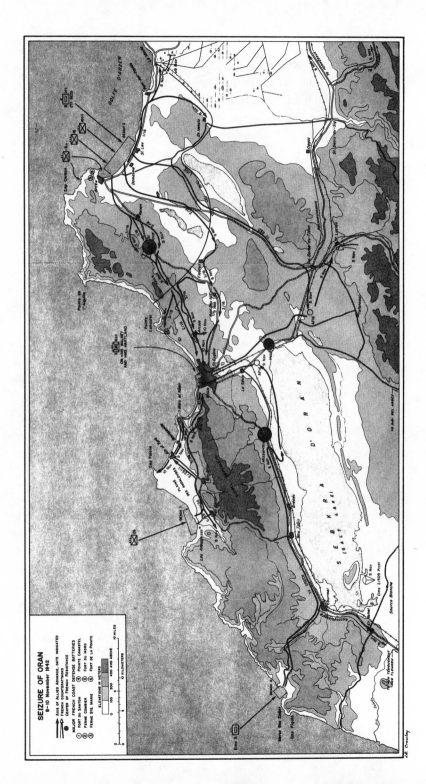

SEIZURE OF ORAN
8–10 November 1942

AXIS OF ALLIED ADVANCE, DATE INDICATED
FRENCH COUNTERATTACKS
CENTER OF FRENCH RESISTANCE
MAJOR FRENCH COAST DEFENSE BATTERIES
① FORT DU SANTON   ④ POINTE CANASTEL
② FERME COMBIER   ⑤ FORT DU NORD
③ FERME STE. MARIE   ⑥ FORT DE LA POINTE

ELEVATIONS IN METERS

400 AND ABOVE

0   100   200   400   600
KILOMETERS

0   5   10 MILES

J.E. Crawley

Muffled curses erupted, damning the "idiots" on high who had demanded that the fireworks gimmick be used.

Despite the blackness and the confusion, Colonel Greer had his 18th Combat Team untangled sufficiently by 4:00 A.M. to send Lieutenant Colonel Courtney P. Brown's 3rd Battalion into Arzew to relieve Darby's Rangers. At a French naval base southwest of the harbor, elements of Brown's battalion were raked by automatic weapons and halted their advance to pound the defenders with mortars. The naval officer commanding the base surrendered. Thirteen seaplanes, fueled, loaded with torpedoes, and warmed up to take off, were captured intact. Presumably the warplanes were preparing to strike at the British fleet squatting off Oran.

In the meantime, Colonel Greer sent his 1st Battalion under Major Richard Parker plunging inland along the coastal road hell-bent for Oran. At the town of St. Cloud, which lay in the center of an open agricultural area astride the main road about one-third of the way to Oran, Parker's men ran into a hornet's nest when their leading elements were charged by five French armored cars just east of St. Cloud. After a brisk firefight all five vehicles were knocked out by antitank rifle grenades. The green Americans, ashen-faced and grim, stared as though mesmerized at the bloody, mutilated corpses of the Frenchmen sprawled grotesquely and hanging out of their wrecked armored cars. Many of Parker's men were sick to their stomachs.

Major Parker rapidly reorganized his battalion to push on toward Oran. Apparently there would be no resistance ahead, for an American armored reconnaissance car had driven through St. Cloud and returned unmolested, its crew reporting the town of 3,500 was deserted. But in the meantime, a strong force of riflemen and machine gunners of the 16th Tunisian Regiment and elements of the Foreign Legion had slipped into St. Cloud and taken up positions inside sturdy concrete houses that provided ready-made pillboxes. When Parker's men approached the town, they were met by a torrent of rifle and machine-gun fire and pounded by shells fired by the 75- and 155-millimeter guns of the 68th African Artillery Regiment in position northwest of St. Cloud. Under heavy fire for the first time and caught out in the open, the Big

Red One battalion hastily pulled back to regroup. Clearly, St. Cloud, blocking the road to Oran, was strongly held and would be a tough nut to crack. Before launching another assault, Major Parker radioed for reinforcements.

On beaches just to the left of Colonel Greer's landing, 5,608 men of Colonel Henry B. Cheadle's 16th Regimental Combat Team of the 1st Infantry Division landed with virtually no opposition and cleared out a small bridgehead for the 3:00 A.M. arrival of the 1st Armored Division's Combat Command B, led by Brigadier General Lunsford E. Oliver.

Oliver's 4,772-man armored force had the mission of seizing the La Sénia and Tafaraoui airfields, south of Oran, in the event Lieutenant Colonel Ed Raff's paratroopers needed help in that task. The French had a large number of fighter-bombers at these two facilities which loomed as a serious threat to Allied ships offshore. The French pilots were experts, and their Dewoitine fighter planes were faster and more maneuverable than the carrier-based Allied aircraft. (Other elements of Lunsford's Combat Command B were landing many miles to the west of Oran at Mersa bou Zedjar, and they would also race for La Sénia and Tafaraoui.)

Meanwhile, off Les Andalouses west of Oran, the 26th Combat Team, 1st Infantry Division, under Brigadier General Teddy Roosevelt, was slowed by unexpected developments before the assault waves cast off. The ladders thrown down the sides of the *Monarch of Bermuda* had rungs two feet apart (instead of the normal one-foot space), so the heavily burdened infantrymen took twice as long as planned to struggle into their assault craft.

Due to the delay aboard the *Monarch of Bermuda*, the first wave hit the Les Andalouses beaches 20 minutes late. But no one was complaining. The beaches, where in peacetime the wealthy of Europe had taken the Mediterranean sun, were deserted. Not a shot had been fired.

The only "casualty"—and he suffered nothing worse than a cold dunking—was General Teddy Roosevelt himself, who had planned to drive right off his big steel invasion barge onto the shore. The ramp was let down too soon, and in the darkness Roosevelt, his driver, and their jeep plunged into eight feet of water.*

Shortly after landing at Les Andalouses, Lieutenant Colonel Kenneth Campbell in the darkness literally stumbled onto an Arab sleeping on the beach. The groggy man, recovering from his initial shock of awakening to find American soldiers milling around the once-deserted shoreline, told Campbell that there were French soldiers in a building atop a nearby hill. The colonel pulled out his Colt .45 and alone slipped up to the darkened structure. He slowly pushed open the door and was greeted by a chorus of loud snores.

Campbell shoved his pistol back into its holster, tiptoed into the building, flipped on a dim light, and awakened the French soldiers. The sleepy-eyed Frenchmen were startled to see an armed American hovering over them. Colonel Campbell, who spoke fluent French, passed his pack of Camel cigarettes around, chatted briefly, then told the soldiers to put on their clothes.

"You're now prisoners of war," Campbell stated almost apologetically.

Along the Les Andalouses sector, the tranquility, the moonlight, and the dancing shadows all joined to create an eerie climate for these American soldiers new to war. "This place gives me the goddamned creeps!" a Big Red One GI whispered to a comrade. No one spoke above a whisper. Each outfit had been given the password and the countersign before leaving ship. Now, in the ominous shadows, it was difficult to tell who was who, and the soldiers were concerned about getting shot by fellow Americans. During the remainder of the hours of darkness, along the beach and on hillsides around Les Andalouses there was a relentless hissing of whispered passwords directed at each approaching shadow.

About eight miles offshore on the *Reina del Pacifico*, an anxious General Terry Allen was peering toward the beaches, seeking desperately to part

---

* In the Normandy invasion on June 6, 1944, Brigadier General Roosevelt, at his own insistence, was in the first assault craft to hit Utah Beach. Six weeks later he died of a heart attack.

the black veil of night. He glanced at his luminous wristwatch: It was 1:20 A.M. What had happened to Teddy Roosevelt's assault force? It was to have landed at H-hour, 20 minutes before. Suddenly, Allen gave out a sigh of relief. From the dark shore a white flare shot into the sky. It was a signal that the first wave had landed unopposed at Les Andalouses. Minutes later there was another flare, this one red. It indicated that the second wave had come ashore, also unopposed.

A gleeful Terry Allen rushed off to a large wardroom where yet another party was preparing to go ashore. "Boys, I thought you'd like to know that our first two waves landed without opposition," the division commander exclaimed. Then, grinning broadly, Allen added: "I've just sent a signal to the French to put in their first team!"

Within minutes, General Allen began to think that the French had heeded his advice. From the direction of Arzew came the angry sounds of gunfire. The French defenders were battling Colonel Bill Darby's Rangers and elements of Colonel Frank Greer's 18th Combat Team.

Fifteen miles west from where Teddy Roosevelt had taken his early-morning dip, Colonel Paul McD. Robinett's Task Force Green (of Ward's 1st Armored Division) was preparing to leave transports for a landing near the dingy little town of Mersa bou Zedjar. Robinett's armored force was to go ashore at H-hour plus 2 (3:00 A.M.). Suddenly, a convoy of five fully lighted French ships, escorted by an armed trawler and headed eastward toward Oran on a course paralleling the coast, sailed between the British ships lying out in the darkness and the beach target of Mersa bou Zedjar.

On his command ship *Largs*, Lieutenant General Lloyd R. Fredendall, the diminutive, fifty-eight-year-old commander of Center Task Force troops, was in a quandary. What to do about this unexpected development? Fredendall had been a staff assistant to General John J. Pershing in World War I and had spent countless hours over the years studying tangled military problems at staff and command school. But Fredendall had never come across the situation now confronting him: the sudden appearance of a lighted convoy belonging to a nation that could or could not be hostile and directly in the path of amphibious assault troops.

Hastily conferring with Commodore Troubridge on the *Largs*, General Fredendall gave the order: Halt and board the French ships. One ship was stopped and a navy detachment scrambled aboard. But the remaining four French vessels sped eastward, chased through the night by British warships. Reaching the vicinity of Les Andalouses (where Teddy Roosevelt's force had just landed), the fleeing vessels ran onto the British light cruiser *Aurora*, which tried to halt the little convoy. The French vessels quickly reversed course and, with *Aurora* in hot pursuit, ran aground near Cap Figalo. In the confusion, the armed trawler fled, was swallowed up by the night, and escaped.

As a result of the wild sea chase, the run into the beach by Colonel Robinett's task force was delayed for 38 minutes. Then, halfway to shore, an assault boat motor caught fire and spilled fuel over the surface. The gasoline burned brightly for hours, providing hostile eyes for miles with illuminating evidence that an amphibious assault was in progress.

In the confusion generated by the French convoy episode, by the green landing-craft navigators, the darkness, and the surface oil fire that forced wide detours, the assault waves heading for the beaches became tangled. This resulted in the curious situation of the second wave landing ahead of the first wave. But within an hour Lieutenant Colonel William B. Kern, commander of assault troops, signaled that the Mersa bou Zedjar beach was secure.

Two-fifty-five A.M. Undisturbed by the shooting that had erupted earlier on the beaches some distance to the east and west, the city of Oran was sleeping peacefully. An almost breathless hush hovered over the metropolis. Suddenly the tranquility was shattered; the sound of air-raid sirens pierced the night; news of the American landings had apparently arrived in the city. Lights were extinguished.

While the sirens wailed mournfully, the former U.S. Coast Guard cutters, now the HMS *Walney* and the HMS *Hartland*, were knifing through the black waters toward the floating boom that stretched for 200 yards across the harbor's mouth to guard against hostile attacks. On the bridge of the leading *Walney*, Captain Frederic Peters, the retired British naval officer who had volunteered to lead this crucial mission to seize Oran's docks, ordered engines to flanking speed in order to hit the boom with maximum force.

Onward came the cutters, apparently undetected. Crammed onto decks and into holds, some 500 assault troops clutched their weapons, unable to do more until the vessels reached the piers. Squinting intently into the blackness as the two cutters neared the boom, Captain Peters felt a surge of deep alarm—*Walney* and the trailing *Hartland* were missing the harbor gate by more than a quarter mile.

Peters had no alternative: He ordered *Walney* and *Hartland* to make a 360-degree circle at full speed and charge the boom again head-on. The cutters' open throttles and tight turns created a wide phosphorescent wake.

French gunners at the Ravin Blanc battery atop cliffs overlooking the harbor had been alerted by the air-raid sirens and were watching the sky. Then, before their eyes, the sea outside of the boom was suddenly glowing in the dark. A powerful searchlight on the cliff switched on. Its beam scanned the wake, then picked out *Walney*. The element necessary for success of Operation Reservist—surprise—had passed to the defenders.

The big guns of the Ravin Blanc battery, its commander undeterred by the huge American flag painted on the bow of the *Walney*, opened fire. French shells began sending up geysers to either side of the British vessel. *Hartland* remained undetected, but, with surprise lost, the British skippers of the two cutters, Lieutenant Commander P. C. Meyrick and Lieutenant Commander G. P. Billot, expected to complete a half circle and zigzag out to sea and away from the flaming French guns of Oran harbor.

Captain Peters, however, had other ideas: He ordered the *Walney*, still in the grasp of powerful searchlight beams, and the *Hartland* to continue with a *full* circle and head once more for the floating boom. In taking this action, Peters disregarded the signal he had received some 15 minutes previously from General Fredendall and Commodore Troubridge on the command ship *Largs*. The message had indicated that the landings on either side of Oran were going well and instructed the Reservist force: "Don't start a fight unless you have to." To Captain Peters, these last-minute instructions were vague. What was meant by the expression "unless you have to"? He interpreted it to mean "unless you have to" in order to carry out the mission.

With French shells and machine-gun fire concentrating on the brightly illuminated *Walney*, the little ship bore down on the floating boom at full speed, crashed into it with an ear-splitting crunch, and plunged onward to smash through a second barrier of a string of barges. *Walney*, now inside the harbor, headed for its objective, the Môle Centre. At point-blank range, the guns atop the cliff continued to pour shells at the beleaguered little ship. For a quarter mile, *Walney* took this plastering, but abruptly the searchlight shifted to *Hartland* and in moments the trailing vessel was under heavy fire. *Walney* staggered on in total darkness.

Unknown to Captain Peters, two French submarines, the *Pallas* and the *Ceres*, were moored near the Môle du Ravin Blanc, their gun crews ready. When *Walney* was only 200 yards away and exposing her port side, the French submarines commenced machine-gun and 75-millimeter fire. Though struck numerous times, *Walney* continued to creep forward, its decks and holds littered with bodies.

A more frightening danger loomed. From the *Walney* bridge, Captain Peters discerned the silhouette of a large French destroyer. Desperately, *Walney* swung sharply to starboard in an effort to ram, but the French warship loosed a broadside from her big guns at a range of less than 200 feet. The blast riddled *Walney*'s bridge, killing several officers, wounding others, and blowing Captain Peters into the night.

Down in a dark compartment of *Walney*, thirty-seven-year-old Sergeant Ralph Gower of Sacramento, California, was huddled fearfully with comrades he could only sense were around him. It was a horrifying experience there in the inky blackness: hearing the terrific racket of machine-gun bursts and shell explosions and the screams of men whose arms, legs, or pieces of face had suddenly been sliced off, feeling the old cutter being rocked repeatedly by direct hits, yet unable to see what was going on. A shell ripped into Gower's inky-black compartment. To the sergeant, it seemed to explode right in his face. For a fleeting second he was aware of strident screams nearby. The blast knocked Gower cold, and when he regained consciousness he could hardly breathe and thought that he was going to choke to death; the ship reeked with ammonia and cordite fumes and thick smoke.

In his hazy mind, he was puzzled. All was quiet—even tomblike.

Only later would he realize that the shell's blast had left him deaf. Gower struggled over to a steel ladder and somehow pulled his way up it to the deck. He could see that the harbor was laced with streams of tracer bullets, and there were many orange bursts of fire from crashing shells. Yet he could hear nothing.

Groggy and weak, the sergeant saw what he thought were rumpled barracks bags scattered about the deck. These were the dead bodies of American soldiers and British sailors. Gower again lost consciousness.

Reviving once more, he found himself lying on deck by the railing, aware that a heavy burden was preventing him from moving. Then he realized that dead bodies were the cause of his immobility. Apparently in an effort to clear a path through *Walney*'s body-littered deck, someone had thought the unconscious Gower was dead and had dragged him to one side and stacked American corpses on top of him.

Finally pulling himself out from under the pile of mutilated bodies, Gower saw that men up and down the deck were kneeling and blazing away at French destroyers and submarines with rifles and tommy guns, yet he could hear nothing. Lieutenant Colonel George Marshall, who commanded the armored infantrymen, had ordered his men to fight back, but their bullets bounced off the thick-plated warship. Marshall's GIs fired until they fell—dead or wounded.

Walney continued doggedly through the gauntlet toward her objective at the far end of the harbor, the Môle Centre. The cutter was within 300 yards of her goal when a shell exploded inside her boiler room, killing those inside and knocking out power to the screw. Fires blazed up. Ammunition exploded. Bodies were flung about. A crew, exposed to the hailstorm of fire, was blasting away with the *Walney*'s lone 5-inch deck gun when a shell blew weapon and crew to pieces.

Now a twisted, burning, smoke-filled wreck without power, *Walney* drifted under its own momentum toward the Môle Centre as though a supernatural force had willed that this doomed little vessel would reach her destination. But another peril loomed. Alongside the Môle Centre, where *Walney*'s assault troops were to disembark, were berthed the French destroyers *Tramontane* and *Epervier*. As the helpless *Walney* drifted toward them, both warships opened fire from main batteries, machine guns, and antiaircraft weapons. At less than 100 feet, French naval gunners couldn't miss. Point-blank broadsides seemed to lift the smoking, twisted hunk of floating wreckage out of the dark water. But *Walney*, refusing to die, inched onward and collided gently with one of the destroyers. *Walney*—now a ghost ship—had reached her goal, but not a man remained to storm the docks. Those on board who were able to do so had leaped into the Oran harbor waters and were struggling to swim to the piers. A few succeeded and were taken prisoner; most drowned.

Minutes later one final violent explosion shook *Walney;* the smoking cutter capsized and sank, taking the dead and dying with her.

The lone *Hartland* now received the full fury of the guns inside Oran harbor. Trailing *Walney* by 600 yards as the two cutters had neared the harbor gate, *Hartland* had missed the hole torn in the floating boom by *Walney*, run up onto a sloping jetty, and stuck there. The skipper, Lieutenant Commander Billot, tried desperately to back off the jetty. His ship was caught in the full glare of a French searchlight just as she pulled free.

The guns on top of the cliffs and all the destroyers and submarines in Oran harbor directed their fire at the illuminated *Hartland*. Commander Billot was temporarily blinded by a shell explosion, but he remained on the bridge and ordered the beleaguered ship to head for its objective, the Môle du Ravin Blanc, a quarter mile from the harbor gate. A gun crew fired three rounds from the lone 5-inch deck gun, until an incoming shell killed the crew and destroyed the weapon. The sightless Billot shouted for *Hartland* to keep moving, and miraculously, the old cutter reached the Môle du Ravin Blanc.

Just as *Hartland*'s crew began mooring her, the *Ceres* and the *Pallas*, the French submarines that had ravaged *Walney* a short time before, opened fire at less than 200 yards' range. At the precise point on the *môle* where it had been planned for *Hartland* to unload her assault troops, yet another French destroyer, the *Typhon*, was lurking ominously in the dark. The *Typhon*'s powerful guns sent shells screaming into the unarmored sides of *Hartland*, killing scores of American soldiers huddled in terror there. In moments, the ill-fated ship lost its boiler power and steering mechanism and became a sheet of flame from bow to stern.

A helpless, twisted mass of steel, *Hartland* drifted away from the *môle*. A fiery inferno raged below decks, and American soldiers who were not dead or seriously wounded scrambled topside to escape being roasted. There they were raked by machine-gun fire from the *Typhon* and other French warships.

Still at his post, Commander Billot ordered word spread: "Abandon ship!" Half of those aboard were already dead. Despite the machine-gun bullets that swept the decks, many soldiers put lifejackets on the seriously wounded, shoved them overboard, and leaped in after them. Those GIs who were able to swim were promptly taken prisoner.

Manned only by the dead, *Hartland* burned fiercely for 15 minutes, then an enormous explosion ripped her into pieces, flinging huge chunks of steel in all directions. What remained of *Hartland* plunged out of sight and joined her sister ship *Walney* on the bottom of Oran harbor.

By dawn the sounds of battle had subsided, and a stillness settled over heavily defended Oran harbor. Of the 17 officers and 376 men of Lieutenant Colonel George Marshall's armored infantry battalion, 9 officers and 180 men were killed or presumed dead, and 5 officers and 153 men were wounded. United States Navy casualties were 5 killed and 7 wounded; Royal Navy losses, 113 killed and 86 wounded. The "Charge of the 700" had been a bloody debacle.

14

Shootout at Arzew Barracks

On D-day morning, Sergeant Norman Harrington and Private Ned Modica stood in the darkness on the hurricane deck of a troop transport lying offshore from Arzew. They carried pistols, but these were not their primary weapons. Harrington and Modica were Signal Corps photographers, and their hazardous war was fought in the front lines with cameras.

Sergeant Harrington had been a civic leader back home in Easton, Maryland, beginning when he was only sixteen years of age. At seventeen he became the nation's youngest Rotarian. His thirty-five-year-old pal Ned Modica had studied art in Paris for two years before the war and later operated his own photographic studio on New York City's fashionable Madison Avenue.

Now, in the offshore blackness, Harrington and Modica were excited and fascinated by the battle scenes their cameras were recording—crisscrossing patterns of American and French tracer bullets, the sudden brilliant skybursts of white, red, or green flares, the fiery orange balls mushrooming into the black sky as shells exploded.

As the darkness gave way to another Mediterranean dawn, the photographers' transport moved in close to the shore. Hardly had it dropped anchor when a French mortar shell exploded on the hurricane deck, sending Harrington and Modica scrambling for cover. Moments later a second shell blew up the spot where they had been sleeping only a few hours before.

Harrington and Modica stared at each other with a degree of concern. So this is what war is *really* like? They shoot at you even before you get ashore. But there was no time for an exchange of views—the loudspeaker blared out with their numbers; they were going ashore.

Scrambling like trained monkeys down the slippery rope ladders (they were grateful that, unlike the assault troops, they did not have to make this hazardous descent in the dark), Harrington and Modica headed for the beach in a tiny landing boat. They were loaded down almost as much as the infantrymen: three musette bags filled with extra film plus an assortment of cameras. Modica clutched a still camera and two color movie cameras, while Harrington lugged a heavy newsreel job and a still camera.

Reaching shallow water, the photographers eagerly leaped out of the boat—landing waist-deep in the cold Mediterranean. Undaunted, Harrington and Modica began furiously grinding away with movie cameras and rapidly clicking their still jobs, all aimed at the spectacular procession of troops, guns, vehicles, and equipment pouring over the beaches.

When they became numb from being half-submerged in cold water for nearly 30 minutes, Harrington and Modica waded ashore. There they filmed their first blood—a wounded French soldier, still wearing his coveted red fez, being treated by American medics. The cameramen had never seen a wounded enemy soldier before—or was this young Frenchman an enemy? The man's intestines were spilled out on the ground.

Offshore on the *Reina del Pacifico*, General Terry Allen had been pacing about like a caged tiger since 3:00 A.M. He was intent on getting ashore immediately to direct the developing battle. But even the commanding general of the Big Red One had to wait for the vicissitudes of war to run their course: In the blackness, the assault-boat coxswains had lost their way on returning to the transport area after depositing troops on the beach, and many landing craft had staggered around the Mediterranean for hours before finally stumbling onto their mother ships.

It was approaching 6:00 A.M. and getting light before Terry Allen's landing craft finally came alongside. Now a perilous venture was about to unfold—35 staff members, not trained for combat, would have to work their way down long ladders over the side of the *Reina del Pacifico* and into the landing craft. Each staff officer and noncom in General Allen's party waddled up to the railing much like a gorilla, armed to the teeth and loaded down with about 40 pounds of gear.

Each carried a tommy gun, carbine, or automatic rifle, and most lugged along grenades and trench knives or daggers. Strapped over their shoulders were musette bags and gas masks; somehow, under all this gear, they had managed to strap on bulky life preservers.

Led by General Allen, who made the difficult descent like a gymnast, the staff personnel worked down the rope ladders and were packed like sardines into a waiting boat by British officers who operated the landing craft. So tightly had they been shoehorned in that they half sat and half lay on their backs, flat on the deck and more or less in each other's laps.

No passenger was able to move or see anything but the back of the neck of the man in front of him. They could tell when the beach was getting closer, for the rattle of machine-gun fire and the crash of artillery and mortar shells were growing louder. Unknown to General Allen and his staff, minutes after they had cast off from the *Reina del Pacifico*, a French artillery shell had smashed into the command ship.

As Allen's craft neared the beach, the British navy fired smoke shells off to the right to form a screen to protect the Big Red One command group from French machine gunners holding out in a sturdy brick building on a hillside in Arzew. A hundred yards from shore, Terry Allen and his men staggered out of the landing craft and waded ashore in knee-deep water. The general quickly moved inland several hundred yards and set up the division's command post in a wooden schoolhouse.

Meanwhile H. R. "Red" Knickerbocker, a *Chicago Sun* correspondent who had come ashore with General Allen, was watching Americans streaming over the beach, which was littered with gas masks, life belts, and other items discarded by weary and overburdened fighting men. A tall, slender man wearing the uniform of the French Foreign Legion walked toward Knickerbocker. This was strange, the reporter reflected, an officer in the French army strolling about unsupervised in American positions. Weren't the French supposed to be the "enemy"?

Speaking in perfect English, the Foreign Legion captain said, "I think you had better do something about the Arzew Barracks. They are still occupied by Tunisian Fusiliers, and until they are cleared out, the town is not safe." Now Knickerbocker was even more amazed. Here was a French officer of the Foreign Legion suggesting that other French units be neutralized to make it safe for the American invaders.

Suddenly Knickerbocker beamed. "Captain Hamilton!"

The Foreign Legion officer's thin face broke into a wide grin and he reached out for the reporter's hand. "Knickerbocker, my God. I haven't seen you since Saigon!"

It was a homecoming of sorts. Five years before the two had met in Saigon, Indochina (later Vietnam), where Captain Edgar G. Hamilton, the only American officer in the Foreign Legion, had told Knickerbocker of his adventures in the fabled French force which he had joined after World War I. Hamilton now said that the outbreak of the current war had caught him in Algeria, and that the Germans had made sure that he stayed there because they knew he wanted to defect and join the American army.

Learning of Captain Hamilton's report on the Tunisian Fusiliers in the Arzew Barracks, Colonel Fred Butler decided to take matters into his own hands. He collared three sergeants armed with automatic rifles and a machine gun, and, with Captain Hamilton and Knickerbocker trailing, left the Big Red One CP for the short trek to the Arzew Barracks.

Nearing the edge of a drillground, the party paused and surveyed the situation. There was a large white building surrounded by a high wall dotted with rifle slots. Not a human was seen.

"Okay, let's go," the slender, prematurely gray Colonel Butler called out. This was the first "action" he had seen.

"Hold it," Captain Hamilton responded. "There's an entire battalion of Fusiliers in that building, and the fact they aren't firing is a sign they are waiting for a good target." Having taken part in countless battle actions in twenty years with the Foreign Legion, Hamilton added: "If you go across that drillground you are certain to be fired at."

Colonel Butler was unimpressed. "What do you expect in war?" he snapped. "Come on."

Hamilton shrugged and followed Butler and the others onto the drillground. Moments later rifle fire erupted from the upper windows of the barracks, and the group dashed for the cover of a stone wall to the front as French bullets whistled past them and kicked up dust near their madly pumping feet.

Reaching the wall, a young soldier with a Garand rifle, breathing heavily from exertion, called out in an excited voice, "Gee, a year ago back in Brooklyn I never would have believed I could do this." With that, he took aim and, one after the other, fired three clips at Tunisian Fusiliers in the windows.

Attracted by the outbreak of shooting, other 1st Infantry Division soldiers arrived on the scene, took up positions behind the stone wall, and joined in peppering the Arzew Barracks. After several minutes of the brisk firefight—in which Foreign Legion Captain Hamilton joined—the Americans had expended all of their ammunition.

Correspondent Knickerbocker noted that his old friend from Saigon days, a battle-scarred veteran of countless shoot-outs, had been mildly amused at the inexperienced Americans in their first battle action.* Now Captain Hamilton suggested to Colonel Butler that they go to the mayor of Arzew and convince him that he should talk the barracks into capitulating.

Butler pondered the proposal, then said tersely, "Okay, let's go." Maybe the Foreign Leigon veteran knew what he was talking about, after all.

Reaching the *hôtel de ville* or city hall, Colonel Butler found the mayor, Dr. Miguel Maille, upset not only over the invasion of Algeria but more specifically over this intrusion into his private domain. Maille's jaw trembled until his teeth clicked like castanets.

Red-faced and nearly apoplectic, Mayor Maille listened as Colonel

---

* Red Knickerbocker survived the war, but was killed shortly afterward in a plane crash in India.

Butler, speaking slowly in French, told him: "Telephone the Arzew Barracks and tell them I have issued an ultimatum: Surrender or be shelled to pieces!"

Maille, a Vichy-installed functionary, now loosed an outburst over the "aggression" of the Americans and British against French Northwest Africa. Colonel Butler became angry. He cut off Maille in midsentence, glared at him with steely eyes, and exclaimed: "May or Maille, I am telling you for the final time. You will make the telephone call as I ordered, or . . ."

The mayor, trembling all over, reached for the telephone. His hands were shaking so badly that he had to use both of them to hold the instrument. Maille talked for a long time, often so excitedly that Butler could not understand him. All the while the American colonel stood in front of the mayor, stared coldly at him, and periodically patted his holstered Colt .45.

Finally, his hands still trembling, Mayor Maille replaced the telephone on the hook, looked up at Colonel Butler, and, in a tone of resignation, said softly: "The officer requests you come to the barracks and take his surrender."*

At first light on D-day, the British aircraft carrier *Furious* and two auxiliary carriers, lying 30 miles off Oran, were bustling with activity. Eight Albacore dive bombers and six Hurricane fighters flew off the carriers' flight decks, formed up at 5,000 feet over *Furious*, and headed inland. They were looking for a fight, and it would not be long in coming. But first the 14 carrier planes flew along the coast in the Oran sector and showered propaganda leaflets on ten towns and villages.

With the psychological warfare mission out of the way, the British planes banked and headed for the key La Sénia airfield, five miles south of Oran, where they were taken under heavy fire by French gunners on the ground. As the warplanes circled the field, loud explosions rocked them and thick black puffs of smoke mushroomed in the sky. Each Albacore peeled off and, one by one, dived on the La Sénia

---

* General Terry Allen immediately proclaimed Foreign Legion Captain Edgar Hamilton an auxiliary member of the Big Red One.

hangars, loosing their 250-pound general-purpose bombs. Despite the torrent of fire sent their way, the pilots were accurate; altogether 24 bombs struck and wrecked the hangars.

A short time later, another British air attack was launched against La Sénia and also Tafaraoui airfield, some ten miles farther inland. This time French Dewoitine 520 fighter planes were in the air and waiting. As ten Seafires from the *Furious* zoomed in at eye-level to strafe grounded planes and antiaircraft batteries, they were pounced on by the Dewoitines.

For the first time in history, British and French pilots were battling each other in a series of dogfights that ranged over a wide swath of Algeria. High in the sky, the Dewoitines and the Seafires dived and looped in effort to gain an advantage. From the ground could be heard the muted, angry chatter of machine guns whenever an opposing warplane would come into the sights of a pilot.

Pilots on both sides paid a heavy price. Five Dewoitines were shot down, some crashing in flames, while three British aircraft were knocked from the sky and several Seafires and Hurricanes were forced down on land. In this curious twilight war, the French air force bitterly contested attacks on its airfields, but made no effort to strike at the juicy offshore target of scores of squatting British vessels.

Out over the Mediterranean Sea that day, Captain Carlos "Doc" Alden, surgeon of the 509th Parachute Infantry Battalion, gazed with his comrades through the small windows of the C-47 named *Shark Bait* as a rising sun erased the remnants of a rainy night. The paratroopers were startled by what they saw—or didn't see. There were only five C-47s in their group. What had become of the other 33 transport planes that had taken off with them from Land's End, England? A trooper, peering down through the early morning haze, called out, "There's nothing but wet water as far as ya' can see."

"Here's some more good news," said a trooper returning from the pilot's compartment, waddling under his burden of heavy gear. "We're goddamned near out of gas—and the fly-boys don't have the slightest idea where we are."

"Whoever named this crate *Shark Bait* sure as hell knew something we didn't," shouted a voice from the rear.

Captain Alden, who was jumpmaster in the C-47, said, calmly, "Okay, fellows, start inflating those three rubber life rafts. Unless one of you can pee in the fuel tank, we might end up in the drink." Several troopers grabbed hand-operated pumps and began inflating the rafts.

Elsewhere over the Mediterranean, Major Bill Yarborough's C-47 was flying alone. His aircraft was also nearly out of fuel, and the pilots were lost. They had reached a coast line and were following it, and Yarborough was desperately trying to sight a recognizable landmark, but to no avail; the rock terrain was almost featureless. Was this North Africa? Or Spain? Or southern France?

Squinting, Yarborough spotted a distant speck in the cloudless sky. It was coming closer, and presently he made out that it was an airplane coming directly toward his unarmed C-47.

Although the men on board thought that Plan Peace was in effect, they had been mentally conditioned for any eventuality. As the unidentified aircraft bore down on his slow moving plane, Yarborough called out, "All right, men, we're under attack. Take the plugs out of the windows and put the muzzles of your weapons through. Get ready to fire." Yarborough hoped his voice hid his apprehension. It would require a near miracle for a few rifles, tommy guns, and Browning automatic rifles to shoot down a fighter.

Despite the near hopelessness of the situation, Jack Pogue, the battalion communications sergeant, could not resist solemnly licking his thumb and applying it to the front sight of his Tommy gun before poking the muzzle out the open window. Frigid air had filled the cabin, but there was perspiration on the foreheads of the paratroopers as they awaited the split second in which the onrushing plane would be within small-arms range. Few of them could expect to survive this.

Suddenly, Major Yarborough shouted: "Hold it. Hold it! Don't fire! It's one of ours!"

The kneeling men, their weapons resting on the window ledges, could now see for themselves. It was a C-47 from their own flight. "I'll bet that son of a bitch is lonely and looking for company," a voice rang through the cabin. Hearty laughter answered the remark.

The two lost C-47s joined up and flew together for a considerable distance over a heavy cloud bank. Spotting an opening, Yarborough's pilot dived through it and leveled out underneath. "Look!" Yarborough called out, pointing. Parked below was a C-47. Clearly, this must be near the objective south of Oran.

As Yarborough's craft flew closer, he could make out a number of soldiers milling around the grounded C-47, their bayonet-tipped rifles glistening. Happy that his 1,600-mile ordeal was over, the pilot got into position to make a landing next to the aircraft on the ground. The plane trailing Yarborough's ship did the same.

Suddenly the major shouted: "Pull up! Don't land! Those are hostile soldiers down there!"

As the two planes regained altitude, Yarborough spotted another C-47 on the ground—this one moving, gathering speed for a takeoff. Right behind it was a small group of men on galloping horses, riding into the thick trail of dust picked up by the propellers.

Leaving the fist-waving horsemen behind, the plane lifted off and joined Yarborough's two C-47s. The three aircraft flew east in search of La Sénia and Tafaraoui fields.

Yarborough had no way of knowing it at the time, but the hostile soldiers had spotted on the ground were Spaniards. Out of fuel and blown far off course, the troop carrier plane had landed in Spanish Morocco, more than 200 miles west of Oran and its two targeted airfields. The paratroopers and air crew were in the process of being taken into custody for violating neutral territory when the second C-47 had touched down nearby. The pilot of the second plane, concluding that he had just landed in a hostile country, had taken off again immediately, with the mounted, rifle-waving Moroccan tribesmen in pursuit.

In the meantime, daylight had enabled the navigators in a cluster of ten C-47s to orient themselves while still out over the Mediterranean. The group appeared to be almost precisely on course. Flying southward, the ten aircraft crossed the Algerian coast near Oran and headed toward La Sénia for what the men on board thought would be a peaceful landing. French soldiers would greet them with open arms.

As the ten C-47s approached La Sénia airfield, the peace was shattered. French antiaircraft gunners began blasting away. Puffs of black smoke filled the sky. Explosions rocked the planes and tore up the thin-skinned craft with shrapnel.

"A hell of a way to greet your friends," said a shaky voice in one C-47.

"Maybe those dizzy bastards down there don't know Plan Peace is in effect," shouted another.

The ten-plane flight, nearly out of fuel, banked steeply and turned away from the unexpected barrage. Although several C-47s had been punctured by hot shrapnel, no one was hit. They lumbered westward for a few miles and landed on the Sebkra D'Oran, a dry salt-water lakebed 32 miles long and more than 7 miles wide.

Minutes after the first group of C-47s had landed, six more ships appeared overhead, circled, and touched down nearby. All six of the new arrivals, one of which was Captain Doc Alden's *Shark Bait*, were virtually out of fuel.

Alden walked up to a fellow parachute officer and surveyed the landscape, which was barren for miles in each direction. With a straight face he said, "I had no idea that La Sénia airport would look like this. Where are the plane hangars?" The other officer shrugged his shoulders. Clearly the mission had become snarled.

Waiting for orders, Alden flopped onto the hot sand under a C-47 wing and scribbled in his pocket diary: "At something called Sebkra D'Oran. Hopeless mess. Men and no companies. All mixed up together." The sun was beating down. Around the airplanes, paratroopers of the 509th Battalion were removing their Long Johns, cursing the heavy woolen underwear they had praised during the night in the cold C-47s.

At another point on the coast, a frustrated battalion commander, Lieutenant Colonel Raff, was in a C-47 piloted by Colonel William Bentley, who had been designated leader of the airborne task force. Bentley was in charge of the operation until Raff's parachutists were on the ground. Bentley, lost, was flying along the coastline seeking some sign of Oran. Behind him were five other aircraft carrying Captain William J. Morrow and his parachute company.

Colonel Raff was worried. Where were the other 33 C-47s with his paratroopers? Had they gone down at sea? On a mountain range in Spain? Been shot down by Luftwaffe night interceptors? Raff resolved to carry out his battalion's mission of securing La Sénia and Tafaraoui airports, even if he had to do the job with only his six planeloads of paratroopers.

On the Sebkra D'Oran, parachute officers were huddled to discuss the next move when they heard aircraft approaching. They squinted at the sky and saw six C-47s—Raff's group. A radio operator on the dry lake radioed to Colonel Bentley, pilot of Raff's C-47, that the paratroopers and air crewmen on the ground were "under fire" from a force of undetermined size to the north of the parked aircraft.

It was the nervous assessment of men in a combat situation for the first time; in fact, there was no "force of undetermined size," and no firing.

Moments after receiving this radio warning, Colonel Bentley spotted three tanks in the distance, moving toward the C-47s parked on the dry lake. "Those tanks are firing at our guys around the 47s," Bentley called out excitedly. Again, there was in fact no firing.

Not knowing the situation on the ground, Colonel Raff made an instant decision: He and his six planeloads of paratroopers would bail out and attack the tanks. A signal was radioed to parachutists in the other five C-47s: Watch for Raff to jump, then bail out after him.

Hastily selected, the DZ (drop zone) appeared to be a smooth expanse of ground, but actually it was boulder-strewn and hilly. Raff struck the earth with heavy impact. His chest smashed into a large, jagged rock, knocking the wind from him and cracking two ribs. But the battalion leader was ready to lead his lightly armed men against the three tanks.

As the troopers were ready to move forward, one man on a knoll shouted: "Colonel, there's big white stars on those goddamned tanks. They're ours!" The tanks belonged to Lieutenant Colonel John K. Waters's "flying column" of the 1st Armored Division, pushing inland from Cape Figalo where they had landed.*

Minutes later, Major Yarborough's three-plane cluster glided in to a landing on the Sebkra D'Oran. General Mark Clark's airborne advisor strode up to Colonel Raff and asked: "What the hell is going on?" It was the standard question that morning on the Sebkra D'Oran.

"Damned if I know," Raff replied. "But the French are obviously fighting, Plan Pleace or no Plan Peace."

Pondering his next move, Edson Raff worried about the C-47s, carry-

---

* Colonel John Waters was General George S. Patton's son-in-law.

ing 135 of his paratroopers, which were still unaccounted for. Major Yarborough had told him about the C-47 on the ground in Spanish Morocco, but only much later would Raff learn the fate of most of the other aircraft. Three of them, out of gas and far off course, had also landed in Spanish Morocco, where those on board were taken into custody by the Spanish government. One aircraft, after being hopelessly lost over Spain all night, had glided to a landing with empty fuel tanks on Gibraltar. A C-47 trying to make a peaceful landing at La Sénia airfield had been driven off by French antiaircraft fire and had crash-landed near Oran. Two planes had touched down on an airfield in French Morocco to have their paratroopers and crewmen captured by French troops.

Since Plan War was obviously in effect, Colonel Raff's next move was to capture Tafaraoui airport. The paratroopers formed up and, with Major Yarborough in the lead, set out for the grueling 26-mile march eastward across the Sebkra D'Oran, which would be followed by another 12-mile trek southward to Tafaraoui. Raff had intended to lead the march but, due to his painful injury, was persuaded to go on ahead in a jeep borrowed from a just-landed armored unit.

After trudging over the dry lakebed for ten miles, the huffing paratroopers, burdened with heavy equipment, came upon Colonel Raff standing beside a communications truck. He told Major Yarborough, "Just got word an American armored unit has captured Tafaraoui airport and several hundred French prisoners. The tank people want to move on, and we're ordered to hurry there and guard the POWs."

It would take many more hours for the sweating paratroopers to reach the airfield by foot, so Yarborough suggested that gasoline be drained from each C-47 parked on the *sebkra*, ten miles to the rear, and that the consolidated fuel be poured into three planes. These three would take off, land by Yarborough's columns, pick up a company of troopers, and rush them to Tafaraoui.

"Great idea," Raff responded. "Get the ball rolling."

Instructions were radioed back. The three refueled planes took off and landed again beside the marching men. Captain John Berry's company scrambled aboard, and, with Yarborough in the lead plane, they quickly lifted off for Tafaraoui, some 25 miles away.

Standing behind the pilot, Yarborough suddenly saw three Vichy French Dewoitine fighters diving toward them. Moments later, machine-gun bullets were ripping through the three thin-skinned transports. Lieutenant Dave Kunkel, a popular young officer in the 509th Parachute Infantry Battalion, grabbed a light machine gun and rushed to set it up in the open door, but before Kunkel could squeeze the trigger, a burst of fire from a diving Dewoitine struck him in the midsection. Bleeding profusely, Kunkel fell to the floor, the first American paratrooper killed in action.

Under repeated assaults by the French fighters, all three C-47s were forced to crash-land on the barren *sebkra*. Paratroopers and air crews scrambled out C-47 doors, but found no cover on the barren lakebed. As the Dewoitines bore in for the kill, trapped men stretched out flat and buried their faces in the sand. The machine-gunning started up again and cries rang out from parachutists struck by bullets. From others hit, there was not outcry—they had died instantly.

Captain William Moir, one of the two 509th Battalion surgeons, leaped to his feet and dashed from one wounded man to another. A slug grazed the surgeon's head, knocking him into a stagger and sending blood cascading down his face. Moir quickly bandaged his own head and got back to treating wounded men as the French fighter planes continued their remorseless strafing.

Ammunition apparently exhausted, the Dewoitines finally flew off. After the chaos of a moment before, the ugly Sebkra D'Oran seemed as quiet as a morgue. The three downed C-47s were disfigured by bullets, and from one a dead paratrooper hung head-first out of a door, blood dripping down his fingers into bright red pools. As Major Yarborough got to his feet, a paratrooper, his face a bloody pulp, staggered toward him. Laying the man on the ground, Yarborough called out, "Medic! Medic!" There was no response. Several more times he shouted for a medic. He forced himself to look at the hideously wounded trooper and wondered what his name was. Then the injured man whispered something, and the kneeling officer leaned down to catch it: "I am the medic." Yarborough knew this trooper well. Now the man was unrecognizable.

Only the moaning of those mutilated by bullets could be heard.

Yarborough took a quick count of casualties from the strafings: In less than three minutes, 7 men of the 509th Parachute Infantry Battalion had been killed and 27 wounded. It had been a terrible baptism of fire. As ashen-faced survivors of the Dewoitine attack looked at the broken bodies of their comrades, they vowed to wreak havoc on the French.*

Major Yarborough's force now had been whittled down to about 60 paratroopers, but he prepared to push on to the objective of Tafaraoui airfield. Unknown to the parachutists, elements of Colonel Waters's Combat Command B of the 1st Armored Division were converging on La Sénia. The injured surgeon, Captain Moir, was left behind to tend to the wounded and watch over the bodies of the men killed. "I'll send some trucks back to you as soon as I can," Yarborough told Moir, then set off across the *sebkra* at the head of his column.

Back where the C-47s had originally landed on the Sebkra D'Oran, airmen had drained a few gallons of gasoline from other planes, poured the fuel into *Shark Bait,* and lifted off for the 30-mile flight to Tafaraoui airfield. Captain Alden, sitting in the open door with his legs dangling outside and a tommy gun cradled in his arms, was the only passenger. "I'm riding shotgun," he told the air crew.

On reaching Tafaraoui, *Shark Belt* landed routinely but was quickly greeted by loud explosions. A French 75-millimeter battery somewhere in the surrounding hills had brought the C-47 under fire. The pilot taxied hastily behind a small knoll, which offered some protection for the shelling, and Doc Alden jumped to the ground. The 509th Parachute Infantry Battalion—represented by himself alone—was on its D-day objective.

Several miles north of Tafaraoui, Colonel William Bentley, the air corps officer who commanded the Paratroop Task Force, sat in the kitchen of an old farmhouse outside Oran, sipping a cup of coffee and chatting with two amiable French officers. Bentley's plight exemplified the frustration felt by all those who participated in America's first para-

---

* A twenty-two-year-old paratrooper named John Thomas "Tommy" Mackall, seriously wounded in the Dewoitine strafings, died a few days later at Gibraltar. Camp Mackall, a new base for training paratroopers in North Carolina, was named after him.

trooper mission. After dropping its stick of paratroopers, Bentley's plane had run out of gas and crash-landed. The colonel and his air crew were prisoners.

It did not take the French navy long to react to the invasion. Shortly after daybreak, *Llangibby Castle*, which had been carrying elements of the 1st Infantry Division and was now anchored only a mile off Les Andalouses, was suddenly confronted by the warship *La Surprise*. The senior British naval officer in the Les Andalouses landing force, Captain E. V. Lees in the *Glengyle*, radioed an urgent appeal for help. Just as *La Surprise* started shelling the helpless transport, HMS *Brilliant* raced up and opened fire on the French warship. An intense duel between the two raged for a half hour until *Brilliant* sent a salvo into an ammunition hold. *La Surprise* was rocked by an enormous explosion and was soon engulfed in flames and smoke. Within minutes the French warship went under, taking her dead, dying, and wounded to the bottom.

Shortly after 9:00 A.M. the big coastal guns at Fort du Santon began pounding the squatting transports. Seventeen minutes later *Llangibby Castle*, which still had troops aboard, was struck by several shells but managed to limp westward out of range. Hits were also scored on the transport *Monarch of Bermuda*. Many miles offshore, the battleship *Rodney* fired her 16-inch guns; 90 seconds later, sounding like freight trains rushing through a tunnel, 700-pound shells crashed into Fort Du Santon. But the French guns there refused to be silent.

15

The "Lost Battalion" of Algiers

Two hundred seventy miles east of Oran, the ancient Moslem city of Algiers lay under a pale moon as the hands of the clock neared midnight on November 7. Few citizens were stirring. Rumors of war had filled the capital of Algeria and there was a great fear of sudden bombings, but only a few people in this port city founded by the Moors in the tenth century actually knew of the momentous events unfolding along the thousand-mile stretch of coastline. As the city of 300,000 slept, a powerful Allied naval force was lying at anchor offshore.

The city was spread on a hillside overlooking the 16-mile-long Bay of Algiers. A large number of modern buildings and housing projects covered the lower slopes of the hill around the sheltered harbor. Algiers itself had a European flavor, while farther up the hill was the fabled Casbah, the old sections peopled by Moslems who lived in crowded tenements along twisting alleys. These sections surrounded old Arab forts and palaces of former Arab rulers. In daylight, residents of the Casbah eked out an existence by hawking rugs, jewelry, and trinkets in open shops jammed together along the streets.

Some ten miles offshore from a peninsular feature known as Cap Sidi Ferruch was the blacked-out command ship HMS *Bulolo*. Conferring earnestly in her operations room were the two leaders of the Eastern Task Force, British Admiral Harold Burrough, veteran of many Luftwaffe and U-boat assaults on convoys he had led, and U.S. Major General Charles W. "Doc" Ryder, until recently the commander of the 34th Infantry Division. The methodical, low-key Ryder had distinguished himself in World War I and become a lieutenant colonel at an early age on the battlefields of France. In order to preserve the illusion that the invasion of French Northwest Africa was strictly an American venture, Ryder had been named to head the Eastern Task Force. Once Algiers was secure, British Lieutenant General Kenneth A. N. Anderson would take over.

The Eastern Task Force was in fact predominantly British. In addition to British warships, including fighter planes on aircraft carriers, 45,000 British troops (along with 10,000 American soldiers) would be involved. Even the three sectors to be attacked had been given the standard British code names Apples, Beer, and Charlie. At 1:00 A.M. the assault troops would strike at these three points to either side of Algiers, secure beachheads, then close in on the city. Then, at 3:00 A.M., two hours after General Ryder's troops were to storm ashore east and west of Algiers, Operation Terminal would strike. Terminal, in the view of those involved, was an appropriately grim name: They regarded it as a suicide mission. On two British destroyers, *Broke* and *Malcolm*, would be 662 American and 74 British fighting men under command of U.S. Lieutenant Colonel Edwin T. Swenson. British participants in Swenson's force would wear American uniforms.

The *Broke* and *Malcolm*, slightly more sturdy than the ancient Coast Guard cutters involved in a carbon-copy mission at Oran, were to steam at full speed into Algiers harbor to discharge their troops, who would secure dock facilities and prevent French vessels from being sabotaged. In overall command of Terminal was a Royal Navy captain, J. L. St. J. Fancourt.

Neither Captain Fancourt nor Lieutenant Colonel Swenson were any more enthusiastic over prospects for success than were other ranks. Total surprise would be essential, but how could surprise be attained when the landings on both sides of Algiers two hours previously would surely alert the entire French defenses? And if the French chose to fight, getting ashore in and around Algiers could be difficult. Allied intelligence had pinpointed 13 French coastal batteries within the port and strung out on dominating heights on both sides. The most powerful of these guns were at Pointe Pescade and at Cap Matifou, west and east of Algiers, covering two of the three Eastern Task Force landing beaches.

Besides capturing Algiers, invading forces had as secondary goals the seizure of two excellent airfields—Maison Blanche and Blida—outside the port. From these two fields, 39 French fighters and 52 bombers could operate against the invaders. Algiers was also within range of German bombers based in Sardinia—planes that could be expected to attack the British armada offshore or pound the landing beaches.

Shortly after midnight of D-day, a French automobile carrying four passengers and a driver was stealing through the night in the direction of Cap Sidi Ferruch, ten miles west of Algiers. Seated grimly in the back was General Raymond Mast, commander of the Algiers Division, who was a disciple of General Henri Giraud. Before leaving his headquarters an hour previously, General Mast had flashed an order to the 16,000 men of his division: "Do not oppose but assist the American landings." Unbeknownst to General Mast, however, his superior, Lieutenant General Louis-Marie Koeltz, commanding the 19th Région Militaire in Algiers, had countermanded Mast's order and issued one of his own: "Resist any invasion by foreign troops with all the means at your disposal." The conflicting directives resulted in complete confusion among Algiers French forces. Some units received Mast's orders, but not those of Koeltz. Others received only Koeltz's directive. Yet others got both orders.

General Koeltz had also ordered Mast to be arrested for treason and had replaced the Giraud protégé with Major General Pierre Roubertie as commander of the Algiers Division.

General Mast's car reached Cap Sidi Ferruch, and he climbed to a cliff to wait for the arrival of the Allies. He studied his luminous watch— 12:45 A.M. H-hour would be in 15 minutes.*

Around midnight, men in pairs and small groups slipped through the dimly lighted streets of Algiers. Each man carried one or more weapons, and some were armed with grenades. They were members of the pro-Allied underground who had been working for weeks with Robert Murphy in planning for this moment. The mission of the underground warriors: to seize control of key points in Algiers in order to aid the American landings.

One group, led by a husky, black-haired cobbler, Jean-Louis Jourdan, scrambled noiselessly up the steps of the main Algiers gendarmerie, or police station. Inside, they brandished weapons and quickly disarmed several pro-Vichy policemen who were wide-eyed over this unexpected raid. The gendarmes were shoved and booted into cells and the doors slammed shut and locked behind them.

So efficient and well organized had been the Algiers underground, that by 1:30 A.M.—only 90 minutes after BBC radio had broadcast the code words indicating that the invasion was imminent—pro-Allied factors were in control. All telephone service had been halted, outlying police stations had been seized, and Radio Algiers had been taken over. General Henri Giraud's exhortation to assist the American landings was broadcast repeatedly; this was the appeal flashed from Gibraltar a few hours previously, when Eisenhower's aides had noted that the original signal and Giraud's signature seemed to have been in the supreme commander's own handwriting.

Still, the underground knew that they could hold key points for two hours at most. By that time, pro-Vichy soldiers and police would overwhelm them. The lives of the shadow warriors depended on strong American forces being in the heart of Algiers, and soon.

---

* Later General Louis-Marie Koeltz would distinguish himself fighting under Allied command against the Germans. After the war, General Eisenhower was profuse in his praise of Koeltz's fighting qualities.

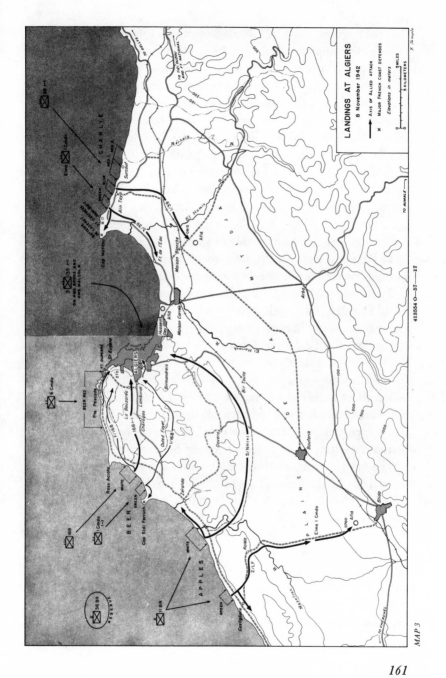

LANDINGS AT ALGIERS
8 November 1942

➤ Axis of Allied attack
✕ Major French coast defenses

Elevations in meters

5 MILES
5 KILOMETERS

MAP 3

161

413554 O—57——17

As assault waves of the 7,230-man British 11th Infantry Brigade neared shore in the Apples sector, 20 miles southwest of Algiers, lights in the little coastal town of Castiglione, population 4,000, were shining brightly. The night was clear, the sea was calm, and men of the East Surrey Regiment, the Lancashire Fusiliers, and the Northamptonshire Regiment scrambled from beached assault boats and began moving inland. Not a shot had been fired. Before daylight British troops secured two key bridges, occupied Castiglione, took over Zeralda and its radio station, and surrounded a French army barracks at Kolea. There, members of General Mast's Algiers Division obeyed his orders, remaining inside as an officer emerged to tell the British that there would be no resistance.

On Beer sector, which included a 10-mile stretch of rugged coastline from Pointe Pescade on the outskirts of Algiers westward to Cap Sidi Ferruch, men of the British 1st Commando led by Lieutenant Colonel T. H. Trevor stormed ashore and began scaling heights toward the guns in old Fort de Sidi Ferruch. The French commander of the strong point, Colonel Alphonse Baril, surrendered before shooting erupted.

Offshore on the *Bulolo*, General Doc Ryder and Admiral Harold Burrough were peering anxiously through binoculars toward the dark beaches. Suddenly they spotted a white flare fired from the shadowy silhouette of a cliff—it was the signal from Lieutenant Colonel Trevor that Fort de Sidi Ferruch had been taken. There was relief on the *Bulolo* that the coastal guns were neutralized. So far the operation had been textbook perfect. Such perfection would be short-lived.

The 6th Commando (British and American) was supposed to seize other menacing batteries on the heights at Fort Anglais, Fort Indépendance, and Fort Duperré. But 6th Commando began having difficulties even before departing the transport *Awates*. Landing craft to pick up the troops had to come from another ship, and the inexperienced coxswains got lost at night and were late in arriving alongside the *Awates*. After the commandos were loaded, engines began to break down on the run into the Beer beaches. Many of the assault boats were old and unseaworthy; they soon filled with water and sank, dumping their occupants into the sea.

Now the first assault waves became scattered, as the half-trained landing-craft navigators lost their way in the blackness. The first men of the 6th Commando were two hours late in reaching shore, and it would be five hours after H-hour before the last would arrive. The plan had been for them to scramble up the heights and surround the big guns at Fort Duperré in the darkness, but it was not until 8:15 A.M., in full daylight, that the 6th Commando encircled the fort. There the commandos came under fire; the French commander had decided to ignore General Mast's order to cooperate in favor of General Koeltz's directive to resist.

Soon nine Albacore fighter-bombers from the carriers offshore were overhead, peeling off one-by-one to dive on the thick-walled old fort and send bombs crashing into it. As smoke and dust cloaked the ramparts, white flags were raised inside the French strongpoint.

At the same time that Lieutenant Colonel Trevor's 1st Commando had landed to seize Fort de Sidi Ferruch, where in 1830 some 37,000 French soldiers had landed to wrest Algeria from its Moslem ruler, Colonel John W. "Iron Mike" O'Daniel's U.S. 168th Regiment (35th Infantry Division) was bogged down. A motor launch, which was to lead O'Daniel's assault waves onto the designated beaches in the Beer sector, got lost, and the 168th Regiment was scattered along 15 miles of coastline. The bulk of O'Daniel's units stormed ashore in Apples sector, far to the west, where they got tangled up in the darkness with elements of the British 11th Infantry Brigade.

Adding to the turmoil, the American regiment's radios had been damaged on landing and were not working. As soldiers milled about along the 15-mile stretch of beach, a few cars and trucks carrying officers raced up and down the roads and the shoreline while shouting unit leaders tried desperately to round up their men.

One of those doing the shouting was Lieutenant Colonel Edward J. Doyle, commander of the 1st Battalion, 168th Infantry, whose unit was to have landed on Beer Green beach. Half of the battalion did arrive there, but Colonel Doyle had been put ashore many miles to the west, in Apples sector. As Doyle looked for his unit, one of his officers, Captain Edward W. Bird, drove off with two British officers to reconnoiter the objective of Lambiridi, the fashionable western suburb of

Algiers. They were fired on as they approached a French barracks on the outskirts, and in the confusion one of the British officers was captured. Under a hail of French bullets, Captain Bird and the other British officer sped away.

Meanwhile, Colonel Iron Mike O'Daniel was having his own problems. The 168th Combat Team leader was to have landed on Beer White beach at 3:00 A.M., but his assault craft had gotten lost and had meandered around in the darkness for several hours until O'Daniel was finally put ashore in the Apples sector. O'Daniel was brought back along the coast to the correct beach, arriving there at 7:00 A.M.—four hours tardy.

Although O'Daniel's regiment was still strung out for many miles, by late morning all three battalions had been sufficiently reorganized to march eastward and start to converge on Lambiridi. Unknown to the approaching Americans, the spy Robert Murphy was being held there in General Juin's Villa des Oliviers.

The trek toward Algiers had been a tortuous one. O'Daniel's men had had to climb to La Bouzarea, a mountain 1,500 feet above sea level, which looked down on Algiers. The regiment's heavy weapons and equipment were late in landing, and when they did arrive the vehicles to carry them could not be located. Machine guns, mortars and shells, metal boxes with small-arms ammunition, and other heavy items had to be lugged by perspiring soldiers who could not keep up with the less heavily burdened rifle companies.

Scouts poking into the outskirts of Lambiridi found the streets empty. Shutters were closed on most of the ornate homes and villas—a sure sign that the families huddled inside were fearful of shooting. As Company K of Lieutenant Colonel Stewart T. Vincent's 3rd Battalion neared the square in the heart of the city, a French armored car suddenly darted out of a side street and opened fire with its machine guns, sending the riflemen running for cover. Then came a torrent of rifle fire from French soldiers concealed in nearby houses. The battle raged in and around the Lambiridi square for more than two hours. A lone French ambulance, a huge red cross painted on each side, front and back, dashed about picking up both American and French wounded.

Meanwhile, aware that the stubborn French force was holding up the advance into Algiers, Lieutenant Colonel Doyle, who had caught up with his 1st Battalion after having been deposited far from its beach, took 25 of his men, worked around Lambiridi to the south, drove on into Algiers, and took over the Palais d'Été deep inside the city. Doyle then headed for the main gendarmerie, which the pro-Allied underground had seized shortly after 1:00 A.M., with about half of his tiny force. The battalion commander hoped to capture the German consul. Doyle and his men had advanced only a few hundred yards through the deserted streets when there was a burst of sniper fire. One bullet killed Doyle, and another man was wounded.

Meanwhile, in the vicinity of Beer sector, General Raymond Mast, unaware of General Koeltz's orders that he be arrested on sight, was agitated to have learned that the invaders had given no special priority to taking over Blida airport, about 25 miles inland. Blida was being held by friendly French forces, Mast told Lieutenant Colonel Trevor of 1st Commando, and General Henri Giraud would land there soon to take command of French forces in North Africa. Unless an Allied unit rapidly occupied Blida airdrome, the situation could change to one of hostility. Mast urged Trevor to rush to Blida and said that he had vehicles available to carry 1st Commando.

Colonel Trevor hesitated. His outfit had already accomplished its primary mission, seizing Fort de Sidi Ferruch. The invasion plan did not call for a quick thrust to the inland airfield. But the British officer consented, and he and most of his men climbed aboard General Mast's trucks at 4:15 A.M. and reached Blida airfield shortly before daybreak. Planes from the aircraft carrier *Argus* had taken up patrol over the field just before the 1st Commando arrived and reported to Colonel Trevor that white flags were flying at the facility.

Leaving his commandos outside the front gate, Trevor began negotiations with the French air force commander at Blida, Brigadier General A. J. de Monsabert, for the peaceful takeover of the facility. Trevor immediately found a change of attitude. In view of conflicting orders from Algiers—don't resist from General Mast and resist from General Koeltz—General de Monsabert refused Colonel Trevor's request to peacefully occupy his airfield.

Trevor shook hands with the French general, returned to his commandos, and deployed them into defensive positions to await reinforcements in the event he was told to attack and capture Blida. The French remained in possession of the field, but General de Monsabert paved the way for the expected early arrival of General Giraud's plane. Allied aircraft would be allowed to *land* at Blida but not to *take off.* It was but one curious twist among many in this twilight war between would-be allies.

It had been about 11:00 P.M.—H-hour minus 2—when a feverish conference had taken place in the operations room of the command ship *Samuel Chase,* lying offshore from Charlie sector 15 miles east of Algiers. A crisis had erupted. U.S. Navy Captain Campbell D. Edgar, commander of Charlie sea forces, and Colonel Benjamin F. Caffey, Jr., leader of the U.S. 39th Regiment (9th Infantry Division) had just learned that the transport *Thomas Stone* had been hit by Luftwaffe bombs and was dead in the water 150 miles northwest of Algiers.

Thomas Stone had been carrying Colonel Caffey's 2nd Battalion, which had been earmarked for the Charlie assault. Now Captain Edgar and Caffey quickly substituted the 3rd Battalion, in floating reserve, for the luckless 2nd Battalion. The hasty revamping would have taxed the ingenuity and skills of even experienced commanders and their naval and ground forces, but there was no other course of action. The switch had to be achieved in total darkness and under the enormous pressure of a rapidly approaching H-hour. Even if the sudden changeover went smoothly, Colonel Caffey would still have to splash ashore almost directly under the guns of the Batterie du Lazaret near Cap Matifou, guns powerful enough to shoot 14 miles.

Valuable time had been lost. Captain Edgar took a calculated risk: He ordered transports to move in much closer to the beaches. While Charlie's first wave was still heading for shore, Captain Edgar picked up a startling item on a shortwave newscast from New York City. The announcer said that Washington had just reported that landings east of Algiers under Navy Captain Campbell D. Edgar had been *successfully accomplished.*

The commotion created by the transports edging closer to the shoreline attracted the inevitable attention of French gunners on the heights at Cap Matifou. Four or five searchlights atop the cliff began playing over the water and found the transports and the British destroyers *Zetland* and *Cowdray*. Lightninglike flashes and loud booms erupted over the heights as the four big guns of the Batterie du Lazaret opened fire. *Zetland* and *Cowdray* quickly returned fire. The searchlights and the mammoth French guns fell silent.

All the while, Charlie landings were proceeding in almost total confusion. Eleven assault boats hit an offshore fogbank and reached the beach two hours late. The first infantry waves from the *Samuel Chase* were to split at an offshore landmark, the Bordelaise Rock, where each group would head for its designated beach. The untried navigators of one group missed sighting the huge rock and continued onward to the wrong beach.

Yet despite the mixup of units, commanders could quickly reorganize because there had been no hostile fire. The 39th Regiment's 3rd Battalion under Major Farrar O. Griggs set out along the coastal road toward Algiers, where it was to establish contact with Allied forces coming into the city from the west, and with pro-Allied French underground forces who were supposed to have control of Algiers by dawn. After a march of six miles, Griggs's battalion neared the resort village of Fort de l'Eau, where a dug-in detachment of French infantry, supported by tanks, brought the advance to a halt.

At the same time, a battalion under Lieutenant Colonel A. H. Rosenfeld scrambled into trucks and set out on a wild road march, hell-bent for the key Maison Blanche airfield, ten miles to the southwest. Nearing the airdrome, the truck convoy was fired on by a handful of French tanks, but the shots were far off target. The hostile tanks quickly spun around and clanked off into the darkness, and Colonel Rosenfeld's men took over Maison Blanche airfield. By 9:00 A.M. the facility was ready to receive warplanes.

While the American assault forces were landing on both sides of Algiers and pushing inland, the British destroyers *Broke* and *Malcolm* were slicing through the Mediterranean toward the north African coast. Crammed aboard were 662 Americans of Lieutenant Colonel Edwin Swenson's battalion and 74 British naval men, destination Algiers. Target time: 3:00 A.M.

As the pair of destroyers neared, the surf was lapping gently against the crescent-shaped sea wall that stretched the entire mile-and-a-half length of Algiers Harbor. Two jetties extending beyond the sea wall left gaps for entry and exit to the harbor, gaps protected by floating booms. The heavily fortified harbor was covered by powerful gun batteries mounted on the Jetée du Nord and the Îlot de la Marine, and on high ground overlooking the port. Just south of the harbor, on a knoll 300 feet high, were medium guns of the Batterie des Arcades. Machine-gun posts were scattered on higher ground rimming the harbor.

Algiers and its harbor were quiet at 4:00 A.M. as the *Broke* and *Malcolm* neared the floating booms, an hour behind schedule. Suddenly the two destroyers were caught by powerful searchlight beams, and other lights throughout Algiers were quickly extinguished. Soon big guns on the heights, particularly those at the Batterie des Arcades, were walking shells toward the brightly illuminated destroyers. Their conning officers were blinded by the glare of the searchlights and, zigzagging to avoid the intense shellfire, missed the entrance twice. Circling for a third try, the *Malcolm* was struck by a shell. Ten men were killed and 25 wounded by the blast and an internal explosion. The badly damaged destroyer then caught fire and her skipper, Commander A. B. Russell, unable to steer her properly, ordered the vessel to pull back out to sea.

As *Malcolm* limped off, *Broke*'s skipper, Lieutenant Commander A. F. C. Layard, circled for a fourth try and crashed through the boom. *Broke* steamed across the harbor, running a gauntlet of shellfire all the way, and berthed along the Môle Louis Billiard. It was 5:20 A.M. and still dark as half of Colonel Swenson's force slipped onto the dock and quickly took possession of the entire *môle*, a petroleum-tank farm, and an electric power station, then headed northward to seize a seaplane base.

The advance was contested only by scattered machine-gun and rifle fire that soon trickled away. Silence fell over the harbor. Unaccountably, church bells throughout Algiers began to peal loudly and kept it up for nearly a half hour.

It appeared that Operation Terminal—previously designated a "suicide mission" by nervous participants—had succeeded, even without the *Malcolm* and its other half of Swenson's battalion. At about 8:10 A.M., a delegation from the Algiers city government, followed by one representing the city police department, approached Colonel Swenson and asked that arrangements be made for the surrender of Algiers. It looked as though the great port would fall without another ounce of blood being shed.

Minutes later this hope was shattered. During the cessation of shooting the French units—described to Swenson as "definitely hostile"—were surrounding the little force of Americans and a few British.

While Swenson was pondering this alarming new development, the big guns on the Jetée du Nord opened fire on the moored *Broke*, driving her to another berth and then to a third which got her out of the direct line of fire. This maneuver took *Broke* a considerable distance from Swenson's foot soldiers. Now another gun opened up on *Broke*, and several shells crashed into her. Skipper Layard made a crucial decision: If he was to save the destroyer, squatting there like a duck on a pond while hunters on all sides took aim at her, *Broke* would have to try to make a mad dash for the open sea.

Commander Layard sounded the ship's siren—the recall signal—and about 55 infantrymen and a few British soldiers nearby dodged machine-gun bullets and scrambled aboard. Most of Colonel Swenson's force would have required several minutes to reach the *Broke*, and Swenson felt he and his men would have a better chance of surviving if they remained in place. After all, it appeared that Algiers was on the verge of capitulating, despite the menacing presence of hostile French soldiers hemming in the Americans. Swenson ordered his men to stand fast, and at 9:40 A.M. *Broke* cast off and staggered out into the Bay of Algiers.

The destroyer *Zetland*, which had been dueling the Batterie du Lazaret, rushed to the aid of the mortally wounded *Broke*, covered her with a partial smokescreen, took aboard all her passengers, and towed the vessel out to sea.*

While carrier-based British dive-bombers blasted coastal batteries rimming Algiers harbor, several companies of Senegalese troops were closing the noose around Colonel Swenson's men. The Americans,

---

* The *Broke* had been so badly damaged that she sank the next day.

under heavy fire, held off the French colonials, but soon were running out of ammunition. Then a new menace entered the picture: several French tanks, firing directly into Swenson's positions. The Americans had no weapons to use against tanks, were out of touch with any friendly unit or headquarters, and had no hope of reinforcements. Nor was there a sound in Algiers that indicated the main body of Americans had even entered the city. At 12:30 P.M. Colonel Swenson surrendered his force, and America's "Lost Battalion" of Algiers marched off into captivity past sullen Senegalese soldiers. Swenson's force suffered 15 men killed and 33 wounded during the daring operation to seize the harbor. British losses on the embattled *Broke* were 9 killed and 18 wounded.

In the meantime, the cruiser HMS *Bermuda* and a flight of Albacore dive-bombers from the carrier *Formidable* for more than an hour pounded the unyielding French marines defending the Batterie du Lazaret. Then the position was stormed by foot soldiers, and, after a brisk firefight, 50 French marine survivors were taken prisoner.

All the while, General Alphonse Juin and Admiral Jean Darlan were at old Fort l'Empereur in Lambiridi, seeking information on developments in French Northwest Africa and to contact old Marshal Pétain in Vichy for his views. Not far away, the sounds of a heavy firefight could be heard.

At 2:45 on that D-day afternoon, some 14 hours after the first invader had come ashore, Darlan and Juin were at last convinced that the Allies were indeed landing in force and would soon be in control of Algiers. The two Frenchmen returned to the nearby Villa des Oliviers where Robert Murphy was being held. Darlan gave Murphy a driver and a car flying a large French flag and a white flag, and the American sped thankfully to General Charles Ryder's CP in Algiers.

Murphy was unimpressed with Ryder. The Eastern Task Force commander seemed to be in a stupor. Murphy insisted that Ryder accompany him immediately to Fort l'Empereur, to which Darlan and Juin had returned, but the general began dictating a report to Eisenhower at Gibraltar. Pacing the floor, the impatient Murphy began to think that Ryder, who halted frequently in his dictation, was never going to finish the signal. Then the cause of the general's lethargic actions struck the master spy: Ryder had been without sleep for more than two days and nights.

Finally finished with the Gibraltar report, General Ryder climbed into a staff car with Murphy and they drove rapidly to Fort l'Empereur. With American bombs exploding in the distance, a grim-faced Admiral Darlan issued an order to all French forces in the Algiers region: Cease firing.

16

"The Heart of America Beats for Us"

At Allied advance headquarters deep in the Rock of Gibraltar, tension had permeated the long black tunnels and the warren of tiny rooms that extended to either side. It was 3:02 A.M., two hours after the first waves were to have hit the beaches at Algiers and Oran. Seated glumly at a desk in his cramped, damp, 8-by-8-foot cubbyhole, General Eisenhower was waiting anxiously for the first fragmentary reports from across the Mediterranean.

Eisenhower had done all he could to assure the success of Operation Torch at the least cost in lives to the invaders and to the French defenders. Hours before, he had given the order that set the assault in motion. Now he was powerless to influence its outcome. The plan, an incorrigible and unyielding offspring, had taken control.

Eisenhower picked up a pen and jotted some notes which he headed, "Inconsequential thoughts of a commander during one of the interminable 'waiting periods.' " For 11 months, since being urgently summoned to Washington shortly after Pearl Harbor to begin planning for a Second Front against Nazi Germany, Eisenhower had been carrying an enormous burden that would have broken lesser men. Now he had nothing to do but reflect on paper the chilling concerns that nagged at his being.

"The final result I don't know," the supreme commander wrote of the operation. "How I'd like a few reports [from the landings]."

Eisenhower scrawled that he was "anxiously awaiting word of West Coast operations [Patton's], Oran operations, Algiers operations, movements of Italian air, intentions of Spain." Also: "Giraud manifestly unwilling to enter the theater [French Northwest Africa] so long as fighting is going on. Giraud is difficult to deal with—wants much in power, equipment, etc., Giraud wants flower plants and radios [in his Gibraltar suite], we don't know whereabouts or conditions of airborne force [Colonel Raff's 509th Parachute Infantry Battalion]." General Eisenhower summed up his anxieties by recording, "We cannot find out *anything.*"

Unknown to the supreme commander huddled over his desk a half mile inside solid rock, turmoil had erupted at the entrance to the underground maze. At 4:30 A.M., barely three and a half hours after the first Allied soldier had stormed ashore in French Northwest Africa, air-raid sirens went off over Gibraltar and searchlights began sweeping the black sky. The faint hum of approaching Luftwaffe bombers sent people on the ground into a mad scramble. Those outside raced for the tunnel entrance and those already inside dashed deeper into the Rock.

Taking off from airfields in Sardinia and Sicily, the Luftwaffe flight was on a mission to find out what was going on at Gibraltar. Antiaircraft guns on the Rock opened up with an enormous clatter of fire. Not a bomb had been dropped, and the big German aircraft were swallowed up by the night. All-clear sirens sounded and those headquarters members who had sought even more protection by running deeper into the rock returned to their offices, proud of the fact that they too had been "under fire."

On the night before D-day, hundreds of blacked-out ships of the all-American Western Task Force, which had sailed from Virginia two weeks earlier, were on the Atlantic Ocean heading toward the coastline of French Morocco. At 10:30 P.M. General George Patton was preparing to take a short nap in his cabin on the cruiser *Augusta,* headquarters ship for the task force. On the eve of America's first major amphibious operation, doubts still preyed on Patton's mind. If the French chose to fight—and indications were that they would—how would his half-trained troops react when shooting erupted? General Patton had to remind himself repeatedly: "Never take counsel of your fears!" But he was convinced that there was an influential ally in his corner—God. Earlier that day, Patton had scribbled in his diary: "This morning it is quiet, the sea is calm, almost too good to be true. Thank God. I hope He stays on *our* side."

Lying on his bunk fully clothed in case of a torpedo attack, Patton read once again his printed battle cry that had been distributed to assault troops aboard the transports: "The eyes of the world are watching us. The heart of America beats for us. God is with us. On our victory depends the freedom or slavery of the human race." He laid aside the leaflet, pleased with his prose. It was pure George Patton, warrior. Flipping off the light switch, the silver-haired general was soon sleeping soundly. He would need the rest; in a few hours he would be stepping from a landing craft.

Patton's Western Assault Force, 33,834 men, was a hodgepodge of elements of the 3rd and 9th Infantry Divisions and the 2nd Armored Division, plus assorted field artillery, tank, tank-destroyer, signal, and medical units.* His primary objective was the great port and city of Casablanca, but it was so strongly defended that a bloodbath—or total disaster—was feared from a frontal assault. Casablanca, therefore, was to be seized from behind, by forces landing at three locales to both sides of the big port.

Patton was uninspired by this strategy. His idea for seizing Casablanca quickly and at the lowest cost was to "bombard hell out of it" and then have his troops charge it. "We should plan either to conquer or be destroyed at Casablanca," he had insisted in a memo weeks previously.

Patton had long harbored a concern that turbulent weather along the Atlantic seaboard of west Africa on D-day might keep him from landing

---

* Two years later in Europe, Patton's Third Army would be twelve times this size.

his troops. If it did, and if there were a communications failure with Gibraltar, Patton feared that Admiral Hewitt might divert the large armada away from Casablanca. Therefore Patton had sought authority from General Eisenhower to *order* Hewitt to bombard Casablanca. Eisenhower, well aware of Patton's impetuosity, had told him there would be no bombardment of Casablanca without prior approval of the supreme commander. The excellent port facilities would serve as a major Allied base.

At daybreak on D-day minus 1, Admiral Hewitt's massive convoy had split. Sub–task forces headed for three locales, to either side of Casablanca:

- Operation Blackstone. Under General Ernest Harmon, the hard-riding old cavalryman, his own Combat Command B of the 2nd Armored Division and the 47th Infantry Regimental Combat Team (9th Infantry Division) would strike at Safi, a small port 140 miles southwest of Casablanca.
- Operation Goalpost. Led by tough-minded Major General Lucian K. Truscott, Jr., the 60th Regimental Combat Team (9th Infantry Division) would storm ashore at Port Lyautey (now Kenitra), 60 miles northeast of Casablanca.
- Operation Brushwood. Commanded by Major General Jonathan W. Anderson, who had the distinction of being a Naval Academy graduate with an army commission, elements of the 3rd Infantry Division would assault the beaches at Fedala, a small fishing and oil-storage port only 18 miles northeast of Casablanca.

As Patton was catching a short nap aboard the *Augusta*, General Raymond Noguès, Resident General of French Morocco at Rabat, the Moslem holy city, found himself in a deepening dilemma. Noguès knew that a coup by pro-Allied French officers was being attempted, and he had been informed personally by General Giraud's protégé, General Marie-Émile Béthouart, that a powerful American force was poised off French Northwest Africa. But was this invading army really there? Noguès himself had seen no indication that it was.

When the hours drifted by and nothing happened in his own back-yard, Resident General Noguès became convinced that a gigantic hoax was being perpetrated. He was awed by what he had experienced of the power of Nazi Germany, and he knew that the Allies had bungled every overseas operation attempted—Norway, Crete, and Dieppe among them. What if this was just another British commando raid and he failed to oppose it? That would be just the excuse Adolf Hitler would need to take over French Northwest Africa. Noguès put all forces in Morocco on full alert and awaited developments before he decided which way to leap.

Eight miles from Safi, the dashing cavalryman, General Ernie Harmon —"Old Gravel Voice" to his men—was standing on the darkened bridge of the transport *Harris* peering intently into the night. On the horizon, a muted white glow indicated that lights were on in Safi. A good omen, Harmon reflected. The residents were not expecting company.

As H-hour at Safi approached, Harmon, like his boss Patton, offered silent thanks to the Almighty: the sea was mirror-calm. This November 8 was one of only about 12 days at this time of the year when a placid surf off west Africa might be hoped for. Harmon had been haunted for months by the specter of 12-foot waves on D-day. His target, Safi, was an ancient town with a current population of about 25,000, near an artificial harbor that had lately been used for the export of phosphates. South of the harbor and the newer structures that clustered around it was an old fishing village that extended for a mile along the coastal shelf. Towering cliffs looked down on the city and an old Portuguese fort built in the Middle Ages. On a Safi hillside was a French army barracks, and about a mile and a half inland was an emergency airfield.

Warnings that the Allies had invaded at Oran and Algiers spread rapidly across French Morocco and reached the commanding officer at Safi, Major Pierre Deuve, at 3:35 A.M. local time. Rousted out of bed, Deuve drove in a small car to his command post, a building complex above the port known as the Front de Mer, where he began issuing orders for the city's defense.

Major Deuve's entire force consisted of only 450 officers and men.

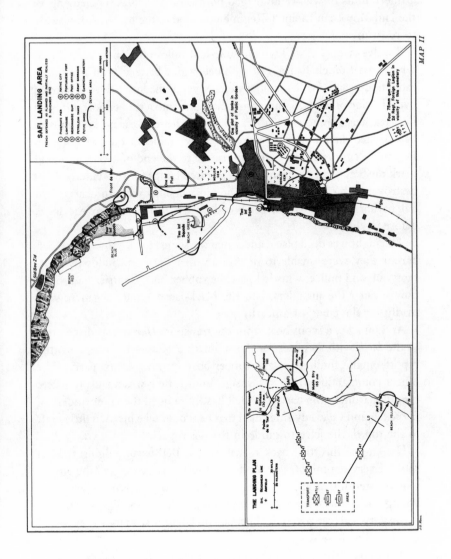

But he had several batteries of fixed coastal guns and other mobile artillery units in well-camouflaged positions. At 4:00 A.M., elements of the 2nd Moroccan Infantry Regiment rushed to the harbor front, ready to resist invading forces.

Twelve-twenty A.M. Two and one-half miles off Pointe de la Tour, where the French had a 130-millimeter gun battery with a modern rangefinder and fire control system, several shadowy figures slipped over the side of the U.S. submarine *Barb* and into a rubber boat. Dressed in black, faces smudged with camouflage grease, wearing knit caps in lieu of steel helmets, these were specially trained scouts of the 47th Infantry Regiment. They were to paddle to the end of a long jetty and mark the Safi harbor entrance with infrared lamps for two vintage 1919 destroyers, *Cole* and *Bernadou*. The old warships were to charge into Safi harbor where 350 troops on board were to seize control of the docks before daylight.

The night was dead black, and when the scouts finally rowed into Safi harbor they were unable to determine their location. Suddenly shots rang out, and bullets whistled past the rubber boat. Sentries had some-how located the intruders, and the black-faced scouts began rowing madly for the cover of a nearby pier.

At 2:00 A.M., a scout boat from the transport *Harris* was dispatched to the *Barb* with an order for the submarine skipper to issue a written report on the findings of the rubber-boat reconnaissance party. The officer commanding the boat, Ensign John J. Bell, was unable to locate the submarine in the darkness. Bell hastily radioed the commanders of *Bernadou* and *Cole*, advising them that he would take his own little craft to the top of the jetty to guide in the destroyers.

His engine throttled back to half-speed, Bell began edging toward shore. Every ten minutes or so, the motor would be cut and the ensign would listen intently. At 4:10 A.M., as Bell's boat neared the jetty, the young navy officer felt a chill surge through him: The lights at the tip of the jetty had just gone out. The men on board braced for the expected gunfire. But there was none.

Bell's boat drifted up to the jetty, and from the direction of Pointe de la Tour the ensign could barely discern the outline of the *Bernadou* edging toward the harbor mouth. The *Bernadou*'s infrared light was visible, so Bell turned his on to guide in the destroyer.

An eerie silence continued to cloak ancient Safi as *Bernadou* entered the mouth of the harbor. If *Bernadou*'s silhouette had been detected on shore, perhaps she had been mistaken for a French warship; weeks before, her superstructure had been altered to confuse the Safi garrison into thinking the vessel was French.

Suddenly the stillness was shattered. French machine-gunners, deployed along the cliffs, began pouring streams of tracer bullets into the *Bernadou*. Moments later they were joined by a 75-millimeter battery at Front de Mer, where Major Deuve was directing the defense of the post, by a 155-millimeter battery hidden south of Safi, and by the 130-millimeter guns at Pointe de la Tour.

The *Bernadou*'s gun crews began firing back as the vessel continued into the harbor. Another of the pyrotechnics with a huge American flag attached was sent up in the hope of lessening the hostile fire. Instead, the light from Old Glory helped French gunners locate the destroyer, and their barrage grew more intense.

Four-twenty-eight A.M. Over the radio net connecting American warships offshore came the words "Play ball, play ball," the signal that the French were resisting and that it was now permissible to fire back. Six miles from shore, the huge guns barked on the venerable battleship *New York*. Brilliant orange flames leaped from her muzzles as salvo after salvo of shells raced toward the big French guns on Pointe de la Tour. One cluster of projectiles crashed into the fire control tower. The cruiser *Philadelphia* pounded the site of the gun flashes south of Safi, and other warships opened up on the machine-gun posts on the cliffs.

For nearly 15 minutes, the dark seascape and the countryside around Safi reverberated with reports of American and French guns. Through it all plowed the *Bernadou*, conned from the bridge by the skipper, Lieutenant Commander R. E. Braddy. By the time the ship neared shore within the hostile harbor, firing had almost ceased.

Four-thirty A.M. Tense men of K Company, 47th Infantry, under Captain Gordon H. Sympson, were deep in the holds of *Bernadou*. It was a gut-wrenching experience, hearing gunfire and not knowing what was going on outside. Suddenly the infantrymen received a terrific jolt—*Bernadou* had run aground on a sand spit. Sympson's soldiers were hurled onto the decks and pitched violently out of bunks. Near-panic broke out among men who thought the ship had been struck by shellfire and would explode momentarily.

Captain Sympson climbed halfway down the ladder into the chamber and called out in a booming voice: "Anybody hurt?" There was no reply. His men simply huddled together. "Okay," Sympson roared, "we've got a job to do. Let's get the hell out of here!"

Rope ladders were flung over the side of the *Bernadou,* and Captain Sympson's heavily laden men climbed down into shallow water and onto the Môle Petite Darse, their target. A few minutes later the men of K Company began driving Foreign Legionnaires back from the waterfront and securing key points in the harbor.

In the meantime, destroyer *Cole,* with Captain Thomson Wilson's L Company aboard, was heading toward the harbor entrance when her bridge spotted what was thought to be the *Bernadou* and turned southward to follow. Actually they had seen the destroyer *Beatty,* moving into position to duel French gun batteries on the high ground.

From his post inside the harbor, Ensign John Bell spotted the *Cole* and felt a surge of anxiety: *Cole* was off course, and if she continued in the same direction would crash into a concrete jetty. Ignoring his own safety, Bell began signaling with his flashlight. The *Cole* continued toward disaster. Then, shouting into his radio, Bell raised the *Cole*'s skipper, Lieutenant Commander G. G. Palmer, who managed to stop his ship only 30 yards before it would have crashed into the jetty.

Ensign Bell guided *Cole* to a pier and the men of Captain Wilson's L Company dashed off to clear the waterfront there. One platoon moved inland for 300 yards to seize a large Shell Oil Company storage facility after first silencing a French machine-gun crew that had opened fire.

At daybreak the harbor, railroad station, post office, and roads entering Safi from the south were held by Americans. The town's police department had been disarmed. But stubborn French forces had concealed themselves on the cliffs east and north of the harbor and continued to pepper the invaders with machine-gun and rifle fire.

One platoon of assault troops from the 47th Infantry, edging up a steep hill to the north, attacked and captured the big guns at Pointe de la Tour. Inside the shattered fire control tower, which had been hit heavily by *New York*'s guns, were the bodies of French gunners, including that of the officer in command of naval elements in the Safi region. Over the tower, which dominated the sea for miles in each direction, the American infantrymen hoisted the Stars and Stripes. As their flag waved majestically in the offshore wind, the platoon of GIs, many overcome by emotion, stood at attention and saluted.

Meanwhile, off Yellow Beach eight miles south of Safi, Major Louis Gershenow's 2nd Battalion, 47th Infantry, was on the transport *Dorothea L. Dix* and preparing to go ashore. Shoehorned into the *Dix* were some 1,450 soldiers, 1,500 tons of vehicles and other cargo, and five light tanks. During the final hour of darkness, a truck being winched over the side swung out of control and crashed heavily into the side of the ship. A can of gasoline on the hanging truck was crushed, spraying fuel onto the hot motor of the landing craft below. A huge explosion and fireball enveloped the LCV, the suspended truck, and the side of the *Dix*.

The men jammed into the *Dix* thought the ship had been torpedoed. Shells in the LCV began to explode, shaking the *Dix* violently. Panic spread to other transports as the tower of flame lit up the dark sky. But the LCV sank, the burning truck was dropped into the water, crewmen extinguished the blaze on the *Dix,* and darkness and relief settled back over the transport area.

The commotion on the *Dix* set back landing operations, and it was not until 8:00 A.M. that leading elements of Major Gershenow's battalion left the ship and headed for Yellow Beach. Not until noon did the entire battalion get ashore. Gershenow's men promptly blew up the coastal railroad, then marched northward through the old fishing village and into Safi.

As assault waves and a few tanks continued to pour into Safi, General Harmon was still pacing the bridge of *Harris*. He was doing all he could as commander of the sub–task force—waiting for reports from the beach. It was almost 5:00 A.M. when the first report reached Harmon— and it was a devastating one: both destroyers, *Bernadou* and *Cole*, had run aground. Their crews and most assault troops had been lost.

Harmon struggled with his emotions, then, 15 minutes later, a second signal arrived: Cancel the first message. Both destroyers were in the harbor, the troops were ashore and the port was rapidly being secured.

At daylight, after hours of concern for his men, Harmon could restrain himself no longer. He climbed down a net, scrambled into a waiting landing craft, and 40 minutes later was striding briskly along a Safi beach. Harmon, who had seen heavy action as a junior officer during World War I, was greeted by the sight of a large number of his soldiers lying face-down, so close to the water's edge that the surf was running up against the soles of their boots. Only an occasional sniper bullet was thudding into the sand around them.

The general winced. Calling over a young captain in charge of the group, Harmon inquired: "Why are your men lying there with their feet in the water?"

"Well, sir," the captain stammered, "because we're under fire."

"Yes," Harmon responded evenly, "I realize you are. But how many people are shooting at you?"

The young officer paused briefly. "About six, sir."

The general then pointed to a building about 200 yards in the distance. "It's obvious the snipers are in there. Send about twelve men to clean out the house, then get going with the rest of your company to your objective."

"Yes, sir," the captain replied eagerly. Within minutes the snipers were flushed out.

Turning to his aide, Captain Thomas Rooney, Harmon remarked, "Those men will be fine soldiers once they have suffered through the stage fright of their first hostile action."

Inspecting the beaches, General Harmon found that he was an armored commander without armor. During the night, eight or ten light tanks had been sneaked ashore on small lighters. One other tank lighter broke down with engine failure, and another got lost and landed several hours late. Those tanks that did get ashore were useless and inoperable due to faulty batteries or drowned engines.

Desperate for armor to help the infantry ward off expected French counterblows, Harmon was relieved to see the *Lakehurst,* a converted seatrain loaded with medium tanks, and the *Titania,* filled with light tanks, edge into the harbor and tie up at adjacent piers. There was trouble immediately. A *Lakehurst* crane had just lifted a medium tank over the side when the winch seized up; frantic engineers could not get the tank up or down. It took five hours to solve that problem. And a hoist on *Titania* had lifted a light tank a foot off the deck when the cable snapped. It took seven hours to locate another.

Beset with difficulties on all sides, General Harmon tried to contact Admiral Lyal Davidson, the Safi naval commander embarked in the *Philadelphia*, to resolve joint problems. He could not reach Davidson, only a few miles off the beaches—ship-to-shore communications had broken down. Harmon, who wanted to be ashore to direct operations personally, had to return to *Harris* in order to communicate with Admiral Davidson.

Hardly had the general climbed over *Harris*'s rail than he was handed an alarming message: Secret sources ashore revealed that more than 70 trucks filled with French fighting men were racing for Safi from Marrakech, 90 miles inland. Harmon thanked his lucky stars for his decision to return to *Harris,* where he could act on this intelligence.

The general found that ship-to-shore radios were again working. He radioed Admiral Davidson, who contacted the aircraft carrier *Santee* 60 miles offshore. Within minutes several flights of dive-bombers from *Santee* were headed for the Marrakech-Safi road, where they intercepted the French truck convoy. For a half hour, the American naval pilots, seeing their first action, strafed the column of trucks. As French soldiers leaped from the vehicles, seeking cover that wasn't there on the bleak terrain, the horror that Major Yarborough had seen on the Sebkra D'Oran was duplicated on a larger scale.

Out of ammunition, low on gasoline, the aircraft headed back to the *Santee*. Left behind were the blackened, smoking hulks of 36 trucks and the bodies of many French soldiers.

Thank God for the United States Navy, General Harmon told his staff officers. The one thousand French soldiers in the truck caravan could have created havoc if they had reached Safi while a disorganized American force was still trying to get ashore.

In the meantime, resolute Foreign Legionnaires were holed up in an old walled barracks near the waterfront. It was 2:30 P.M. and the fight for the barracks had been raging for seven hours. Suddenly three Renault tanks appeared and charged the American positions. Confronted by tanks for the first time, the green GIs didn't try to use the new bazookas that had been issued to them, but relied instead on rifle grenades. Two of the Renaults were knocked out, and the third lost control and crashed into a stone wall; the driver was knocked unconscious.

Without tanks of their own, the infantry GIs turned the Renault guns around and fired them at the barracks. American reinforcements arrived, and 81-millimeter mortar crews under Captain James J. Johnston began pounding the Foreign Legion force. Running out of ammunition, outnumbered, and surrounded, the French commander emerged from the barracks under a white flag. It was 3:30 P.M. The legionnaires were given cigarettes and made prisoners of war in the comfort of their own barracks.

General Harmon, in the meantime, had returned to shore, frustrated over the mechanical difficulties that were preventing his tanks from being unloaded. Harmon, clad in his pink jodhpurs and knee-high riding boots, and others on the dock were the periodic targets of snipers hidden in the cliffs. Twice the annoyed general sent a squad of soldiers to a hillside house from which most of the shooting seemed to be coming. Each time the sergeant in charge reported back: "There's no one there but a harmless man and woman, sir."

Each time the squad had probed the suspected house and returned, sniping had erupted anew. Several Americans on the dock were hit by bullets. Harmon was furious. He collared the commander of a tank, pointed to the house, and bellowed: "Get up the hill to within ten feet of that goddamned house and blow it off the map!"

The tank clanked forward and minutes later its gun roared. The house collapsed in a smoldering heap of splintered wood and masonry. From out of a trapdoor underneath the rubble emerged a French officer and 30 of his men. The hostile group had been hidden in the cellar by the man and woman whose bodies were sprawled in the ruins of their home.

At 8:00 A.M., monitors on Gibraltar picked up a newscast over Radio Vichy: "Admiral Darlan, chief of the French armed forces, and General

Juin are in Algiers, directing the army and navy. . . . Oran and Algiers have been heavily bombarded, with attempted landings in their harbors, but all landings have been repulsed."

During the night, Adolf Hitler's private train rattled through the Bavarian hills on the way to Munich, where he would address the faithful at the celebration marking the 19th anniversary of the 1923 Beer Hall Putsch. It was dawn, with the Führer asleep after all-night military conferences, when the private train was flagged down at a small station outside of Munich.

Walther Hewel, a civilian advisor to the Führer, was summoned to the stationmaster's office to receive an urgent telephone call. It was the Foreign Ministry in Berlin. An excited voice read off a transcript of a BBC broadcast from London, just received and translated:

> *An Allied expeditionary force has landed in North Africa. Powerful American and British armies under Lieutenant General Eisenhower, supported by British and American battleships, have already taken Algiers and are advancing on Casablanca and Oran. All is going well. We come as friends. Only token resistance is expected from the French, whom we have come to liberate.*

Hewel rushed back onto the train to wake Generaloberst Alfred Jodl, Hitler's military advisor, and a hurried conference was held. Should Hitler be awakened and given the startling news? He was essentially a night person, who conducted conferences—during which others were able to interject only an occasional monosyllable—until the wee hours. Then he slept until late afternoon, when a hot shower and an injection by his personal physician readied him for another night of decision-making.

Even Wehrmacht generals had known Hitler's wrath when they had disturbed his sleep on matters the dictator considered insufficently important.* It was decided that General Jodl, who had been at Hitler's

---

* Even when the Allies poured ashore at dawn on D-day in Normandy, June 6, 1944, no one in Hitler's entourage could summon up the courage to awaken the Führer to give him the bad news.

elbow since 1940, would awaken him. Jodl, it was agreed, seemed to have a way for breaking bad news that elicited less of an outburst.

Hitler was astonished by word of massive Allied landings in French Northwest Africa. The machinations of the XX-Committee over many weeks had sent him to bed convinced that the Allied convoys the Germans had detected were bound for the eastern Mediterranean, hundreds of miles from Algiers and Oran. It was in the eastern Mediterranean that most of the U-boat wolfpacks were lying futilely in wait.

Three days before taking off on their history-making mission to North Africa, men of the 509th Parachute Infantry Battalion marched in review for America's first lady, Eleanor Roosevelt. (Phillips Publications)

General Alphonse Juin. (U.S. Army)

General Henri Giraud. (U.S. Army)

Resident General of Tunisia, Vice Admiral Jean-Pierre Estéva. (National Archives)

General Louis-Marie Koeltz.
(National Archives)

Leaflets with a message of friendship from President Roosevelt, signed by General Eisenhower, were dropped just before the invasion. (Author's collection)

Message du Président des Etats Unis

Le Président des Etats Unis m'a chargé comme Général Commandant en Chef des Forces Expéditionnaires Américaines de faire parvenir aux peuples de l'Afrique française du Nord le message suivant:

Aucune nation n'est plus intimement liée, tant par l'histoire que par l'amitié profonde, au peuple de France et à ses amis que ne le sont les Etats Unis d'Amérique.

Les Américains luttent actuellement, non seulement pour assurer leur avenir, mais pour restituer les libertés et les principes démocratiques de tous ceux qui ont vécu sous le drapeau tricolore.

Nous venons chez vous pour vous libérer des conquérants qui ne désirent que vous priver à tout jamais de vos droits souverains, de votre droit à la liberté du culte, de votre droit de mener votre train de vie en paix.

Nous venons chez vous uniquement pour anéantir vos ennemis — nous ne voulons pas vous faire de mal.

Nous venons chez vous en vous assurant que nous partirons dès que la menace de l'Allemagne et de l'Italie aura été dissipée.

Je fais appel à votre sens des réalités ainsi qu'à votre idéalisme.

Ne faites rien pour entraver l'accomplissement de ce grand dessein.

Aidez-nous, et l'avènement du jour de la paix universelle sera hâté.

[signature]

DWIGHT D. EISENHOWER
Lieutenant Général, Commandant en Chef
des Forces Expéditionnaires Américaines.

Hundreds of thousands of leaflets signed by General Eisenhower were dropped over North African towns hours before the invasion. (Author's collection)

Ce tract a été lancé sur tous les centres principaux de la France Metropolitaine.

Français de l'Afrique du Nord:

FIDÈLE à l'amitié traditionnelle et séculaire du gouvernement et du peuple des Etats Unis pour la France et pour l'Afrique française du Nord une grande armée américaine débarque sur votre sol.

Notre mission immédiate est de protéger l'Afrique française du Nord

AU VERSO

SUITE DE LA PREMIÈRE PAGE

Ce tract a été lancé sur tous les centres principaux de la France Metropolitaine.

contre la menace d'une invasion italo-allemande. Notre but principal est le même qu'en 1917, c'est-à-dire, l'anéantissement de l'ennemi et la libération complète de la France envahie.

Le jour où la menace italo-allemande ne pèsera plus sur les territoires français nous quitterons votre sol.

La souveraineté de la France sur les territoires français reste entière.

Nous savons que nous pouvons compter sur votre concours pour frayer le chemin qui mène à la victoire et à la paix.

Tous ensemble, on les aura!

DWIGHT D. EISENHOWER,
Lieutenant Général,
Commandant en Chef des
Forces Expéditionnaires Américaines

Lieutenant Colonel Edson D. Raff led America's first paratrooper mission. (U.S. Army)

Captain Carlos C. "Doc" Alden, 509th Parachute Infantry Battalion, first paratrooper to reach the airborne's D-day objective. (Author's collection)

Men of the 509th Parachute Infantry Battalion quickly assemble after dropping on Youks-les-Bains airfield near the Algerian-Tunisian border. This photo was taken with a small box camera by Lt. Archie Birkner just after he parachuted to earth. (Author's collection)

An American paratrooper offers a light to a captured French sailor. (U.S. Army)

Captured French sailors salute as they march past American paratroopers. (U.S. Army)

Prime Minister Winston Churchill, who promoted Operation Torch. (U.S. Army)

Lieutenant Colonel William O. Darby,
Ranger force leader in Arzew landings.
(U.S. Army)

Lieutenant Colonel Lyle W. Bernard's
3rd Division battalion assaulted
Fedala. (U.S. Army)

Colonel John W. "Iron Mike"
O'Daniel (here a brigadier general)
led combat team in attack on Algiers.
(U.S. Army)

Major General Ernest N. Harmon, commander of Safi assault. (U.S. Army)

Major General Lucian K. Truscott, Jr., led assault on Port Lyautey. (Photo taken after promotion.) (U.S. Army)

U.S. Major General Charles Ryder, commander, Eastern Task Force. (U.S. Army)

Americans in support units wade ashore near Oran. The transport in the background had daringly edged to within a few hundred yards of the beach. (U.S. Army photo)

A transport's assault boats form up for the run into the Safi beaches. (U.S. Army)

American troops hit the beaches near Algiers. The Stars and Stripes was carried by a soldier (left) to discourage the French from firing. (National Archives)

British assault troops going ashore outside Algiers. (Imperial War Museum)

Near Safi, General Ernest Harmon's reinforcing waves hit the beach on the morning of D-day. (U.S. Army photo)

Elements of the 3rd Infantry Division sloshed ashore near Fedala. (U.S. Army)

British aircraft carrier Argus *operating off the North African coast.*
(Imperial War Museum)

American reinforcements land near Algiers. (U.S. Army)

American soldiers interrogate a French prisoner in fighting around Oran. (U.S. Army)

American soldiers walk down Oran street after city was secured. Curious civilians line the curbs. (U.S. Army)

An American rifleman dashes ahead under fire as French evicted from the building look on nonchalantly. (U.S. Army)

The 60th Regiment, 3rd Infantry Division, suffered 225 casualties in the final charge that seized the thick-walled Casbah (left), which guarded river and ground approaches to Port Lyautey. Perched on a hill, the bastion for three days defied air, sea, and ground efforts to capture or destroy it. (U.S. Army)

Major William P. Yarborough (right) summons medics moments after a French ambulance has been strafed. The French driver on the ground was killed when he dashed back to let the wounded men out. (Author's collection)

(Above) General Dwight D. Eisenhower lays down the law to French Admiral Jean-François Darlan. (U.S. Army)

(Left) Admiral Andrew B. Cunningham, RN. (Imperial War Museum)

(Above) Rear Admiral Harold Burrough, RN. (Imperial War Museum)

(Right) Rear Admiral Thomas Troubridge, RN. (Imperial War Museum)

In the fighting against the Axis in Tunisia, General Alphonse Juin (left) confers with General Henri Giraud (right). In center is General Jean Catroux. (U.S. Army)

The French battleship Jean Bart, *hit by U.S. Navy Wildcats at her berth in Casablanca harbor. (U.S. Army)*

President Franklin D. Roosevelt pins the Distinguished Service Cross on Major General Mark W. Clark for activities connected with Operation Torch. (U.S. Army)

17

"Be Warned: They Are Alert on Shore!"

It was 10:00 on the night of D-day minus 1 as General George Patton's Goalpost sub–task force closed in on the Atlantic coastline of North Africa. In a few hours, the embarked troops under General Lucian Truscott would be storming the beaches at Port Lyautey and adjoining Plage de Mehdia, some 60 miles northeast of Casablanca. Stars shone over a seascape that was black and foreboding.

Forty-seven-year-old Lucian Truscott, who was known as one of the army's finest polo players, was on the bridge of the transport *Henry T. Allen*, reviewing the problems facing him on the eve of battle. Navy officers on board had admitted to Truscott that, with the sketchy and outdated navigational charts they were using, the assault waves might end up as far as three miles from targeted beaches. The navy had emphasized to the Goalpost troop commander the unlikelihood that they could navigate to a specified dot on the map in the dark at a specific hour after sailing some 3,000 miles of ocean.

At 10:15 P.M. the lights of a large town were seen to starboard. What town was it? One officer mumbled that it might be Rabat, 20 miles south of the objective at Port Lyautey.

Suddenly lookouts reported the outline of a submarine off the bow, one that the convoy's commodore, Harold Gray, had sent ahead to scout the shore at the targeted beaches and to try to locate the mouth of the Sebou River, which was in the center of the objective. The sub's skipper signaled that the *Henry T. Allen*, Goalpost's command ship, had strayed out of formation and was dangerously close to shore. Indeed officers on the *Allen*'s bridge could detect the dim silhouettes of sand dunes and cliffs. Gray ordered the *Allen* back out to sea to locate her position in the convoy. A short time later the ship halted.

There was a bustle of activity on the Allen's quarterdeck as navy officers dashed from side to side, peered off into the murky blackness, and conversed in nervous tones.

Finally Truscott turned to convoy commander Gray and in a tone just short of exasperation inquired: "Well, Commodore, where are we?"

Gray was clearly nervous and replied: "Well, General, to be perfectly honest, I am not right sure exactly where we are."

Truscott winced. Now he was nervous too.

The general glanced at his watch. The convoy was already an hour behind schedule. How would this affect the carefully timed assault operation? A short time later Truscott felt a partial surge of relief: The dim outlines of other vessels could be discerned. The *Allen* was not alone.

Port Lyautey, the second most important anchorage in French Morocco, lies six miles inland, on the Sebou River. Just before the westward-flowing Sebou empties into the Atlantic, it loops to the north and back in a horseshoe bend. Along the western, or descending, leg of the horseshoe was the Casbah, a citadel guarding the river approach to Port Lyautey. To the southwest of the Casbah was the resort Mehdia Beach, and some three miles north of Port Lyautey lay an excellent airport, which was the prime objective of Goalpost. The airdrome's concrete runways and its modern hangars lay on low flats next to the river, looked down upon from the north by 100-foot bluffs.

Invading troops starting toward Port Lyautey from the coast would be confronted by a lagoon which ran parallel to the shore for almost 4 miles, fringed by pine woods and steep ridges. There was only one narrow corridor, a mere 200 yards wide at points, through which troops and vehicles could pass—under the muzzles of six 138.6-millimeter guns located on high ground. The entire region was dotted with automatic weapons, antiaircraft guns, and elaborate connecting trenches.

Port Lyautey and its prized airdrome would be tough nuts to crack. "It would be hard to pick out a more difficult place to assault in all of west Africa," a harried planner had said weeks before. But the airfield had to be taken: 76 fighter planes from the carrier *Chenango* were to land there no later than the end of D-day in support of the attack on Casablanca itself. Also arriving would be heavy bombers.

Truscott's plan of attack would be to land his equivalent of four battalions at five points along the Atlantic shore, beginning at H-hour at 4:00 A.M. Coastal guns were to be neutralized before dawn, after which four groups would advance inland.

Once assault troops were ashore, a detachment of 75 specially trained raiders would try to reach the airfield by sailing up the Sebou River on the ancient destroyer *Dallas*. This mission would be full of risks. A sandbar at the river's mouth limited entry, and a mile upstream a barrier blocked further progress. French artillery and machine guns were sited to cover the Sebou, and gunners in the thick-walled Casbah could look down on the channel.

Lucian Truscott held out little hope for a peaceful occupation of his objectives, but he would do what he could to win French cooperation. He had drawn up a letter to the French commander at Port Lyautey and had it translated into French and ornately hand-lettered on a scroll. The impressive document was secured with a bright ribbon. Two volunteers would land with the first wave, jeep through French lines under a flag of truce, and try to deliver the Truscott appeal.

At midnight, the blacked-out convoy was lying some eight miles offshore—hopefully, offshore from the targeted beaches. No one knew for sure. Wherever they were, the transports had anchored out of position, and in a keenly honed operation where it was crucial that each ship be in its proper location, no one vessel knew the position of any other ship, nor was certain of its own.

General Truscott's worries multiplied when the ship-to-ship radios refused to work. What were they doing on the other transports? Waiting for orders? Or would they proceed with the amphibious landings? The harried Truscott, with time running out, needed answers.

Along with an aide, Truscott climbed down a rope ladder and into a small boat. Groping through the blackness and dodging landing craft milling aimlessly about, he somehow managed to locate, one by one, each of the five transports carrying his troops. Arriving at the side of each vessel, he tried to communicate with shadowy forms on deck, but nervous officers refused to respond to this man who hailed them out of the darkness and claimed to be General Truscott. So he had to take the time to climb up rope ladders on each transport and hastily go over last-minute revised plans with troops commanders. Due to the monumental confusion, the general postponed H-hour 30 minutes, to 4:30 A.M.

Having made his rounds (and considering it miraculous that he had stumbled onto all five transports) a weary Truscott returned to the *Allen* at 3:30 A.M. His hopes that he might still achieve surprise by reaching the shore before daylight were dashed by Truscott's chief of staff, who rushed up just as the general climbed back over *Allen*'s railing. "Boss," said Colonel Don E. Carlton excitedly, "listen to this." It was President Roosevelt's rebroadcast to the French people, calling for their cooperation. The broadcast was to have been aired along Patton's Western Task Force region at the original 4:00 A.M. H-hour, at the precise minute American troops were to be hitting the beaches. Now, Truscott felt, it would be miraculous if the French defenders were not on full alert. Lights in the town thought to be Port Lyautey were still glowing, but minutes later five French cargo vessels steamed in a column out of the mouth of the Sebou River, their lights burning brightly. The ships moved westward directly through the Goalpost convoy. One of the steamers, the *Lorraine*, flashed a blinker signal in French: "*Be warned. They are alert on shore!*"

As a young navy officer on the *Allen*'s bridge translated the message, the five French vessels continued to the southwest on a course paralleling the coastline. Only much later would those in the Goalpost group learn the fate of these Good Samaritan ships: east of Casablanca, American destroyers, protecting a convoy that was landing troops at Fedala, fired at them and forced them aground.

Off Lyautey, men of Colonel Frederick J. de Rohan's 60th Infantry Regiment (they called themselves the Go-Devils) had been standing nervously for more than three hours on the decks of the transports *Allen*,

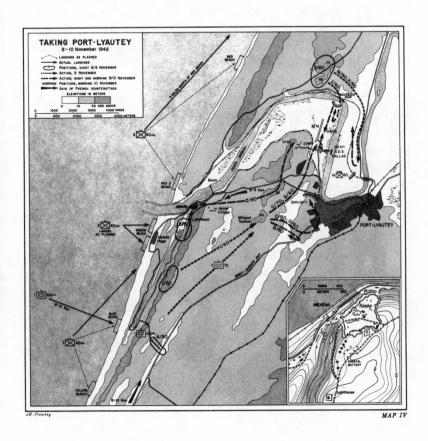

TAKING PORT-LYAUTEY
8-10 November 1942

LANDINGS AS PLANNED
ACTUAL LANDINGS
POSITIONS, NIGHT 8/9 NOVEMBER
ACTION, 9 NOVEMBER
ACTION, NIGHT AND MORNING 9/10 NOVEMBER
POSITIONS, MORNING 10 NOVEMBER
AXIS OF FRENCH COUNTERATTACK
ELEVATIONS IN METERS

J.R. Crowley

MAP IV

Clymer, Susan B. Anthony, Algarab, and *Florence Nightingale,* waiting for lost landing craft that were milling around in the blackness. Suddenly the lights on the horizon went out.

At 5:40 A.M. the first wave of Major John H. Dilley's 2nd Battalion was nearing Green Beach at the mouth of the Sebou River. The abrupt beams of French searchlights made the Go-Devils crouch instinctively. Several of the assault boats were picked up by the probing lights, and moments later a brilliant red flare burst over the shoreline—a signal to all defenders that invaders were nearing the beach.

There was a sudden cacophony as French coastal guns opened up on the transports and warships. American naval guns returned heavy fire, causing the searchlights to go out and temporarily silencing the shore guns. On the run into the beach, Major Dilley's first wave had gotten lost, and his second wave landed first.

With the arrival of dawn, two French Dewoitine fighter planes took off from the Port Lyautey airdrome, the primary target of Goalpost, sped the few miles to the shoreline, and began a strafing run along Green Beach. Dilley's men pushed their faces into the wet sand, but many of them were hit.

A few miles to the south, Major Percy DeW. McCarley's 1st Battalion got ashore unopposed at Blue and Yellow beaches, but McCarley recognized no landmarks. He studied his map. His entire battalion had been put ashore more than a mile and a half from its designated beaches.

A considerable distance to the north, Lieutenant Colonel John J. Toffey's 3rd Battalion bogged down in confusion before it even left the transport area. Toffey's landing craft had tried to form up around the control ship *Osprey,* but in the dark the maneuver deteriorated into a jumble of milling boats.

Finally, though Toffey's assault boats were in no recognizable order, the signal was given to head for shore. At 6:35 A.M.—in daylight—the leading wave neared the beach. Four French fighter planes strafed and dropped several bombs; near misses swamped two landing craft, dumping the heavily loaded Go-Devils into the cold Atlantic water. Members of the 692nd Coast Guard Artillery (Antiaircraft) shot down two of the French warplanes and pounded each other on the back at their first kill.

On the beach, Lieutenant Colonel Toffey calculated that his battalion had been put on land five miles from its designated beach. Undaunted, he began the task of untangling the squads, platoons, and companies that had landed piecemeal. Ahead lay an arduous cross-country march of five miles to the airport objective. Machine guns, mortars and shells, bazookas, rockets, ammunition boxes, and a wide assortment of heavier gear would have to be lugged by hand, up one ridge and down the other and over terrain thick with scrub.

In the meantime, Colonel Demas T. "Nick" Craw and Major Pierpont M. Hamilton, air corps officers assigned to General Truscott's headquarters, had climbed down rope ladders on the *Clymer* and headed shoreward with the first wave. In their dress uniforms, with leather and brass gleaming, they appeared out of place in the cramped assault boats with GIs clad in battle dress. Craw and Hamilton each wore aviator wings and rows of ribbons earned in World War I. Both officers spoke fluent French. Hamilton had spent many years in France, and Craw had a wide acquaintanceship among French officers from duty in Greece and the Balkans. They had volunteered to try to get through hostile lines and reach the local commander, Colonel Charles Petit, with General Truscott's appeal to cease firing and cooperate with the American *libérateurs*.

As dawn broke, the pair of couriers arrived at the mouth of the Sebou River—just in time to be greeted by several Dewoitines strafing the beach. Heading inland in a jeep flying a huge white flag, Craw and Hamilton reached the Casbah without incident. There French troops directed the Americans to Port Lyautey, as though the appearance of armed foreign officers were an everyday event. On the outskirts of town, the jeep rounded a sharp bend in the road, and nervous French machine-gunners up ahead opened fire on the approaching vehicle. Colonel Craw was killed instantly; Major Hamilton had not been hit and was taken prisoner.

Hamilton, shaken by the unexpected violence and by the death of his partner, was escorted to Colonel Petit's Port Lyautey headquarters. The French commander received the American cordially and expressed deep regret, which Hamilton thought was sincere, over the killing of Colonel Craw. But he would make no commitment to order a cease fire, even though he declared his distaste to be fighting "our American friends."

What was lacking to halt the violence was an order from the French commander's superior. Unless and until such authorization was received, Colonel Petit said, his soldiers' honor required him to keep fighting. Hamilton's request to return to his own lines was "regretfully" denied, and Petit ordered the American officer held in protective custody.*

At the precise time that Major Hamilton was parlaying with Colonel Petit, hundreds of miles away in Vichy the American chargé d'affaires, S. Pinkney Tuck, was being received by Marshal Henri Pétain, the eighty-four-year-old head of France's puppet government. Tuck read a personal message from President Roosevelt to the white-haired hero of World War I. It was an official announcement that the *Americans* were conducting a preventive occupation of French Northwest Africa to thwart Hitler's doing so, and asking Pétain not to oppose it.

To Tuck, Pétain seemed confused. The Vichy head of state made no reply. An aide handed Pétain a prepared statement that he promptly signed and handed to the American *chargé d'affaires:* "It is with stupor and sadness that I learned of the aggression of your troops against North Africa. I have read your message. You invoke pretexts which nothing justifies. . . . France and her honor are at stake. We are attacked; we shall defend ourselves; this is the order I am giving."

Tuck put the response in his briefcase and rose to depart. In good spirits, and with the greatest amiability, the confused old marshal insisted that Tuck remain for a while and chat. Pétain's subject: the glory days of World War I.

In the meantime, French coastal guns around Port Lyautey resumed the occasional shelling of American vessels. At midmorning, when follow-

---

* Both Colonel Craw and Major Hamilton were later awarded the Congressional Medal of Honor for their mission. After the war, Hamilton rose to brigadier general.

up waves were still disembarking from the transport *Allen*, several shells exploded a few hundred yards from the ship. Moments later the voice of Commodore Gray blared over the loudspeaker: "Cease unloading. Clear away landing craft. Stand by to move out to sea!"

General Truscott was shocked—and angry. He rushed to Gray and protested vigorously. A heated argument erupted. Truscott shouted that the remaining troops on board were vitally needed on shore. "We have to take chances!" the general exclaimed. Gray finally agreed, and ordered unloading to continue—for the time being.

In the anchorage area off Port Lyautey, jittery American lookouts who were in a combat situation for the first time sounded air-raid warnings every few minutes—a development that disrupted operations. Not a single aircraft was sighted.

At about 10:00 A.M. a twin-engine airplane did appear from the north, flying low and heading directly for the transports. No air-raid alarm was sounded—there had not been time. Spontaneously every gun within range opened up and a torrent of flying steel crisscrossed the sky.

The plane headed directly for the *Allen*; on board someone shouted, "My God, cease firing! Those are British markers on it!"

Once started, the firing proved impossible to close down. Within a few hundred yards of the *Allen*, the riddled aircraft burst into flames and crashed. Small boats were rushed to the spot, but no survivors were found. Only later would it be learned that the RAF plane had been sent from Gibraltar to report on progress of the Western Task Force landings.

On shore there was monumental confusion. Heavy surfs had hindered the landing of crucial artillery, tanks, ammunition, and supplies. What did land was often on the wrong beach. Ship-to-shore communication had become snarled, which made it impossible for naval guns to effectively support troops clinging to shallow beachheads and being bombarded by French 75-millimeter batteries.

Major John Dilley's 2nd Battalion, which had landed near the mouth of the Sebou River and quickly secured Mehdia against negligible opposition, was still disorganized. But Dilley ordered an attack against his battalion's primary objective, the heavily defended Casbah, which stood atop a steep, brush-covered ridge. Dilley's leading elements paddled rubber boats across the lagoon running parallel to the shore and advanced through heavy brush for 600 yards. Suddenly the green soldiers in their first attack halted: Huge naval shells were screaming into the ridge only 200 yards to their front. Rattled by the shelling from "friendly" guns, Dilley's men scrambled to the rear in considerable disarray.*

Major Dilley rushed from the beach to his forward positions; by now the naval gunfire had ceased. Looking through binoculars, the battalion commander scanned the lighthouse that was perched on the nearest shoulder of the ridge leading to the Casbah. Dilley could see only a few French sailors. He ordered the attack resumed.

Picking their way up the brush-covered slope, the Americans were met by automatic-weapons and rifle fire from the lighthouse. Men of E Company flopped to the ground and lay there face down, unable to move. Lieutenant Charles Dushane, Corporal Frank L. Czar, Private First Class Theodore R. Bratkowitz, and another private suddenly got to their feet and rushed forward into the hostile fire. Crossing barbed-wire entanglements, they dashed inside the lighthouse. Shots rang out, then silence. Moments later the Americans and 12 prisoners emerged.

Other French defenders had hastily pulled back from the lighthouse, and E and F companies teamed up to clear the trench system which connected this strongpoint with the Casbah. Fighting had been brief but bloody; many French and American dead and wounded were sprawled around the trenches. Colonel de Rohan, commander of the 60th Infantry Regiment, arrived at the lighthouse and found his infantrymen stalled, unsure of what to do next. Rohan ordered them to attack the Casbah once more.

One company was left to secure the lighthouse positions and the remainder of the battalion set out for the glowering fortress. Shaken by their first combat, Dilley's men began to straggle, and then communica-

---

* Much later GIs would coin a phrase for a spontaneous retrograde movement of this type—bugging out.

tions with the rear echelon and supporting artillery went out. But in approximate company strength, the Americans entered a small collection of buildings known as Cactus Village and were met by a torrent of fire from elements of the Moroccan 1st Infantry Regiment.

French 75s poured fire into American ranks, and then three Renault tanks began clanking toward the beleaguered Go-Devils. Already decimated by casualties and a large number of stragglers, without tanks or artillery support, Dilley's men began scrambling piecemeal for the rear. In the face of heavy fire by advancing Moroccan infantrymen, Lieutenant Dushane and Corporal Czar rushed to a nearby antitank gun which the French had abandoned after removing part of its breech. Czar aimed the antitank gun at the hostile force and Dushane set it off repeatedly by firing a bullet from his tommy gun at the percussion cap at the base of each shell.

Now the attackers concentrated their fire on Dushane and Czar, but the two Americans continued to shoot the gun. They knocked out a tank and caused the accompanying infantry to waver, then to halt. Lieutenant Dushane was aiming his tommy gun at the base of a shell when a French bullet struck him in the head. He toppled over dead. Corporal Czar, unable to shoot the antitank gun alone, crawled away under a hail of fire.

At 1:30 P.M., General Truscott and a few staff officers headed for Green Beach at the mouth of the Sebou, landing there at about 3:00 P.M. The waves had turned angry, and as Truscott's jeep left the landing craft it bogged down in powdery sand and would remain there all night. His was not an isolated predicament. Surveying the shoreline in each direction, Truscott saw that scores of other vehicles were also mired and abandoned.

Armed with a two-way radio that refused to work, the general climbed into a halftrack and set off inland. He came upon two tanks and a tank destroyer and ordered them to accompany him. One tanker accidentally squeezed off a burst from a machine gun, and the bullets whistled past within three inches of Truscott's head.

Nearing dense woods, Truscott left the halftrack and, with two aides, continued on foot. For an hour the perspiring general tramped ahead through thick brush and rugged terrain. Reaching the vicinity of the lighthouse and Cactus Village, Truscott encountered a grim-faced Colonel de Rohan. The regimental commander said that Major John Dilley's battalion, in its baptism as an attacking force, had been decimated, with companies chopped down to 40 or 50 men each.

Truscott was doubtful of this gloomy report. There had been heavy fighting on the approaches to the Casbah, he could see; many American and French bodies were strewn about. But Truscott concluded that most of Major Dilley's "casualties" were stragglers—frightened young soldiers who had taken cover from the violence and refused to budge.

"Colonel," Truscott told de Rohan, "I want you to use your headquarters troops to search every house in this area."

An hour later, more than two hundred stragglers had been rounded up.

It was dark and hushed as Lucian Truscott arrived back at the beach command post, which consisted of a radio and a pole with the Blue Beach flag. The only person at the CP was a half-awake operator listening for radio messages that never arrived—the communications set (and Truscott) was out of touch with vessels offshore and with troop units on land.

Where were the officers? Truscott presumed that the lumps he saw dimly on the gound were the officers—deep in exhausted sleep. Shadowy figures wandered the blacked-out beaches. There were shouts and curses. Repeatedly Truscott heard calls of "George" and "Patton," the night's password and countersign.

Seated on a sand dune, cold, wet, miserable, and frustrated, Lucian Truscott felt terribly alone. All around him were hundreds of men, yet he felt isolated and powerless to influence the chaotic situation. In his anxiety and personal discomfort, Truscott violated his own strict order: He lit a cigarette. It was a relief to see orange glows in the darkness, an indication that other offenders around him were also violating his no-smoking-at-night order. There was nothing as lonely as a black, hostile beach.

As Truscott sat, a shadowy figure approached him from the direction of the shore, acting suspiciously, halting every few steps and looking in each direction. He stopped in front of Truscott, and in some sort of accent said: "Hey, gimme a cigarette."

The commanding general handed one over and heard him say, "Goddam. All wet. Gimme light too."

Without identifying himself, Truscott held out the lighted end of his cigarette just as two of his officers leaped forward and poked tommy guns into the stranger's stomach. One of them called out the password—"George!"

Came back instantly: "George? Me no George! Me Lee, cook, Company C, 540th Engineers!" Lee, a talented cook, had been deposited on the black beach, and was searching for his outfit.*

Lucian Truscott, sensing that the ingredients were present for a major American disaster, was concerned about a dawn attack on his southern flank by a French armored column reported to be approaching along the concrete road from Rabat. Truscott did not have a single foot soldier in reserve—a nightmare to any battle leader.

Now he received his first bit of good news: An aide had been sent to locate Lieutenant Colonel Harry H. Semmes and Semmes was now standing before the general. Truscott told the leader of the 3rd Armored Landing Team (2nd Armored Division) to take the seven of his tanks that had reached shore, head for the southern portion of the beachhead, and block the Rabat–Port Lyautey road along which the French armored column was approaching. "Get in position before dawn," Truscott said.

Leaving word for his other tanks to join him when they landed, Colonel Semmes hopped through the turret hatch of his own tank and led his clanking column off toward the south. Arriving about an hour later at a blocking position one mile south of infantry outposts, Semmes deployed his tanks and waited.

The young armored commander was worried: It was too dark to issue

---

* Lucian K. Truscott, Jr., *Command Missions*. Later Truscott "stole" Lee to be his own cook, and the cook was pirated in turn by General Patton.

orders to his tanks by arm signals, nor could he communicate with them by radio—his equipment had been ruined by salt spray during the crossing of the Atlantic. If the French struck before dawn, each of Semmes's tank commanders would be on his own.

18

The Warships Slug it Out

At 8:30 A.M. on D-day, General Dwight Eisenhower, bleary-eyed from 36 hours without sleep, was still in his cubbyhole office deep underground on Gibraltar. "I've seen larger telephone booths," a staff officer whispered to another. For seven hours the supreme commander had been breathing bad air and awaiting reports from the beaches. Since 2:45 A.M., only 75 minutes after H-hour, fragmentary signals had been tumbling in from Generals Lloyd Fredendall and Charles Ryder off Oran and Algiers. But now, four and a half hours after the Western Task Force was to have stormed the beaches, there had been only silence from General Patton.

In the signal center on the Rock, Colonel Darryl F. Zanuck, a Hollywood producer famed for his epic historical films, was helping process the incoming reports when he was summoned by Eisenhower—for about the tenth time in four hours. The terse script had been the same each time.

"Anything from Patton?"

"Not a word, sir."

Colonel Zanuck returned to his post.

Eisenhower scrawled in his personal diary: "Battles are raging, and we seem to be in control of most of Algiers and Oran. But the Casablanca theater [Patton] is ominously silent."

A short time later, some word arrived from a curious source—pro-Allied French officers at Safi. They reported to Gibraltar by radio that General Ernest Harmon's assault force had secured most of the old port and that the French defenders were being overwhelmed.

In the meantime, General Henri Giraud appeared back at Allied force headquarters in the Rock after several hours of sleep. For nearly two hours he conferred with Eisenhower and General Mark Clark, and as favorable reports continued to arrive the French general displayed a change in attitude. Giraud was now eager to cooperate.

Within minutes the broad outline of a deal was worked out: Giraud would be flown to Algiers as soon as American troops secured the city, where he would become commander in chief of all French forces in Northwest Africa. He also agreed to try to halt resistance at the earliest possible moment. This was a humbling concession for Giraud who, only a few hours before, had demanded that he be appointed commander of all Allied forces in Northwest Africa and had threatened to "view the operation as a spectator." Now, with Allied success apparently in the offing, the reluctant French general had reevaluated his position concerning his soldier's honor.

But there was still no word from General Patton. Why was he keeping Eisenhower from learning of the progress of the Western Task Force? There was ample reason: Patton's communications system had collapsed.

Patton's nerve center for the entire Western Task Force assault was Radio One, the message center of the flagship *Augusta* which was supposed to handle all his messages. But Radio One was crammed with 26 radiomen operating 11 receivers, 3 decoding and encoding machines, and assorted other equipment. In this crowded situation, Radio One soon became hopelessly snarled. Patton's incoming and outgoing messages began to pile up.

It was one difficulty after the other. At another control center on the *Augusta* where nine men were assigned to operate the Western Task Force's tactical radio net, the crew turned out to be so inexperienced that they had to be relieved a few hours after H-hour. When the equally green relief crew did finally send out a few messages over the tactical net, they proved to be worthless—all were in the wrong code. At one point a young operator intercepted an uncoded French signal, a potential intelligence bonanza. It described what actions were being taken in Casablanca to meet the invasion. Instead of passing the message on to his superiors, however, the radioman recorded it in his log and filed it.

The *Augusta*, with Patton and Admiral Kent Hewitt aboard, was with the Brushwood Sub-Task Force, commanded by General Jonathan Anderson, off Fedala. Anderson's men would go ashore there as a preliminary to seizing the main prize, Casablanca, 18 miles to the southwest.

Due to mixups in ships finding their spots—two transports had anchored six miles from assigned positions—H-hour twice had to be postponed. It was not until 4:45 A.M. that the first waves were sent in.

General Anderson's 3rd Infantry Division assault troops were to go ashore along a four-mile stretch between Cape Fedala and the Pont Blondin, a sector known as the River of Morocco. Cold, soaked by ocean spray, the men huddled in assault boats had no time or inclination to reflect on the fact that they would be landing at a renowned resort that sported a magnificent hotel, a race track, a casino, a golf course, beautiful gardens, and broad palm-lined streets.

When the first wave was a mile offshore, searchlights were pointed skyward at Cape Fedala and at Cherqui, on the heights to either side of Fedala. From the transport *Leonard Wood*, General Anderson could see them, and he felt incomparable relief: Vertical searchlight beams had been specified by General Eisenhower in his radio broadcast as the signal to indicate the French would not resist the landings.

But it was all a mistake. The French, thinking they might be under attack by air, had initially aimed their lights upward to look for hostile warplanes. Shortly afterward, the brilliant lights came down to play over the water. Onward came the assault craft, many held in the searchlight beams and peppered by machine-gun fire. Chaos erupted.

Boatloads of troops were scattered up and down the black coastline, sometimes miles wide of their objectives. The surf swept many boats out of control. Some were hurled against rocks and either capsized or

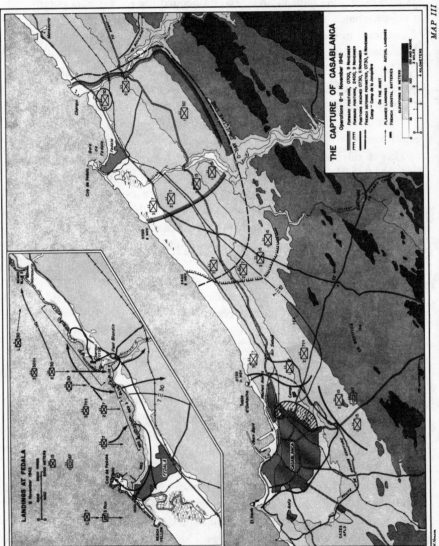

LANDINGS AT FEDALA
9 November 1942

THE CAPTURE OF CASABLANCA
Operations 8–11 November 1942

Forward positions, 0700, 9 November
Forward positions, 2400, 9 November
Positions reached perimeter, 0730, 11 November
French defense perimeter, 0730, 11 November
Camp — Camp de la Jonquière
On the inset
Planned landings — Actual landings
French Coastal batteries

ELEVATIONS IN METERS

MAP III

smashed into pieces. Heavily laden soldiers, pitched into the cold Atlantic, were drowned.

Boats hit rocky reefs instead of sandy beaches and defied efforts to retract them. Passengers striking out for shore badly cut their feet, hands, arms, and legs on razor-sharp rocks. Survivors of these mishaps reached the beach but without weapons, radios, and other essential equipment.

Daylight revealed a scene of enormous carnage for miles along the rugged coastline at Fedala. One hundred sixteen assault boats had departed from the transports *Leonard Wood, Thomas Jefferson, Charles Carroll,* and *Joseph T. Dickman.* Now 62 of them were splintered wrecks.

Reorganizing rapidly, elements of Lieutenant Colonel Roy E. Moore's 1st Battalion, 7th Infantry, charged into Fedala against sporadic machine-gun fire. One platoon surrounded the fashionable Miramer Hotel, home base for the German Armistice Commission, whose members the GIs wanted desperately to capture. Groups of Senegalese soldiers—Fedala's garrison—sat on curbs and watched the Americans bolt into the Miramer to find that their quarry had fled. While the GIs were scrounging through the three floors that had been occupied by the Germans, shells from American warships began screaming into Fedala. Two of the projectiles struck the hotel.

"Let's get the hell out of here!" a voice inside called out. His comrades needed no urging, and they dashed outside to rejoin their company.

About a mile from the Miramer, a convoy of three German staff cars raced out of Fedala. Rounding a street corner, the fleeing vehicles came upon an American platoon. Brakes squealed and the cars lurched to a halt. *"Komm heraus, Schweinehund!"* called out a GI, pleased to have had the chance to use the German he had been honing for weeks. Ten impeccably attired members of the German Armistice Commission emerged slowly with their hands in the air.

Lieutenant Colonel Moore had arrived at Boulevard Moulay Youssef, the first street in Fedala, and had gone on to set up 1st Battalion headquarters near the the Miramer Hotel. Warships promptly resumed shelling the town, and Moore sent Captain Everett W. Duval, the battalion executive officer, or second in command, back to the beach to get the navy to cease firing. Duval located Brigadier General William W. Eagles, assistant commander of the 3rd Division, and Eagles immediately radioed the command ship *Leonard Wood:* "Cease shelling Fedala."

Concerned that the signal was phony, some sort of enemy trick, General Anderson on the *Wood,* asked for a verification of the message. General Eagles, tall, mild-mannered, bespectacled, shot back in exasperation: "For God's sake, stop shelling Fedala. You're killing our own men and friendly French troops. Shells are falling all over town. If you stop they will surrender."

The bombardment of Fedala finally lifted.

Since shortly after daybreak, navy Wildcat dive-bombers from the big carrier *Ranger* had circled threateningly over Casablanca, a bustling city of 257,000 residents—the jewel of colonial France, described by one Torch planner as "half Arabian, half European, and half Hollywood." Spotter planes, catapulted from the old battleship *Massachusetts* and the heavy cruisers *Wichita* and *Tuscaloosa,* were hovering at a lower altitude should the naval bombardment of Casablanca be ordered. One squadron of fighters from the *Ranger* was cruising over two airfields at Rabat, and another squadron was in position over Cazes airfield outside Casablanca. Not a shot had been fired at the invading warplanes.

Just before 7:00 A.M., Casablanca harbor erupted in a mighty crescendo of noise. French antiaircraft guns had opened up, and the circling American pilots were buffeted by explosions. Black smoke dotted the sky. French Dewoitines, flown by experienced pilots, roared in, and soon fierce dogfights were raging over Casablanca.

Ordered to strike if French reaction was hostile, the American Wildcats pounced on predesignated targets. They bombed and strafed airfields, coastal batteries, and antiaircraft positions, taking time in between to duel with persistent Dewoitines. By noon, the French air force around Casablanca and Rabat had been virtually destroyed, its planes shot down or left burning on the runways of airfields.

At about the same time that American warplanes went into action, French coastal guns on the heights at Cape Fedala, the Batterie du Pont Blondin, and the Batterie du Port opened fire on the ships offshore and pounded the beaches where 3rd Infantry Division men were coming ashore. Once the French had thus tipped their hand, the cruiser *Brooklyn* and four destroyers began exchanging shells with the coastal guns. The destroyer *Murphy*, less than three miles offshore, was first straddled by a salvo, then several shells tore into her, killing and wounding several men and forcing her to limp out to sea.

Minutes later, the *Brooklyn* gained a measure of revenge: A salvo from her big guns hit the fire control apparatus within the fortifications of Batterie du Pont Blondin at the eastern end of the Bay of Fedala. The concrete-encased nerve center was destroyed. Another *Brooklyn* shell smashed into a gun emplacement, knocking out the big weapon, igniting powder bags, and killing or wounding some 30 Frenchmen.

While the *Brooklyn* was pounding the Batterie du Pont Blondin, elements of Lieutenant Colonel Lyle W. Bernard's 2nd Battalion, 30th Infantry, had virtually surrounded the gun position. Company and platoon leaders were in charge in Colonel Bernard's absence. (His battalion had landed on its designated beach, but a lone assault boat had strayed and deposited its passengers three miles away. Those passengers were Bernard and his command group.)

As soon as the naval gunfire lifted, Captain Mackenzie E. Porter's men of Company H scrambled to their feet, charged the Pont Blondin gun battery, and captured it from the dazed defenders.

At about 8:00 A.M. Lieutenant Colonel Fred W. Sladin's 1st Battalion, 30th Infantry Regiment, was marching southward toward its objective on the high ground. Suddenly scouts ahead of the main body threw up their hands, a signal to halt. The GIs hit the ground. In the distance an electric passenger train was approaching along tracks parallel to the battalion's route. Sladin's men took positions on either side of the tracks, and when the train neared they leaped out with weapons leveled at the wide-eyed engineer. Sparks flew from the rails as the train braked noisily to a halt. In the manner of a robbery in the days of America's Old West, the train, heading from Rabat to Casablanca, was boarded and searched. Some 75 French army, navy, and air force officers, bound for their duty stations, were taken prisoners. The satisfied GIs trudged on to their objective; never in their wildest dreams had they anticipated capturing an enemy train.

On the *Augusta*, the snarled radio network had prevented General Patton from getting reports on the fighting. A few minutes before

8:00 A.M. Patton was ready to head for the Fedala beachhead with a few members of his staff. Their personal effects, including the Western Task Force commander's celebrated pair of ivory-handled pistols, were placed in a landing craft, swinging from davits.

Just as Patton started to climb into the little boat, there was a terrific roar and the *Augusta* shook violently from bow to stern. The destroyer had opened fire on a French light cruiser and six destroyers that had come out of Casablanca at speed and were heading for the vulnerable transports.

The muzzle blast of the first round fired by *Augusta*'s after turret blew Patton's dangling landing craft to pieces. George Patton cursed the destruction of the boat; the naval artillery duel would postpone indefinitely his trek onto the beaches. He was only partly mollified when handed his prized pistols—someone had retrieved them just before the landing boat was blasted apart.

Even at this late hour some of the French did not know whether the ships landing invading troops on French soil were German, American, or British. And they did not care. The French navy's centuries-old honor dictated.

The pride of the French navy, the *Jean Bart*, with its huge 15-inch guns, was moored in Casablanca harbor. But it had opened fire at the warships offshore, and the Americans had replied. Within 20 minutes, American shells had crashed into the stationary *Jean Bart*'s main batteries, silencing her big guns. (But two days later they would be back in action.)

Now, just as General Patton was about to head for shore, the French warships, led by Rear Admiral Gervais de Lafond in the destroyer *Milan*, had sortied from the relative safety of Casablanca harbor to do battle with the invaders. Under cover of a thick smokescreen and undaunted by repeated attacks from the *Ranger*'s Wildcats, the French destroyers opened fire on the American warships nearest to them, sent two shells into the destroyer *Ludlow*, and forced the destroyer *Wilkes* to pull back out to sea.

The French ships, dodging in and out of smokescreens to shoot, fought a shrewd and stout-hearted battle. But the guns of the cruisers *Brooklyn* and *Augusta* along with several destroyers were too powerful for Admiral de Lafond's flotilla, and it pulled back into Casablanca harbor, unable to get at the transports.

At 9:35 A.M., however, the French tried once more. Three French destroyers and eight submarines slipped out of the harbor and were soon joined by the cruiser *Primauguet.* In an hour of furious sea battle, the French ships worked their way to within five miles of the transports. A few American warships were struck by shellfire and torpedoes, but with the heavy support of bombing and strafing by Wildcats, the tide of battle turned.

Admiral de Lafond's flagship *Milan,* mortally wounded, ran aground on Roches Noires and burned furiously. The destroyers *Boulonnais* and *Fougueux* blew up and sank. *Brestois* and *Frondeur* were sent to the bottom by Wildcat bombs, and the *Primauguet* took a bad beating before limping back to a jetty at the entrance to Casablanca harbor.

The *Ranger* quickly launched several squadrons of Wildcats to finish off the blackened and smoking *Primauguet.* With the battle-cry "Get the *Primauguet!*" ringing on their interplane network, the navy pilots sped to the scene, peeled off and began pounding the wounded warship. French sailors stood on the decks and fired machine guns at the diving Wildcats, but the cruiser was struck by several bombs, shuddered violently, and uncontrollable fires broke out. Hundreds of her crewmen leaped overboard to escape the raging inferno. The *Primauguet* refused to die easily. She would smoulder all night, her various magazines exploding periodically.

Also in trouble was the American destroyer *Wichita.* She had received several direct hits from a powerful shore battery, and 14 of her men had been wounded.

While the sea battle unfolded off Casablanca and Fedala, Colonel William H. Wilbur, an officer on Patton's staff, was engaged in a crucial—and perilous—mission: trying to get the French commander in Casablanca, Admiral François Michelier, to accept an American occupation without prolonged resistance. Wilbur would have his work cut out for him: Michelier was one of the pro-Vichy hardliners.

Colonel Wilbur had his problems even before reaching shore with one of the early waves at 5:30 A.M. In his landing craft was an amphibious jeep equipped with a radio, a large United States flag, and an equally big white flag. In his pocket, Wilbur carried a letter signed by General Patton and approved by President Roosevelt, directed to the Casablanca commander.

Approaching shore, Colonel Wilbur's craft was picked out by a searchlight; then a 50-caliber machine gun began spitting bullets that bounced off the front of the boat. On land, the amphibious jeep refused to start. After an intense search, the colonel located another jeep, commandeered it, transferred the two flags, and set out with his driver for the 18-mile trip to Casablanca.

He reached French army positions where officers directed him toward the big port. Wilbur sped there, followed by a French captain in a civilian car.

Colonel Wilbur entered headquarters of the crack Casablanca Division, where he was confronted by its commander, Brigadier General Raymond Desré. The Frenchman was told by Wilbur that he had a letter from President Roosevelt, but Desré would not accept it, protesting in a coldly correct manner that Admiral Michelier was in command in Casablanca. Wilbur placed the letter on General Desré's desk and departed.

The French captain who had been following in a civilian car volunteered to escort the American colonel to the admiralty, where Michelier had his office. Just as Wilbur reached the reception room, American shells and bombs began exploding in the area, angering a French officer who refused to allow Wilbur to enter Admiral Michelier's office.

Wilbur insisted that he had to see Michelier, and twice the hostile officer disappeared into the admiral's office, apparently to obtain directions. When Wilbur was told for the second time that Michelier refused to see him, the American kept demanding an audience. Red-faced with anger, the nearly apoplectic Frenchman exploded. He pointed at the door and shouted: "Get the hell out of here!"

Colonel Wilbur and his driver departed for the Fedala beaches. Along the way they encountered numerous groups of armed French soldiers and sailors; some stared impassively, some looked hostile, others smiled broadly and waved.

On arrival back at the Fedala beaches, Colonel Wilbur tried to locate a boat to take him out to the *Augusta* for a personal report to General Patton on the truce excursion. He became aware that the menacing

French gun battery atop Cape Fedala was firing at ships offshore, and he determined to knock out the big guns. The colonel rounded up four tanks under Lieutenant John M. Rutledge of the 765th Tank Battalion and Captain Albert Brown's A Company of Lieutenant Colonel Moore's infantry battalion.

Colonel Wilbur leaped on top of the first tank and, crouching and clutching a tommy gun, waved the tank-infantry force forward. At 10:30 A.M. Wilbur had his impromptu battle group deployed in front of the Cape Fedala battery's fire-control center, a concrete structure on a small hill.

Between the building and the American tanks and infantry was open ground, and the French center was heavily protected by barbed wire. Captain Brown's infantrymen opened a fusillade against the fire-control center, and one of Lieutenant Rutledge's tanks crashed forward through the barbed-wire entanglements. The tank turned over, and, as it lay there helpless, French machine-gunners raked it with bullets.

As the defenders were giving their full attention to the American tank, Captain Brown waved his riflemen forward. They leaped to their feet, charged up the hill, and burst into the fire-control center, capturing the French soldiers there. Brown's men then hurried on to seize the gun battery that had been pounding ships offshore.

Colonel Wilbur entered the gun position, and the French officer commanding the complex insisted that a formal ceremony be conducted to transfer proprietorship. As American and French soldiers, who less than an hour before had been firing at each other, stood shoulder to shoulder at present arms or hand salutes, the French tricolor was lowered from a pole, and Captain Brown hoisted the Stars and Stripes in its place.*

At the racetrack on the outskirts of Fedala that morning, Captain Herman E. Wagner's C Company of Moore's battalion was pinned down and was being raked by a group of heavy antiaircraft weapons at the far end of the oval where, in more peaceful times, thoroughbreds had raced. A few GIs crawled forward, and a lieutenant and a sergeant fired several bazooka rockets that exploded inside the French positions.

---

* For his truce mission into Casablanca and other D-day exploits, Colonel William H. Wilbur received the Congressional Medal of Honor.

A white flag was waved vigorously at the hostile gun site, and the American lieutenant and sergeant, in their first combat situation, got to their feet and walked forward to receive the surrender. A burst of machine-gun fire erupted from the French position, and the two Americans toppled over dead.

Watching comrades were shocked and furious. They promptly began blasting the antiaircraft-gun crews, and a short time later another white flag appeared. This time the GIs—learning fast—remained under cover and shouted for the Frenchmen to come out with hands in the air.

It was approximately 12:30 P.M. when a frustrated George Patton, puffing on a long black cigar, climbed over the railing of the *Augusta* and into the small boat that would take him ashore. Immaculately dressed, as always, with cavalry boots shined and two oversized stars gleaming on the front of his helmet, Patton stood ramrod-straight as his craft cast off. Lining the railings of the *Augusta*, scores of sailors let loose with rousing cheers. Patton grinned broadly, waved, and clenched his hands overhead in the traditional boxer's salute to victory.

When he reached shore, his frustration intensified. Radio communications were so snarled that he was still nearly helpless to influence events. Most unit radios had failed due to assorted mishaps. Soaked by sea water in landing, the power-supply cords and contacts had shorted, and the radios died. Signal operations collapsed. There were signalmen without their equipment, and elsewhere piles of radios were stacked up with no one to operate them. Much of the gear had never reached shore and was still buried under supplies still aboard ships. Cipher machines (for encoding and decoding secret messages) had been landed far away from units for which they were intended. Unknown to General Patton, similar maddening communications difficulties were being encountered ashore by his other two sub–task forces—General Harmon's at Safi and General Truscott's at Port Lyautey.

In Munich, Adolf Hitler had reacted with speed and foresight. He ordered a signal sent to Field Marshal Albrecht Kesselring, Wehrmacht commander in chief in the Mediterranean region, ordering him to start rushing troops into Tunisia, also a French colony, in order to form a strong bridgehead into which the retreating Afrika Korps could withdraw for a last-ditch stand against the Allies.

Acting with customary alacrity, Kesselring within hours had Luftwaffe fighters and bombers and transports loaded with crack *Fallschirmjaeger* (paratroopers) arriving at El Aouina airdrome, near Tunis. Kesselring sent along his elite headquarters guard to protect the landing strips. French troops promptly ringed the airfield to keep the German invaders there. But General der Flieger (Flying General) Bruno Loerzer, commander of II Fliegerkorps in Sicily, rushed to the scene, drove through the French cordon under a flag of truce, and called on Vice Admiral Jean-Pierre Estéva, French Resident General for Tunisia.

After a tense confrontation, General Loerzer obtained from Admiral Estéva a guarantee of at least a passive French reception of German forces wherever they would arrive in Tunisia, including at the two big ports of Tunis and Bizerte. Estéva knew that his lightly armed and ill-equipped troops would be no match for the power of the Wehrmacht.

19

A French Surrender Hoax

At Gibraltar early on the morning of November 9—D-day plus 1—
General Mark Clark was preparing to fly to Algiers on a crucial assignment: He would meet with Vichy French leaders in Northwest Africa
in an effort to halt the bloodshed, secure the powerful French fleet for
the Allies, and get on with the war against Germany. Clark had no
illusions that his task would be a simple one. He would be going directly
into the center of feuding French factions and no doubt would be called
to account for the invasion of French territory.

Earlier Clark had asked Governor General Mason-McFarlane to draw
out General Henri Giraud's views on Admiral Darlan. Giraud bristled
at the mention of Darlan's name but grudgingly conceded that "a place
might be found" for Darlan if such an action would mean getting the
French fleet. Darlan's place, it was clear, would be one subordinate to
General Giraud's.

Unknown to Mark Clark, only a few hours before in Algiers Robert
Murphy had sounded out Admiral Darlan on Giraud, who had commanded the French Seventh Army against Hitler's legions in the 1940
debacle. "Giraud," the admiral had huffed, "might be capable of leading
a division."

At about 9:00 A.M. General Giraud had lifted off in a Hudson bomber, bound for Blida airfield south of Algiers where British Lieutenant Colonel Trevor and his commandos were still deployed outside the front gate. The airport commander, General de Monsabert, would clearly not allow the British on the premises without a fight. Clark was to follow promptly in the *Red Gremlin* with the rest of his staff in the *Boomerang*. Weather suddenly closed in and Clark's takeoff was delayed until noon.

So that there would be no misunderstanding of Clark's authority as he prepared to plunge into the French political mess in Algiers, he would carry a terse message signed by General Eisenhower. He was empowered to make any necessary decisions in the name of the Allied supreme commander. Any arrangements that General Giraud wished to take up with Allied headquarters were to be conducted through him.

Earlier that D-day plus 1 at Tafaraoui airport, some 12 miles south of French-held Oran, dawn found Captain Carlos "Doc" Alden sleeping on the floor of his C-47, *Shark Bait,* which had landed there the evening before. Alden had been the only member of the airborne force to reach the Tafaraoui objective on D-day.

At 6:35 A.M. Alden was awakened by a French fighter-bomber that zipped in low over the airfield and dropped a single bomb that rocked *Shark Bait.* The battle surgeon instinctively reached beside him for his pistol and holster. Gone. Alden thought he knew the identity of the culprits—scores of Arabs were wandering around the airfield.

Alden ate a can of cold beans that, to his surprise, the thieves had overlooked, then went for a stroll and discovered that the 509th Parachute Infantry Battalion, engaged in a grueling all-night march through the Sebkra d'Oran, had not yet arrived. But later that morning Major Bill Yarborough and his column of paratroopers trudged wearily into Tafaraoui after a 12-hour march with only one short rest break. It was a feat that could have been achieved only by men in superb physical condition. So gummy was the *sebkra* surface that it had taken a conscious effort to pull one foot after the other for more than 25 miles, and the troopers were loaded down with machine guns, ammunition, bazookas and rockets, personal weapons, and other heavy accoutrements of war.

The long march, the lack of sleep, the tiring 1,600-mile flight, and the trauma of their bloody first battle all had taken a toll on the exhausted paratroopers.

About noon, a motley fleet of trucks, automobiles, busses, and assorted conveyances looking much like a gypsy caravan chugged into Tafaraoui. Commandeered from civilians, the rolling stock brought Lieutenant Colonel Ed Raff and the remainder of his 509th Parachute Infantry Battalion to Tafaraoui. Their arrival was formally recognized by French 75-millimeter batteries in surrounding hills—the guns bombarded the airport.

Learning from Major Yarborough of the two score wounded paratroopers left on the *sebkra* with the other battalion surgeon, Captain Bill Moir, Doc Alden rounded up several medics and five derelict French trucks and sped to the scene. The wounded men were gently loaded into the vehicles, and the little convoy headed back for Tafaraoui. On the way, a roving fighter-bomber swooped down and strafed the convoy, damaging two vehicles but hitting no one. As the warplane flew off, the Americans cursed and shook their first—it was a British Spitfire.

With a large force of paratroopers on hand to guard some 300 French prisoners taken by Lieutenant Colonel John Waters's tankers in the capture of Tafaraoui the previous day, Waters's flying column clanked off to the north to seize La Sénia airport, only five miles south of Oran. Waters received an urgent signal: Return to Tafaraoui as rapidly as possible; a French armored column was seven miles to the east of the airfield and heading in its direction.

Already, General Jimmy Doolittle's warplanes of the Twelfth Air Force were using the field, and the facility had to be held at all costs. A reconnaissance platoon of Waters's tanks, led by Lieutenant William Beckett, collided with the French armored column heading for Tafaraoui and opened fire. A short time later Captain William R. Tuck's tank company and a platoon of tank-destroyers reached the scene. A full-fledged shootout erupted, and for nearly two hours the bleak terrain echoed with the roar of gunfire.

As suddenly as it began, the tank fight ended. Those French tanks that survived limped away. Left behind, blackened smoking hulks, were 14 French tanks. The serious threat to Tafaraoui airfield had been smashed at a cost of one American soldier, one tank, and one halftrack.

Meanwhile a flying column belonging to Colonel Paul Robinett's Task Force Green, which had come ashore west of Oran, barreled into La Sénia airfield at 10:00 A.M. After a brief fight, the French garrison capitulated. Many warplanes based at the field had already flown away, probably to bases in French Morocco. Other aircraft were parked around the field and in hangars.

Lieutenant Colonel John Todd, leader of the light tanks and self-propelled guns that had seized the airport, signaled higher headquarters: "La Sénia taken. Sixty airplanes captured. Over 300 prisoners taken."

It was the initial assessment of a green commander flushed with victory. An hour later those figures were revised downward to 159 prisoners, who had 64 rifles and 4 machine guns among them, and "several" aircraft.

Todd had not lost a man in seizing the important objective, but minutes later his occupying force had to scramble for cover: French guns located near Valmy began heavily pounding La Sénia airfield, making its use a precarious venture.

At daybreak that morning of November 9, about five miles east of Oran, Colonel Frank Greer, leader of the Big Red One's 18th Infantry Regiment, was making last-minute preparations for an attack on the pretty little village of St. Cloud. The innocent-looking town of 4,000 residents was lethal and blocked the coastal road leading from Arzew to Oran. Inside St. Cloud's thick-walled houses—each a ready-made bunker— were a large number of Algerian mercenaries, young fighting men who were anxious to demonstrate their battlefield tenacity, even if it meant killing their friends the Americans.

The attack on St. Cloud jumped off at 7:00 A.M. One of the assault groups in the forefront was a company of Bill Darby's Rangers led by Lieutenant Gordon Klefman (the other Ranger companies were mopping up in Arzew). Klefman and his men had advanced to within 400 yards of St. Cloud when they were raked by heavy machine-gun and rifle fire, and pounded by artillery. Deploying his men, Lieutenant Klefman led one platoon in a bold charge across open ground into the teeth of intense machine-gun fire, while the rest of the Rangers hit the Algerian strongpoint from the flanks.

Shouting at the tops of their lungs, the Rangers burst into the French position with grenades and tommy guns. Lieutenant Klefman, out in front, pitched a grenade at a machine-gun nest, blowing up the weapon and its crew—but not before a burst was fired that riddled Klefman at point-blank range. He died almost instantly. Killed alongside him were Privates First Class Alder L. Lystrom and Elmer I. Eskola, who were lunging with bayonet-tipped rifles at French gunners when they were cut down. But the furious attack by Darby's Ranger company was costly to the defenders. Dead and wounded Algerians were strewn about the strong point, and survivors surrendered the position.

Elsewhere in and around St. Cloud, Colonel Greer's men of the Big Red One were fighting in equally vicious little battles. Small groups forced their way into the town but were driven out by heavy fire. Signal Corps photographer Ned Modica had slipped into the front lines and was so engrossed in taking shots of the spectacular fighting that it took him a few moments to notice that someone was leaning on him. From the corner of his eye he saw the tiny American flag on the man's sleeve. Without turning his head, Modica said, "It's getting goddamned hot around here, isn't it?"

At that moment, under the intense pressure of heavy French fire, Americans all around scrambled to their feet and ran toward the rear. Modica said to the soldier leaning against him, "Let's get the hell out of here!" When the photographer spun around to run, the soldier collapsed to the ground—dead.

At his CP, Colonel Greer was furious over the tenacious fight put up by the French and the heavy American casualties. He vowed to "wipe the goddamned town off the map" and declared that St. Cloud would be plastered with 1,500 shells in 30 minutes, beginning at 2:00 P.M. Only then would Greer risk another infantry assault.

Minutes later General Terry Allen jeeped up in a cloud of dust. Told of plans to wipe St. Cloud off the map, the 1st Infantry Division commander said evenly, "No, we are not going to plaster the town. We are going to bypass it [to the south]."

Allen had concerns beyond reducing the bloodletting between American and French soldiers. A heavy bombardment of St. Cloud would kill large numbers of civilians and would hand anti-Allied groups a propaganda bonanza. It would also steel the French will to fight.

General Allen directed that St. Cloud be contained by one battalion, and that plans be made to go around the town and attack Oran itself at dawn.

By midnight of D-day plus 1, Oran was hemmed in on all sides by American forces, and its two main airfields, Tafaraoui and La Sénia, were in American hands.

While the great port of Oran was in its death throes, far to the west at dawn on November 9 Lieutenant Colonel Harry Semmes was scanning the Rabat–Port Lyautey road. His tanks had reached the positions from which they would protect General Lucian Truscott's southern flank. Now Semmes tensed. Approaching him were an estimated two battalions of French infantry supported by 14 to 18 Renault tanks. Outnumbering the American tanks by more than two to one, the World War I–vintage French tanks deployed into clusters of twos and threes to get into position to fire their small 37-millimeter guns.

Colonel Semmes shouted an order to begin firing, and within ten minutes four of the Renaults were smoking, blackened hulks. Machine guns on the American tanks cut down numerous French infantrymen whose bodies were strewn among the burning Renaults. French tankers blasted away with supposed armor-piercing shells of less than 37-millimeter size only to see the projectiles fail to penetrate Semmes's tanks.

Soon two spotter planes began hovering over the scene of the shootout and sent directions offshore to the destroyer *Savannah*. Within minutes the *Savannah*'s big shells were exploding around the French force. Surviving Renaults and French infantrymen broke off the attack, pulled back along the Rabat road, and disappeared over a ridge.

A hush fell over the tank battleground. Lieutenant Colonel Semmes, pleased with his men's performance in their first combat, hopped down from his tank. He had picked off two of the Renaults himself. Removing his leather tankers' helmet and lighting a cigarette, Semmes inspected his tanks and found that they had been struck repeatedly without damage. Returning to his own tank, the battalion commander swallowed hard: Two armor-piercing shells were imbedded in its armor.

At 7:00 that morning, two of General Jonathan Anderson's 3rd Infantry Division regiments, Colonel Robert C. Macon's 7th and Colonel Thomas Monroe's 15th, jumped off west of Fedala in what was to be a coordinated attack designated to slam on into Casablanca from the east and the south. The assault was halted in its tracks, not by hostile fire but by a critical shortage of vehicles, supporting guns, and communications equipment.

The 10th Field Artillery Battalion's radios had been lost or ruined in the landing, and the 39th Field Artillery Battalion had no vehicles; they were lost or had not arrived as scheduled. One jeep was all that was available to haul another four-gun battery. A cannon company, a self-propelled battery, and an antiaircraft outfit did not have their guns. Colonel Monroe's 15th Infantry Regiment's total transport consisted of five jeeps. The cause of this agonizing shortcoming: Unloading operations along the Fedala beaches had bogged down and were in a chaotic state.

Patton rushed to the shore at Fedala, and was appalled by what he saw. Landing craft were coming in, being unloaded, then sitting idle while coxswains waited for someone to tell them what to do next. GIs doing the unloading milled about, uncertain of their roles. Even the officers stood around without purpose.

An occasional French artillery round exploded in the vicinity, and at 8:00 A.M. a flight of Dewoitines swooped in to strafe the shoreline. Although shells and machine-gun bullets were missing the beaches by wide margins, hundreds of men in the unloading crews would dash long distances for cover.

Patton knew the men were green, and, to show his contempt for French marksmanship, he stood upright out in the open until the flurry of shooting halted. Most of the unloading crews began remaining at their jobs.

By midafternoon, the 3rd Division's missing artillery pieces and many vehicles were finally coming in over the beaches. So three Cub spotter planes were launched from the carrier *Ranger* with instructions to land on the Fedala racetrack to serve as the artillery "eyes." The Cubs' course took them a short distance from the anchored ships, and the flimsy aircraft were rocked suddenly by nearby explosions: Gunners on the cruiser *Brooklyn* were firing at the planes. Then guns on several other vessels joined in.

The slow-flying little aircraft were nearly concealed from sight by thick puffs of black smoke. Winging through the curtains of fire, the three Cub pilots breathed sighs of relief on nearing the shore, out of range of the warship guns. Relief was short-lived: On crossing the beaches, the three spotter planes were raked by American antiaircraft guns on land. One Cub was riddled and plunged to earth, killing the pilot. The other two craft, their fuselages and wings punctured by scores of bullet and shell-fragment holes, landed on the Fedala racetrack as planned.

At the same time, the Fedala civilian telephone company came under new management—members of the 239th Signal Operating Company took over the switchboard. Through the civilian network, an effort would be made to coordinate another attack on Casablanca. When 3rd Division elements had jumped off that morning, there had been no communication between command posts and units because no telephone wire had been strung. Wire and related equipment had not yet landed, and no one knew where these essential items were. When the advance on Casablanca resumed, 3rd Division commanders would have to go into a house or store to contact subordinate units or higher headquarters through the Fedala civilian switchboard.

Shortly after 3:00 P.M., the ornate Miramer Hotel in Fedala gained a prestigious new clientele to replace the German Armistice Commission, the longtime occupants who had abruptly departed the day before. The Miramer was taken over as headquarters of Patton's Western Task Force. Renewed efforts were made to establish communications with Gibraltar, but wireless traffic was snarled by an unknown hostile station—German or French. The station was sending messages to Patton's headquarters and indicating that they were coming from Eisenhower, while at the same time the bogus source was dispatching signals to Gibraltar as though they had originated from Patton.

While communications had broken down almost entirely within the Western Task Force and between Patton and Gibraltar, all bogged down in a morass of ruined equipment, inexperienced personnel, and lost shipments, an OSS spy who could have resolved the communications debacle was sitting idle by his powerful radio set in Casablanca. Code-named Ajax, the OSS agent controlled the nerve center of a clandestine radio net of 24 stations that spread the width of French Northwest Africa.

The OSS, with a great deal of foresight, had established the secret network in recent weeks to counter just such a difficulty as now faced the Western Task Force—a total breakdown in communications. But Ajax merely sat hunched over his set, waiting for a call over the signal he had specified. Ajax, prior to D-day, had gotten into a dispute with signal corps officers in Torch headquarters over what communications procedures to use. Ajax insisted that his be followed, but American officers were equally stubborn in demanding that theirs be used. Now, even in this crisis, neither of the disputants would budge.

At 10:00 A.M. on D-day plus 1, General Lucian Truscott was inspecting frontline positions on the southern flank of his Port Lyautey beachhead when electrifying news reached him: A French lieutenant, speaking perfect English, had reached Green Beach with a message that the commander of the Casbah wanted to negotiate a surrender of the fortress. A capitulation of this strongpoint would save lives on both sides and would open the way to the airfield. In their elation over the news, neither Truscott nor any of his officers reflected on a curious factor: The French lieutenant had somehow passed through American lines unscathed without carrying a white flag or any other indication that he was on a truce mission. Nor did the untested Americans consider another strange matter: Hardly ever would a truce emissary enter hostile lines alone.

General Truscott immediately contacted Colonel de Rohan and instructed the regimental leader to send the French lieutenant back to the Casbah, together with an American officer, to arrange for a noon peace parlay. Then Truscott hurried back to his CP in Mehdia, where he and his staff conferred excitedly over plans for the meeting with the Casbah's commandant. Truscott took a few minutes to shave and brush the mud and dust from his uniform.

The general and his staff waited . . . and waited some more. Noon came. No word from the French. Truscott was growing uneasy. What had caused the delay? Truscott grew suspicious about the episode. The French commandant had not put his message in writing, nor had the French ceased firing during the entire period. But Truscott convinced himself that the French had been acting in good faith, so he quickly dictated a letter to the Casbah commander expressing regret that Americans and Frenchmen, friends of long standing, were fighting and killing each other. He said that he would be willing to meet at any time during daylight to discuss a cease-fire.

Truscott gave the letter to two of his officers with instructions to deliver it personally to the Casbah commander. Approaching the gray old fortress with a huge white flag, the two American couriers were fired on. They scrambled back to friendly lines, clutching the undelivered letter.

Only much later would Lucian Truscott and others learn that the French lieutenant had become separated from his men in fighting near Green Beach and was in danger of being captured. So he strolled along the shore line and concocted the cease-fire story that got him escorted back to his own lines.

Lucian Truscott was chagrined over having been victim of a hoax by a young French officer. What anguished him more was that the Frenchman had obtained a vast amount of intelligence on American positions during his sojourn behind hostile lines. A vital lesson had been driven home to Truscott: American generals were green also. He vowed never again to allow wishful thinking to color his battlefield judgments.

At noon on November 9 in his office in Munich, Adolf Hitler was yelling at his closest military confidants, Field Marshal Wilhelm Keitel and Colonel General Alfred Jodl. In the previous two hours, Hitler's response had switched from one of praise for "our French friends" for the tenacious fight put up by French warships at Oran and Casablanca, to one of denouncing the "born traitors" of France. He had by now grown deeply suspicious that the French leaders in Northwest Africa were conniving at a deal with the invaders. He was particularly livid at General Henri Giraud, who only the previous day he had thought to be at home in Lyons, France, under scrutiny by the Abwehr. Hitler shouted that Giraud had given his written promise not to take any action against Germany, and now the French general had slipped into the Allied den and let broadcasts be made in his name. When Italian Foreign Minister Count Galeazzo Ciano appeared for an appointment in midafternoon, Hitler renewed his vocal attacks against the "French traitors." The Wehrmacht, he told Count Ciano, was already massing on the demarcation line between occupied and unoccupied France, and within the hour Hitler would give the order sending his armed forces racing southward all the way to the Mediterranean Sea.

Back at Algiers at noon on November 9, a French official working with the Allies received a telephone call from the beleaguered Admiral Jean-Pierre Estéva, resident general of Tunisia where the Germans were pouring in troops and warplanes. "I now have a guardian," Estéva stated. Then he was cut off. The message was clear: Admiral Eséva was being held hostage by the Wehrmacht. However, General George Barré, the French ground commander in Tunisia, apparently had been free to take action. Under his orders, French forces in Tunisia began to withdraw westward into the mountains, toward the invading Allies in Algiers and French Morocco.

On Gibraltar, at about noon of D-day plus 1, the long silence from General George Patton was broken. The Western Task Force leader reported tersely that "resistance has been overcome on the beaches (at Safi, Fedala, and Port Lyautey]." General Eisenhower eagerly radioed back for details. He received no reply.

At Algiers on the afternoon of November 9, General Henri Giraud was in seclusion at the Arab-quarter residence of a friend, Jacques Lemaigre-Dubreuil, conferring with Robert Murphy. Murphy cautiously broached the fact that Admiral Darlan was in Algiers, expecting a show of agitation from Giraud. There was none. Giraud calmly responded that perhaps Darlan, like himself, had been working behind the scenes to aid the Allied invasion. Murphy thought this relatively placid response showed that the first hurdle toward resolving French political disputes may have been surmounted.

A few minutes after 5:00 P.M. General Mark Clark's B-17 bomber, the *Red Gremlin*, escorted by 13 Spitfire fighters, touched down at Maison Blanche airport on the outskirts of Algiers. The *Red Gremlin* had just come to a halt when a tremendous racket erupted: antiaircraft guns opening fire on a flight of 12 German JU-88 bombers that were over the airfield at 6,000 feet. The black-bodied aircraft were obviously not after Maison Blanche—nor General Clark—because they flew through a thick curtain of fire and began dropping bombs on crowded Algiers harbor. British Spitfires arrived and buzzed around the Luftwaffe bombers with machine guns blazing. At Maison Blanche, hundreds of Americans dashed out into the open, gazing skyward and cheering on the friendly fighter planes. At least two JU-88s took hits and crashed.

While the uproar was at its most intense, General Clark climbed into a British Bren-gun carrier that had come out to the *Red Gremlin*, and as the vehicle sped toward the main airport building the American general watched the fascinating pyrotechnics in the sky. It was nearing dusk, and the orange balls of exploding shells reminded Clark of a string of Christmas-tree lights.

Just as the Bren-gun carrier reached the main building, Clark looked back just in time to see three bombs explode in brilliant orange—less than 100 feet from the *Red Gremlin*. Then the general heard a loud noise overhead; a JU-88, hit by flak and trailing a plume of smoke, was coming down like a rocket directly at Clark and a few of his staff in another vehicle. The Americans got their legs over the side, but before they could dash away the bomber exploded about 1,000 feet overhead and virtually disintegrated.

General Clark and the others pulled in their legs, which seemed to them to have turned to jelly, and drove off for Algiers. The little convoy weaved through the narrow, winding streets and up a steep hill to the fashionable St. George Hotel, which would become Allied Force headquarters.

Clark immediately conferred with General Ryder, the Eastern Task Force commander. Ryder was grim and haggard. "I'm glad you're here," he told Clark. "I've stalled them off about as long as I could."

"They" were leaders of the feuding French government and military factions, all of whom had been clamoring for some sort of a settlement of the tangled situation. Clark and Ryder, professional soldiers, were ill prepared to negotiate political disputes. Now they found themselves in the center of a complex controversy.

Hardly had Mark Clark entered his suite in the luxurious St. George than he recieved a shock: General Giraud, on whose magic name the Americans had counted to halt the fighting, was being rejected by all the powerful French figures in French Northwest Africa. They would have nothing to do with Giraud, none would even meet with him, and many considered him a traitor to France.

Clark was absorbing this jarring development when Robert Murphy burst into the St. George: "Where are your tanks?" he wanted to know. Murphy wanted a show of strength, a parade of tank and infantry forces through Algiers to influence French leaders still on the fence.

Clark was irritated. "Okay, if you insist," he said. "I'll have all *three* of our available tanks put on a show."

Murphy had not realized that American armored strength around Algiers was minimal, and that what tanks had landed were occupied in missions outside the city.

Clark had ordered a heavily armed contingent of American soldiers placed around the St. George, mainly as a display for French leaders. Now Clark decided to go to bed; he had had only a few winks of sleep in 60 hours and was past exhaustion. Before climbing into bed, General Clark said to an aide, "What a mess. Why do soldiers have to get mixed up in things liked this?"

20

Bloody Clash at the Casbah

It was an hour before midnight on November 9. The tiny schoolroom was lit by a single gasoline lantern hanging from the low ceiling. At a desk beneath it was General Terry Allen, his face framed in the beam of the light, his form in darkness. Around him, their figures in shadow, stood some ten staff officers. It had just been decided that the Big Red One would jump off in an assault on Oran at 7:15 A.M., with tanks to follow 15 minutes later.

Allen gave to Colonel d'Alary Fetchet the unenviable task of personally carrying the battle orders to the 16th and 18th Regiments. This would mean jeeping in blackness, sleet, and gusting winds to locate two commanders on the move at undetermined roads through a battle area now designated as "fluid," meaning that opposing forces were mixed together and neither side knew exactly where the other side was.

Colonel Fetchet, along with a driver and a correspondent, H. R. Knickerbocker, hunched over in the back seat with a carbine between his knees. Knickerbocker was supposed to be "riding shotgun," so felt that it would be better if he kept to himself the fact that he had never fired a carbine and did not know how to load one.

Fetchet reminded the driver that the password was "Heigh-yo Silver," after which the jeep's occupants were to respond "Away!" the exclamation made popular by the Lone Ranger. Fetchet wanted to make sure that the countersign "Away!" would be shouted loud and clear, for the jeep no doubt would be challenged by large numbers of trigger-happy young sentries.

Distant flares and artillery made for an eerie trip. The farther the jeep advanced, the fewer sentries there were. Obviously, Colonel Fetchet and the others were nearing the front. From out of the dark a sentry shouted, "Better not go up there, they're machine-gunning the crossroads."

Since only French machine-gunners were up there, Colonel Fetchet ordered the driver to head in another direction. The group drove for two hours, getting increasingly nervous. Fetchet had the uneasy feeling that the jeep had gotten far out in front of the friendly troops. Suddenly they came upon the rear of a column of men trudging in the sleet and cold along a muddy road crisscrossed with ruts.

It was part of the 16th Infantry. Nearby in the shadows were two trucks crammed with groaning French soldiers who had been wounded in heavy fighting a short time before. Fetchet and Knickerbocker dismounted, picked their way through the darkness, and found Colonel Henry Cheadle, the regimental leader, in his command car. Fetchet handed General Allen's orders to Cheadle and said, "You are to attack at 7:15 A.M. and take Oran tomorrow." (By now, "tomorrow" was already today.)

Colonel Cheadle protested: "My boys are exhausted, they've had no sleep for forty-eight hours and nothing to eat in two days."

"Makes no difference," Colonel Fetchet responded. "The general says you've got to attack with everything you've got!"

Fetchet, Knickerbocker, and the driver drove away. The sleet was more intense, the wind gustier, it was blacker and colder. One hour later, almost by a miracle, the 18th Infantry CP was located. Colonel Frank Greer and his staff were deep in exhausted sleep, sprawled in command cars and jeeps. It was 4:00 A.M.

Colonel Greer was awakened and handed the attack orders. Understandably in the circumstances, Greer was in a foul mood. The two colonels had a shouting match, and as Fetchet began to leave Greer said in a calm voice, "We'll jump off at seven-fifteen as ordered."

A young major emerged from the shadows. "How in the hell can we attack?" he yelled. "The men haven't had any sleep and only one can of rations to eat all day!"

Fetchet climbed into his jeep and disappeared into the blackness.

At dawn on D-day plus 2, Oran was about to be struck from three sides: Allen's Big Red One from the east, elements of Brigadier General Lunsford Oliver's 1st Armored Division from the south, and General Teddy Roosevelt's 26th Combat Team from the west. (A Spitfire had swooped over Roosevelt's CP to drop a terse order from General Allen, "Shoot the works at once!")

Offshore from the doomed city, the menacing guns of the big warships *Rodney, Jamaica,* and *Aurora* were loaded, and crews were standing by to fire if needed. Dive-bomber pilots on the carrier *Furious* were ready on call to lift off and pound Oran's defenses.

As promised, Colonel Greer's exhausted fighting men jumped off—right on the button at 7:15 A.M. An artillery piece near the CP unexpectedly fired a registration round, causing several officers, mistaking the loud report for an incoming shell, to flop face-down in the dirt. They got to their feet sheepishly and dusted off their clothing.

The 18th Regiment's advance was over an open field, and within 40 minutes the first batch of prisoners, four French officers and some 25 native soldiers, were marching past the CP to the rear.

Correspondent Knickerbocker caught a ride to an advance aid station where there were 30 American wounded. Some had on muddy, blood-soaked bandages. An ashen-faced youth of no more than 18 years of age was brought in, and Knickerbocker knelt beside him. "Where'd you get hit?" the reporter asked softly.

"A bullet in the stomach," the boy replied weakly.

A medic came up to inject pain-relieving morphine. Moments later the boy died with a gasp. A muddy blanket was pulled over his head.

Now the front of the attacking 18th Infantry was a solid crescendo of machine-gun fire and crashing artillery shells. The French were putting up a savage fight. An increasing number of men with the Big Red One on the shoulders of their combat jackets were being brought to the rear on litters. Some soldiers were unconscious; they were the lucky ones. Most were blood- and mud-caked and grimacing from pain.

All around the outskirts of Oran a series of nasty little fights had erupted as American infantry and tanks pushed forward. Elements of the 1st Armored Division under Lieutenant Colonel John Waters, General Patton's son-in-law, pushed across a dusty plain and without realizing it barreled on into Oran from the south. Waters's leading tank got lost in the maze of narrow, winding streets, ran into a pair of French 75s, and before the surprised gun crew could react, ran over the hostile guns and crushed them.

Continuing onward, the lone tank spotted a roadblock of vehicles, crashed into it and struck an unyielding concrete pole. The jolt killed the engine and painfully cut the four men inside the tank. But the crew managed to restart the motor and the tankers drove off to join their outfit.

A short distance away a tank force led by Lieutenant Colonel John Todd broke into Oran at the same time that Waters's column was crashing into the city. Just before 11:00 A.M. Todd's tankers reached the Château Neuf, headquarters of General Robert Boissau, commander of French forces in the Oran region.

Some of Colonel Todd's tanks pushed on to the harbor to prevent destruction of facilities there, and an infantry force under Lieutenant Colonel William Kern rushed to Camp Philippe where it released some 500 American and British prisoners.

Meanwhile Lieutenant Colonel Waters's tankers cruised Oran unmolested except for an occasional sniper bullet. One tank company headed eastward where it joined up with Allen's Big Red One, which now marched into Oran without the need for heavy artillery fire and air support. But just west of Oran, General Teddy Roosevelt's 26th Regimental Combat Team ran into a hornet's nest when it tried to take Fort du Santon. Warships shelled the thick-walled bastion, and dive bombers pounded it, but each infantry attack was repulsed by withering French fire.

Inside the big port city, American tanks scrambling noisily through the streets had so frightened residents that the mayor of Oran, without seeking military authority, came out waving a huge white flag and told 1st Infantry Division officers that he was surrendering the city. In the meantime, General Lloyd Fredendall, commander of Center Task Force, climbed upon Lieutenant Colonel Waters's personal tank and rode piggy-back into the heart of the city to the Château Neuf. There General Terry Allen strode up to Fredendall in the turreted courtyard and reported that General Boissau had flashed a cease-fire order to all his troops, including those at coastal batteries. General Fredendall then entered the Château Neuf to negotiate armistice arrangements. He found Boissau in high good spirits, clearly relieved to have an enormous burden removed from his shoulders.

It was agreed that the French flag would continue to fly over Oran with a smaller white flag just below it. Americans would occupy key points and French troops would remain in their barracks but retain their weapons. In this curious twilight war between Americans and French, the defeated General Boissau was to remain in command of the city and be responsible for policing it.

Now General Fredendall and his party withdrew, and the Center Task Force headquarters was set up in the luxury of the Grand Hotel in Oran. On leaving the Château Neuf, the Americans took an important Allied comrade with them: Royal Navy Captain Frederic Peters. He had led the charge into Oran harbor by the ill-fated *Walney* and *Hartland*, and was thought to have been killed, but had been fished out of the water by the French and held as a prisoner of war.

Tens of thousands of wildly cheering residents swarmed into the streets. One of the first American tanks pulled up to a halt in the city square. A curious throng quickly gathered around, not knowing whether the tank was French, British, American, German, or something else.

When an American officer finally stuck his head out through the turret opening someone called out in French, "What country are you from?" The officer did not speak French and replied in English. The crowd recognized his American accent and a tumultuous cheer rocked the square. The citizens waved arms and shouted in frenzied joy: *"Vive les Americaines! Vive les États Unis! Vive la Liberté!"**

At Port Lyautey, 60 miles northeast of Casablanca, the night of November 9 was black. Rain and sleet were pouring down on General Truscott's soldiers, who earlier in the day had been repulsed repeatedly in efforts to storm the Casbah guarding river and land routes inland to the key objective, the Port Lyautey airfield. At the close of this D-day plus 2, not only was the airfield still in French hands, but the cable barrier across the Sebou River had not been severed to permit passage of the *Dallas* and her 75 raiders.

It was 9:30 P.M. when a small party of American naval men and soldiers climbed down a rope ladder on the transport *Clymer* and headed for the mouth of the Sebou. Their mission was both difficult and perilous: to cut the river barrier. Feeling its way through the blackness, the little boat reached shore at the designated point, but the demolition party could not locate Lieutenant Colonel Frederic A. Henney, commander of the 15th Combat Engineers, as planned. Henney was to lead the demolition mission.

Young navy Lieutenant M. K. Starkweather took charge and ordered the little craft to continue up the Sebou. Much to the surprise of the party, not a shot was fired at them as they sailed through the dark. When they reached the boom, the cable was rapidly cut. Starkweather sent a man under the water, and he bobbed back up, shivering, to confirm that the barrier had indeed been severed.

Moments later the peace was shattered as French sentries on both sides of the Sebou began firing at the Americans in midriver. "Let's get the hell out of here!" Lieutenant Starkweather called out, and the boat began a hasty withdrawal down the Sebou. French sentry bullets had hit several men, but none were wounded seriously.

---

* Later, crackerbarrel philosophers among the GIs analyzed the tumultuous reception: 60 percent was based on the Frenchman's love for cheering any passing show, 20 percent was due to a feeling that France would soon be liberated, 15 percent because citizens felt they would now get more to eat, and 5 percent because they were genuinely glad to see Americans.

At 4:30 A.M. the weary demolition party climbed back up the rope ladder on the *Clymer*, convinced that they had opened the way for the destroyer *Dallas* and its 75-man raider detachment to reach the critical airfield.

In the meantime, Major Percy McCarley's 1st Battalion, 60th Regiment, jumped off in the blackness and the sleet. Its orders: Seize the airfield. The battalion soon got lost. At 1:00 A.M. leading elements ran into a machine-gun ambush, and in the ensuing confusion McCarley's force split into three groups. However, the major portion of the scattered battalion continued toward the airport and at 4:30 A.M. reached a blacked-out building which was thought to be a French barracks.

The barracks was surrounded stealthily and machine guns were posted at exit roads and paths. Then an American officer shouted a call for surrender and waited. Inside, some 75 occupants set down their wine glasses and headed for the door. The GIs standing outside with their weapons leveled discerned a single column of dark figures coming out with hands in the air, but they were all civilians. This was not a barracks but a popular café.

After Major McCarley's battalion had stumbled into the machine-gun ambush and been scattered, he and the few men he had with him reached the south edge of French-held Port Lyautey, reversed course, and continued looking for their battalion. Just as the first hint of daylight began to show, the major and his men ran into a force of Foreign Legionnaires and were taken prisoner.*

At 5:30 A.M. on November 10—D-day plus 2—the twenty-two-year-old destroyer *Dallas* began edging toward the mouth of the Sebou River. On board were the 75 raiders who were to seize the Port Lyautey airfield. Significant tides and a rough surf were encountered, but the *Dallas*'s skipper, Captain Robert J. Brodie, got the old vessel to the river mouth, helped not a little by a riverboat pilot named Jules Malavergne who had been smuggled out of Morocco by the OSS and rushed to the United States in time to accompany General Patton's convoys. *Dallas* sailed upstream to the barrier that had been severed by Lieutenant

---

* Later that day, when his Foreign Legion captors halted in a march to eat, Major McCarley dashed into nearby woods and escaped.

Starkweather's men, whereupon a new difficulty arose. The buoys holding up the cut cable were anchored, and the boom refused to swing all the way open. Skipper Brodie had just given the order to ram the barrier at full speed when the *Dallas* was detected and shells from the Casbah above started hitting the water nearby. The ship smashed through the boom and continued up the Sebou; so far she had not been hit.

It was now fully daylight and other French guns joined in. From nearby hills, machine gunners raked her decks as her officers concentrated on the run upriver. She squeezed by a French ship, *St. Amiel*, which had been scuttled in midriver to hinder passage, and at 7:20 A.M. *Dallas* crunched to a halt on a sandbar. She had come to rest in shallow water near the eastern edge of the Port Lyautey airfield.*

The raiders scrambled into rubber boats, paddled the short distance to shore, and charged onto the airfield; by 8:00 A.M. the Americans had it in hand. Army fighter planes from the carrier *Chenango* soon landed on the pockmarked runways and began preparing to support the looming assault on Casablanca.

During the hours of darkness, two French soldiers had slipped into American lines and been taken promptly to General Truscott's CP in Mehdia. The Frenchmen were known to the Americans as the "Bordeaux Boys"; defending soldiers who wished to cooperate with the invaders had been instructed in Allied broadcasts to use the code word "Bordeaux" when they approached American positions. The pair told Truscott that an American colonel (Nick Craw) had been killed while carrying Truscott's message to the French commander in the region, and that an American major (Pierpont Hamilton) had been captured. The French, they said, were holding Major Hamilton in Port Lyautey because they were afraid of American reaction if he were sent back with the news that an officer had been killed while flying a flag of truce.

In the hours before dawn, General Truscott had told Colonel de Rohan's operations officer to round up whatever men he could from the

---

* Considering the number of shells fired at the *Dallas*, which could not take evasive action, her reaching the airport was almost miraculous, U.S. Navy officers later agreed.

beaches and to flush out French snipers from a thick woods between Mehdia and the Casbah. A hodgepodge of some 80 men were collected—air force mechanics, clerks, drivers, cooks—and formed into squads. As this crew headed out for the woods, Truscott was accosted by an air force mechanic lugging a tommy gun. "General, we've never shot these things before. Couldn't we try them out to see how they work before we have to fight?"

A good idea, Truscott agreed. So the instant infantrymen faced a sand dune, were told how to load and fire their weapons, and blasted away for several minutes before setting out for the woods to take on the snipers.*

Also during the night, General Truscott had ordered Colonel de Rohan to seize the Casbah "the first thing in the morning." At dawn that day, November 10, Major John Dilley's 2nd Battalion jumped off to take another crack. Fighting was bitter, but by 9:30 A.M. Dilley's dogfaces, as American foot soldiers liked to call themselves, had driven French machine-gunners and riflemen outside the Casbah back into the fortress.

A pair of 105-millimeter guns were rolled forward and several rounds were fired point-blank at the gates, but the barriers refused to budge. Reinforced by about 125 engineers led by Captain Verle McBride, Dilley's men twice charged the gates but were driven back by automatic-weapons and rifle fire.

A radio message was transmitted and within minutes navy Wildcat fighter-bombers were circling over the Casbah. One after another the Wildcats dove on the fortress, bombing as close as they could to the massive gates. With smoke and dust still pouring out of the Casbah, Dilley's foot soldiers charged the heavily damaged gates once more and got inside. Some 250 French soldiers quickly surrendered. Most of the French coastal guns had either been knocked out or seized, and the capture of the Casbah broke the back of French defenses in the Port Lyautey region.

---

* Lucian K. Truscott, *Command Missions*.

Now Major Dilley counted noses. His casualties in taking the Casbah had been heavy—more than 225 men dead or wounded. French losses had also been considerable.

General Truscott, who had arrived in time to see the charge that carried through the Casbah's gates, had little time to savor the victory. An urgent radio signal reached him: A large force of French cavalry was heading for the beachhead's right flank. The general hopped into a jeep and sped off for the threatened locale, where he discovered the source of the alarming report: Four bedraggled French soldiers had ridden horses into American lines to surrender.

While French defenses were rapidly disintegrating and hundreds of the defenders were streaming in as prisoners, a group of American infantrymen captured the French commander of the Port Lyautey region, Colonel Charles Petit, who had gone out from his command post in the town of Port Lyautey in a desperate effort to reorganize his forces. At his own suggestion, Colonel Petit was paroled in the custody of Major Pierpont Hamilton, the D-day courier who had been held "in protective custody" at Petit's headquarters. This resulted in a unique situation: Colonel Petit had returned to his CP to be taken prisoner by an American officer who had been his captive.

Colonel Petit sent a signal to his remaining resisting units: Cease firing. As the darkness of D-day plus 2 blanketed the Port Lyautey region, there was only occasional sniper fire. This apparently was coming from Arabs who had stolen rifles and ammunition from American stockpiles and were trying out the weapons—with Americans and Frenchmen alike as random targets.

One hundred forty miles southwest of Casablanca, General Ernest Harmon's Combat Command B of the 2nd Armored Division had been heading north after dark on November 9, bound for his next objective, the port of Mazagan 90 tortuous miles away. Once Mazagan was seized, Harmon's force was to push on up the Atlantic coastline and join in the assault on Casablanca.

Ernie Harmon was traveling in the dark in more ways than one. Due to chaotic communications in the Western Task Force, he had no idea of what was happening around Casablanca. Nor did he know what opposing force, if any, he would encounter at Mazagan (later El Jadida). The night was so black and stormy that his tanks and light vehicles (he had no trucks) kept slipping into ditches alongside the narrow, slippery, high-crowned road.

In his thrust to Mazagan, General Harmon was taking a calculated risk. His tanks would soon become thirsty and require thousands of gallons of gasoline. He had no way to carry this fuel with him, nor was there any known source for gasoline between Harmon and French-held Casablanca. The navy agreed to send a destroyer, loaded with the crucial gasoline, into Mazagan harbor. But what if the vessel were sunk? Or if the French were to bitterly contest Mazagan, so that the destroyer could not enter the harbor? Harmon and his tanks would be stranded in hostile country midway between Safi and Casablanca.

The 2nd Armored convoy would inch ahead, then come to a halt for minutes at a time. During one such jam-up, an angry General Harmon worked his way forward to find that several soldiers had fallen asleep in a vehicle that was blocking the road. It seemed that the only problem Harmon did not have was stragglers. Rumors had swept through the armored force that bands of Arabs roamed in the dark, stripping battlefield wounded and torturing and emasculating prisoners.

As dawn was breaking, the column reached Mazagan without a shot being fired at it. The force halted and Harmon immediately gave orders for attacking and seizing the port. Shortly afterward, at 6:30 A.M., General Harmon received a radio message from Patton—the first communication he had had with the Western Task Force commander. The signal deeply concerned Harmon. Although it was marked URGENT, Patton's message had been sent the day before. The order directed General Harmon's force to attack the southern exits of Casablanca at 11:00 A.M. It was already 6:30 A.M.—and Harmon was 45 miles from Casablanca. He would need several hours just to take on fuel from the destroyer he hoped would be in Mazagan harbor. Harmon tried to contact Patton to advise him of the impossibility of his executing the order, but his radio went dead.

At Gibraltar that morning of November 10, concern over the absence of any word from General Patton's Western Task Force had given way to suspicion that Patton was relishing his enforced isolation and had made no real effort to establish communications with Gibraltar. General Eisenhower could do little more than hibernate in his office inside the Rock and fret. Not only was he in the dark about Patton's progress— or lack of it—but he had little idea what was going on with Fredendall's Center Task Force or Ryder's Eastern Task Force. Staff officers were obtaining most of their information from an unlikely source—Radio Vichy. It was from Radio Vichy that Eisenhower first learned of Oran's surrender.

By that afternoon, Eisenhower was able to get a signal through to General Patton at the Miramer Hotel in Fedala, outside Casablanca— one of the few signals that Gibraltar had been able to put through. Patton put on his spectacles and read Eisenhower's message:

"Dear George: Algiers has been ours for two days. Oran defenses are crumbling rapidly with navy shore batteries surrendering. Only tough nut left to crack is in your hands. Crack it open quickly. Ike."

Patton took off his spectacles and flipped the message onto his desk. The signal left him confused, a mixture of anger and bewilderment. Was this message from the supreme commander a friendly acknowledgment that Eisenhower understood Patton's difficulties, or was it a harpoon from on high prodding Patton to get moving?

Whatever the supreme commander's motive (and Patton decided it was well-meaning) the Western Task Force leader issued immediate orders for an all-out assault on Casablanca the following morning. Indeed, the heavily fortified crown jewel of colonial France would be a tough nut to crack—and Georgie Patton intended to be the one to crack it.

The general contacted his former sparring partner, Admiral Kent Hewitt on the *Augusta*, to arrange for massive naval gunfire and heavy dive-bombing attacks from the carrier *Ranger*. He told General Anderson that his 3rd Infantry Division was to smash on into Casablanca at all costs. Patton had long been convinced that the way to capture Casablanca was to "beat the hell out of it and then rush in." Concerned that Eisenhower might veto his plans, he decided to use the excuse of faulty communications for not clearing it with the supreme commander.

He would launch his all-out assault, seize Casablanca, and say to Eisenhower: You wanted it. Here it is.

General Patton concluded arrangements for the attack and set H-hour at 7:30 A.M. the following day, November 11. Then he went to bed. Before closing his eyes, an errant thought drifted into his mind: The attack could be a bloody one, and it would be taking place on Armistice Day, which marked the cessation of hostilities in World War I—the "war to end all wars." November 11 would also be his fifty-seventh birthday.

In London that night of November 10, Prime Minister Winston Churchill was addressing a gala dinner for the lord mayor of London. Churchill was in good spirits and spoke in a triumphant vein. He paid homage to General Harold Alexander and his "brilliant lieutenant," General Bernard Montgomery, for "very largely destroying" Rommel's Afrika Korps. "Now this is not the end," the prime minister cautioned. "It is not even the beginning of the end. But it is, perhaps, the end of the beginning." Turning to Operation Torch, Churchill praised President Roosevelt as "the author of this mighty undertaking" and suggested that he had been Roosevelt's "active and ardent lieutenant."

This revelation would come as a surprise to the American president, who along with generals George Marshall, Dwight Eisenhower, Mark Clark, and others had been against Torch almost up to the date of its launching.

21

"French Troops Will Cease Hostilities"

General Mark Clark, refreshed after several hours of sleep, was deliberately stern-faced as he strode into a conference room in Algiers's old St. George Hotel to confront a galaxy of French generals and admirals. It was 9:00 A.M. on November 10. The room overlooked a beautiful garden of flowers and palm trees, but the mood was strained as Clark took his seat at the head of a long conference table.

Mark Clark, customarily gracious and friendly, had purposely changed personalities. He would become Mark Clark, shouter and table-banger. He felt he had to impress on the French delegation that America meant business. As General Eisenhower's deputy, the relatively youthful general was charged with a task that few men in history had faced: He was to fight the French armed forces if need be, but, if possible, he was to prevent a bloody, prolonged clash with them so as to get on with the war against Hitler's and Mussolini's armies.

For nearly a minute, Mark Clark said nothing; he sat in his chair and looked over the French officers, most of whom outranked the Allied deputy commander. The Frenchmen squirmed uncomfortably under the scrutiny of this gangling American of whom, until the day before, they had never heard. To Clark's left sat Admiral Darlan, Marshal Pétain's number-two man who, Clark noticed, had watery eyes and seemed nervous, uncertain, and ill at ease. Repeatedly during the conference Darlan would pull out his handkerchief and mop his forehead. He fumbled with the papers in front of him and shifted constantly in his chair.

On Clark's right, General Alphonse Juin, commander of French forces in Northwest Africa, sat in silence and contributed nothing to negotiations.* Also present were General Louis-Marie Koeltz, who two days previously had ordered his French forces to resist the invasion; Vice Admiral d'Escadre Moreau, naval commander; Admiral Raymond Fenard, secretary general of the North African government, who two nights previously had sat with Robert Murphy when the American underground chief was a prisoner in General Juin's villa; and General Pierre Mendigal, air commander in North Africa.

Clark regarded Admiral Darlan with distaste, considering him a crass opportunist. After the fall of France in 1940, Darlan had collaborated with the Nazis as a leading figure in Marshal Pétain's government. Now, with the Allies on the verge of establishing some momentum, Darlan had shown signs of being willing to step aboard the Allies' bandwagon.

Staring coldly at the short, stubby, perspiring Frenchman at his left, General Clark said to his translator, the underground chief Robert Murphy, "Tell Admiral Darlan that we have work to do to meet the common enemy [Germany]. Is he ready to sign the terms of the armistice? It will cover all French forces in North Africa. It is essential that we stop this waste of time and blood."

Darlan hemmed and hawed, taking out his handkerchief again. Finally he said that he had sent an outline of the terms to Vichy, but that there would be no reply until the Council of Ministers met there that afternoon.

---

* General Juin later would become one of Mark Clark's best battle commanders and closest friends, but following this conference Juin returned home to tell his wife that he and his associates had been browbeaten by "a big American who does nothing but shout and pound the table."

Clark, red-faced with anger over this obvious stall, banged the table with his fist. "Do you understand," the American asked icily, "that relations between France and the United States were broken off [by Pétain] in the last twenty-four hours?"

Darlan, fumbling with his papers, looked down at the table and said that he had no official confirmation. "I have been given strict orders [by Vichy] not to enter negotiations until orders arrive from Marshal Pétain and the Council of Ministers," he said.

Again, Clark's fist struck the table, and Admiral Darlan quickly added, "However, my associates and I feel hostilities are fruitless."

Much of Clark's histrionics were calculated to galvanize the stone-faced French leaders into action, but they were also the result of his frustration over the fact that he could not escape the necessity of dealing with this officer whom the Allies had dubbed the "Little Fella." Without exception, French commanders had refused to bring their forces over to the side of the Allies without authorization that came from the head of the Vichy government, Marshal Pétain, through the commander of his armed forces. Pétain's picture, after all, was given a place of prominence in almost every private home, and public buildings displayed huge likenesses of the number-one Vichyite along with extracts from his speeches and statements.

Admiral Darlan, despite his perspiring and nervous demeanor, proved to be a tough, nimble-minded adversary. Both men knew that Darlan was holding a number of aces. The French realized above all that the Allies could never turn eastward and fight Germans in Tunisia while at the same time having to maintain order among 21 million Arabs and hundreds of thousands of Frenchmen in Algeria and Morocco. Only a cooperating French establishment could do that.

As the morning wore on and Admiral Darlan refused to order French forces to cease fighting, Clark threatened to jail Darlan, and followed this with an even more radical proposal: He would lock up all the French generals and admirals and form a military government in Algeria and Morocco. Darlan merely shrugged his shoulders as if to say: "Go right ahead."

Finally, Admiral Darlan asked if he could meet alone with his commanders, and Clark and other Americans left the room. When the general rejoined the conference, Darlan surprised him by wordlessly handing over a proposed order that the admiral was willing to send out over his signature: All French ground, sea, and air forces were to cease firing immediately, return to their garrisons and "remain neutral." Darlan's officers would retain their commands, and political authority in Algeria and Morocco would not be changed. Clark read the order without change of expression. Inwardly he was elated. This was even more than he had hoped for. But he sternly warned Admiral Darlan that the proposed order would have to be approved by General Eisenhower. This gesture was not, of course, for show. Clark knew that the supreme commander would be quick to reach for his pen.

When the meeting broke up, Clark and Murphy remained for a private talk with Darlan. Clark said he hoped that the admiral could gain for the Allies the powerful French fleet based at Toulon in unoccupied southern France. Darlan doubted if he could produce it. "I can assure you one thing," Darlan said solemnly. "It will never fall into German hands."*

Robert Murphy, who had been told by Eisenhower that he could now drop his *nom de guerre,* Lieutenant Colonel McGowan, escorted Admiral Darlan to his car. Before getting in, the little admiral turned to the American and said evenly, "Would you please do me a favor, Mr. Murphy? Please remind Major General Clark that I am a five-star admiral. He should cease shouting at me and treating me like a junior lieutenant."

Murphy agreed. But he knew that Clark would continue to shout if it ended the bloodshed and let the Americans get on with the war against Hitler.

In Vichy, Marshal Pétain gave his approval to Admiral Darlan's ceasefire order. But Pierre Laval, the premier of France considered by the Allies to be an arch-collaborator with Nazi Germany, heard the ceasefire news over Radio Vichy as he was driving toward Munich for a

---

* Admiral Darlan kept his word. A short time later the magnificent French warships at Toulon were scuttled to keep them out of the clutches of Adolf Hitler.

conference with Hitler. Laval rushed to the nearest telephone, called Henri Pétain, and persuaded the old marshal to disavow Darlan's order.

At Gibraltar that afternoon, Eisenhower's chief of staff, General Al Gruenther, and other officers were monitoring Radio Vichy when electrifying news came over the air: The befuddled Marshal Pétain had rejected a North African armistice and fired Darlan, who was to be succeeded by General Auguste Noguès, Resident General of Morocco. Noguès at that moment was desperately trying to ward off General Patton's thrusts toward Casablanca. Pétain's action threw yet another complication into the French political mess.

In Algiers, Admiral Darlan's spirits were crushed at the news that Pétain had bounced him from his post. Apparently seeking to get back into Pétain's good graces, Darlan flip-flopped once more. He told an irritated General Clark, "I must revoke the order that I signed this morning."

"Like hell you will!" the American shouted. "There will be no revocation of your orders."

"Then I must consider myself a prisoner."

"That's okay with me," Clark snapped.

Admiral Darlan, his face impassive, was led away to be locked up in a comfortable home in an Algiers suburb, surrounded by a platoon of American soldiers who knew only that they were guarding "some French big shot."

Hundreds of miles to the west of Algiers, men of Company G, 30th Infantry, were peering through the blackness at an outpost near Fedala. It was 2:00 A.M. on November 11. The GIs were especially alert. They had heard a report earlier in the night that a small force of Berbers, fierce warriors from the mountains of Morocco feared for their skill with long, razor-sharp knives, had infiltrated American positions, silently hacked up four soldiers, and melted into the night.

Suddenly the stillness at the G Company outpost was shattered. The startled GIs heard the strident notes of a bugle in the blackness, then discerned, behind oncoming headlights, the outline of an automobile flying a large white flag. As the car neared the outpost, the Americans could make out a dark figure standing on the running board, blowing relentlessly on the bugle. The Americans held their fire as the automobile jerked to a stop.

Out hopped two French officers and two enlisted men who requested to see "the commanding general." The group was escorted to the Miramer Hotel, Western Task Force headquarters, where General Patton was awakened. Patton dressed quickly and rushed downstairs and into a smoking room. It was an eerie setting. Illumination came from a single candle thrust into the mouth of an empty champagne bottle, and shadows flickered off the walls. The immaculately groomed general, wearing what his devoted staff called his number-three frown (he had several of varying intensity), was approached by a French officer wearing a black leather helmet. The grimy-faced visitor saluted sharply, introduced himself as Commandant Philippe Lebel, Third Moroccan Spahis, and handed Patton a message. It was scrawled on a single sheet of paper over the signature of General Georges Lascroux, ground force commander in Morocco.

"On receipt of this order," Lascroux wrote, "French troops will cease hostilities with American troops. French commanders will take immediate steps to notify American outposts."

Without change of expression, Patton stepped to one side to hold a whispered conversation with two key staff officers, Brigadier General Geoffrey Keyes and Colonel Hobart S. Gay. The pair suggested that the assault against Casablanca, now only some four hours away, be called off. Patton shook his head, declaring that this had happened in 1918 in a similar situation when the Germans sent out cease-fire feelers.

Patton returned to the French officer: "Lebel, if I accept this order at its face value and call off a highly coordinated attack, what is my guarantee that it will be obeyed by the French navy?"

The Frenchman replied that Admiral Michelier's chief of staff knew him personally, and if permitted he would go immediately to the admiralty in Casablanca to secure a guarantee that the French navy would not shoot.

Patton, seated at a small table, was silent for several moments in intense reflection. "Okay, Lebel, I'll accept your word and let you go,"

Patton stated in an even tone. He paused and then his high-pitched voice rose an octave: "Tell Admiral Michelier that if he doesn't want to be destroyed he better quit at once."

Turning to Colonel John P. Ratay, his assistant intelligence officer, Patton said, "Ratay, you'll accompany Commandant Lebel into Casablanca. Unless the French navy abides by this cease-fire order, the attack jumps off as scheduled."

"Yes, sir," the colonel responded as he headed for the door. Patton called out, "And Ratay . . ."

"Yes, sir."

"Don't get yourself shot in the ass."

Patton scribbled a note in his almost illegible handwriting: "If you receive message from me in the clear *Play Ball* cease all hostilities at once." He handed it to his signal officer, Colonel Elton F. Hammond, with instructions to send it to all units and to Admiral Kent Hewitt on the *Augusta*.

Rising from his chair, Patton motioned to Colonel Gay. "Come on, Hap," he declared. "Let's go to Anderson's [3rd Division] CP. It's too sticky in here to sweat out this goddamned thing!" It was 4:15 A.M. Indeed, George Patton did have to sweat it out. For an hour at the forward CP, he paced like a tiger, all the time puffing on a cigar. Then a second interminable hour ticked past with no word from Colonel Ratay and Commandant Lebel. A gray dawn was breaking and already Army P-40s from the just-captured Port Lyautey airdrome and Wildcat dive-bombers from the carrier *Enterprise* were circling ominously over Casablanca. Offshore, Kent Hewitt's warships had moved into position with big guns loaded and their crews standing by for the order to fire. At the Miramer Hotel in Fedala, Colonel Hammond was hovering nervously by the radio receiver, anxiously waiting for word from Casablanca.

At 6:48 A.M. the radio set crackled and Patton's excited voice came over the air. "Hammond," the general bellowed, *"call it off!* The French navy has capitulated. But you'll have to work fast; there are only a few minutes left."

Patton turned to General Jonathan Anderson and ordered him to rush his 3rd Infantry Division into Casablanca. If anyone tries to stop him, Anderson was to "kick hell out of them." Within minutes the fighting men of the Rock of the Marne division were heading for the big port city. They drove past contingents of armed French soldiers and sailors who merely stared curiously at the Americans loaded down with combat gear. Not a shot was fired.

While Patton's men were pouring into Casablanca, General Eisenhower that morning was deep inside the Rock of Gibraltar, skimming through London newspapers that had just been flown in. It was heady stuff to the former Kansas farm boy; the name Eisenhower was plastered over the pages, a far cry from a little over a year earlier when a newspaper picture caption had identified the then-obscure staff officer as Colonel D. D. Ersenslager.

The supreme commander was sitting in his underpants. He had spilled ink on his trousers, and an aide, Captain Ernest "Tex" Lee, was laboring to remove the stain. Lee's efforts were in vain; the aide to one of the world's most powerful men could not locate the few ounces of gasoline needed to complete the stain-removal mission.

At 7:30 A.M. a signal officer rushed into Eisenhower's cubbyhole and handed him a hand-printed message: "Word just received from General Patton of surrender of French at Casa." There were broad grins all around.

The brief exhilaration was tempered as the morning wore on and a litany of ominous signals kept pouring into Gibraltar: One hundred German aircraft and gliders have landed at El Aouina airport in Tunisia . . . 500 German paratroopers flown in there . . . ten Luftwaffe planes carrying tanks land . . . Germans cut Algiers-Tunis railroad . . . transport *New Zealand* sunk by U-boats . . .

General Eisenhower at this point was keeping a close watch on the French fleet in Toulon. Hitler's armies had begun racing south into unoccupied France early that morning and should reach Toulon by nightfall. What would the French admirals do under present circumstances? Through the prodding of Mark Clark in Algiers, the captive Admiral Darlan had issued what amounted to a mild invitation to the Toulon warships to come over to the Allies. But on the Rock, Eisenhower's close aide, Lieutenant Commander Butcher, scrawled in the supreme commander's diary: "Will it [the French fleet] join us in North Africa or will it play ostrich and let Hitler have it by default? Fleet personnel hate the British and don't think Americans are so hot, either."

In the Miramer Hotel in Fedala late that morning of November 11, American and French commanders gathered to smoke the peace pipe. General Patton, Admiral Kent Hewitt and other Americans were in high good spirits, elated to have the fighting halted. Admiral Michelier, the hardline Vicyite, was grim, even sullen, and fidgeted nervously. The amiable Kent Hewitt put out his hand to Michelier, and the Frenchman hesitated several moments before he responded with a limp clasp.

The opposing commanders milled self-consciously about the room, but the meeting never began; General Noguès, Resident General of Morocco, failed to appear. More tension. Finally both groups went to the *Augusta*, where Hewitt played host at a sumptuous meal. The wine flowed, the talk became more jovial, and Admiral Michelier began to thaw.* Patton was at his charming best, regaling Michelier with war tales in fractured French and treating the admiral with great deference. Michelier was the same man Patton for days had branded as "that goddamned bastard." Havana cigars were brought out along with brandy, and the wardroom was soon one large cloud of smoke. The lively gala had to conclude and all present returned to the Miramer Hotel to await the arrival of General Noguès. Out in front of the old building was a neatly dressed honor guard of American soldiers, drawn up on Patton's orders for the arrival of Noguès. Patton had explained that there was "no use knocking a man when he's down."

Precisely at 3:00 P.M., General Noguès made his belated appearance. It was an arrival that in pomp and circumstance would have done justice to an ancient Chinese potentate. French motorcycles, their drivers in shiny black leather helmets, thundered up to the front of the Miramer. Behind was a long black limousine, and as the American honor guard presented arms, General Noguès emerged. With him were General

---

* Later General Patton would write that the French leaders "drank up $47 worth of our wine—but it was worth it."

Lascroux and the chief of French air forces in Morocco, General La-houelle.

General Keyes met the French dignitaries and escorted them to a conference room, where Patton praised the French for the "courage and skill shown by your armed forces." Noguès was unmoved by the flat-tery. His face remained grim and cold. Admiral Michelier, who had the advantage of considerable wine and brandy to cheer his outlook, sat with a fixed smile on his face.

General Patton ordered Colonel William Wilbur to read the terms of a stringent treaty, one that had been prepared by diplomats in the U.S. State Department who were far removed from the realities of the situa-tion in French Northwest Africa. At the conclusion of the reading, Noguès's face became more icy. The set smile vanished from Michelier's face. These terms, dictated as though France were a vanquished foe, were unacceptable, both leaders declared coldly.

Noguès angrily played his trump card. In an ice-tinged voice, he pointed out that without French cooperation—that is, if the United States insisted on inflicting such a harsh treaty upon French Morocco —then the American army would be powerless to drive eastward and confront the Germans in Tunisia. He stressed that the entire task of preserving order among 21 million Arabs, Berbers, Jews, and other nationalities, along with protecting a thousand miles of supply lines to Tunisia, would fall solely upon the Americans.

It was a powerful argument that struck George Patton between the eyes. He rose and called for the treaty, which was handed to him by Colonel Wilbur. Patton dramatically held up the sheets of paper and slowly, a strip at a time, tore the treaty into ribbons. Then he launched into an emotional speech, lauding the tradition of the French army and recalling that he had been a student at army schools in France. "We all belong to the same profession," he said in his improvisatory French, leaving most American officers wondering what he was saying, "and your word is as good as your written signature."

He paused briefly for effect. Then: "I propose until final terms are arranged by higher headquarters, that you return all your men and arms to the proper stations, that you take your sick and wounded with you and your dead. Give me your word that you will not bear arms against our forces and that you immediately return any of our men who may be prisoners and our dead, and that you will make every effort to maintain good order in Morocco."

Patton sat down and surveyed the gathering. Tension had vanished as if by magic. French faces brightened. Even General Noguès managed a trace of a grin.

Patton could not resist a final spontaneous gesture. "There is, however, an additional condition upon which I must insist," he said solemnly.

Tomblike silence fell over the room. French smiles disappeared, and all eyes went apprehensively to the grim-faced Patton.

"It is this," said the American general, breaking into a wide grin—"that you join me in a glass of champagne."

Even as French officers in Northwest Africa ceased struggling with their consciences and halted the shooting, the Allied race to beat the Axis into Tunisia had begun. On November 11, elements of the British 78th Division under Major General Vyvyan Evelegh splashed ashore near the port of Bougie, 100 miles east of Algiers. The British convoy carrying this force used the sheltered Bay of Bougie in which to anchor—with the permission of the French officer in command.

Almost at once, waves of Luftwaffe bombers, based in Sicily and in Sardinia, began pounding the squatting Bougie convoy. They sank the transports *Karanja, Cathey,* and *Awatea,* and the antiaircraft ship *Tynwald,* and damaged the monitor *Roberts.*

At dawn the following day, two British destroyers, guided by a friendly local French pilot, slipped into the port of Bône, 125 miles east of Bougie, and put ashore the 6th Commando. At this point, the Allies had reached the eastern boundary of Algeria and were 185 miles west of Torch's primary goal, the port of Tunis in Tunisia.

On the night of November 11, 15 transports and cargo ships of Admiral Kent Hewitt's Western Task Force were riding at anchor off Fedala. American skippers were comforted by the knowledge that the vulnerable vessels were being protected by a cordon of warships and a mine field. Undeterred by these odds, however, the captain of the German *U-173* worked his way through and torpedoed and sank the transport *Joseph Hewes*. In quick order *U-173* torpedoed but failed to sink the destroyer *Hambleton* and the oiler *Winooski*, then slipped back out to sea.

Another submarine, the *U-130*, launched an even more devastating assault, torpedoing the transports *Tasker H. Bliss*, *Hugh L. Scott*, and *Edward Rutledge*, killing over 100 Americans. Later the destroyer *Electra* was torpedoed 16 miles off Casablanca.

In the Rock of Gibraltar, the Luftwaffe and U-boat attacks tempered the elation over the cessation of fighting in Algeria and French Morocco. One ominous factor stood out: Hitler's war machine was still powerful and resolute. The tortuous road to Berlin would be a long and bloody one.

Epilogue

Five-star General Auguste Noguès flew on November 12 from Morocco to Algiers, where French leaders were closeted with General Mark Clark in an effort to hammer out a workable agreement for Algeria and French Morocco. Clark, who in only three days had absorbed a crash course on international intrigue, initially joined underground chief Robert Murphy in a scheme to replace Admiral Darlan with General Henri Giraud. The effort fell apart because Giraud wanted no part of politics.

General Noguès readily agreed to Admiral Darlan's being installed as head of government and insisted that he himself should be commander of military forces in French Northwest Africa. He refused to have anything to do with Giraud, whom he regarded as a traitor along with Generals Mast and Béthouart.

Finally, General Alphonse Juin stepped into the breach and brought Noguès around to agreeing that Giraud could be commander in chief, but only if he took his orders from Darlan in the name of Marshal Henri Pétain. Noguès presented another significant condition for his agreement: that arch-rival General Charles de Gaulle, Prime Minister Winston Churchill's candidate for taking over in French Northwest Africa, be prevented from as much as setting foot on that continent.

The next afternoon, November 13, General Eisenhower met with Darlan, Noguès, Giraud, and Juin at Algiers's St. George Hotel and gave his official blessing to an arrangement in which Darlan would be head of government and Giraud would be commander of armed forces. There was no surrender in French Northwest Africa, no transfer of sovereignty, simply a permanent cease-fire. To a man, French ground, sea, and air commanders had obeyed Admiral Darlan's order to break off hostilities and to make French troops, weapons, and facilities available to the Western Allies for pursuit of the war against a common foe —Nazi Germany.

General Eisenhower and his deputy Mark Clark had agonizingly decided to go along with Darlan as head of state due to a fact that cut through the welter of French political problems: Admiral Darlan was the only man in a position to save countless American, British, and French lives, ensure full cooperation with the Western Allies in the looming fight against the Germans in Tunisia, and prevent an incalculable amount of sabotage and obstruction to Allied operations.

At once an uproar exploded on the homefronts as left-wing circles in the United States and Great Britain denounced the cease-fire arrangement. It was tagged with a disparaging label: the Darlan Deal. Many editorial writers in the United States and Great Britain deplored General Eisenhower and General Clark's "getting in bed with the arch Nazi collaborationist," as one paper characterized it. In the U.S. Congress and in Parliament, the chambers echoed with bitter denunciations by liberal legislators.

As abuse was heaped on them over the Darlan Deal, Eisenhower and Clark took a measure of solace from the strong support given to their cease-fire agreement by President Roosevelt. The American chief executive went to considerable effort to point out to the press and to the homefront that the arrangement worked out in French Northwest Africa had been based on some uncomfortable exigencies both there and in France.

Four days later, under a pounding from many newspapers, Roosevelt began to waver. The Darlan Deal was just a "temporary expedient," he stressed. In Great Britain, however, Winston Churchill had endorsed it even though he had privately bitterly opposed a Darlan deal from the beginning.

On December 24, the hullabaloo came to a sudden halt. In Algiers on that Christmas Eve afternoon, Admiral Darlan returned to his office from a luncheon and was approached by twenty-year-old Fernand Eugene Bonnier de la Chapelle. The youth had been active in the underground, and in the early morning hours of D-day he had been among the pro-Allied group of young Frenchmen who had surrounded General Juin's Algiers villa where master-spy Robert Murphy was being held prisoner.

Without a word, Bonnier shot Darlan at point-blank range with a pistol. Bleeding extensively from the mouth, the admiral collapsed in the doorway of his office and died a short time later.

Bonnier de la Chapelle was caught by guards as he tried to flee the building. He was tried by a hastily convened court-martial, found guilty, and executed by a firing squad two days after the murder.

Circumstances surrounding Admiral Darlan's assassination have remained cloudy to this day. At the time, and in later years, it was recognized that young Bonnier de la Chapelle could not have acted alone, that a conspiracy had been involved. Who were these conspirators? Why had they decided to have Darlan murdered? Why had the gunman been executed so quickly, before he could be extensively questioned about accomplices? No one in official position had been too distressed over the little French admiral's passing from the scene, perhaps because he had taken on his new duties with total dedication to the Allied cause, and with his customary vitality.

In the four-day war in French Northwest Africa, the bloodletting had been heavy, even though General Eisenhower had sought to play down the casualties in order to keep French emotions from flaring into even more resolute hostility toward the invaders. American forces suffered 1,404 casualties, including 556 killed, 837 wounded, and 41 missing. Great Britain had sustained nearly 300 casualties, and the French estimated their losses at more than 700 killed, 1,400 wounded, and 400 missing.

In addition, the French air force in Northwest Africa lost scores of aircraft and pilots, and the proud French navy had many warships sunk, including 10 destroyers, 4 submarines, and the cruiser *Primauguet*. As a result of Hitler's decision to occupy all of France, a move triggered by Operation Torch, the French fleet based on Toulon and other ports in southern France was scuttled: a battleship, 7 cruisers, 24 destroyers, 10 submarines, and 19 other assorted vessels. The French submarines *Casabianca, Glorieux,* and *Marsouin* joined the Allies in Algiers.

After the war, American generals admitted candidly that it had been providential that the French had chosen to fight. Operation Torch became a gigantic combat laboratory where generals and privates alike learned the bitter lessons of warfare before having to take on the powerful and battle-tested Wehrmacht. Even the supremely self-confident General George Patton learned that there was much more to leading a large fighting force than dashing ashore and swearing loudly.

The inexperience of the half-trained Torch force, the catastrophic collapse of communications, the inadequate weapons, the unseaworthy ships, the gigantic snarls in beach-unloading operations, the equipment that failed, and the manner in which the entire operation had of necessity been thrown together all contributed to the invasion coming precariously close to foundering. General Patton gave a revealing analysis three days after the shooting ceased. "It is my firm conviction that the great success attending this hazardous operation . . . could have been possible only through the intervention of Divine Providence."

The tinkling of champagne glasses and the litany of toasts between French and American military leaders by no means settled the political mess in French Northwest Africa. Soured by the turn of events, the unpredictable General Auguste Noguès proved to be vindictive. It was learned that he intended to bring to trial as "traitors to France" General Émile Béthouart and other officers who had been working with the Allies to smooth a path for the invasion. Noguès, Allied intelligence officers concluded, intended to have Béthouart shot.

Patton was especially incensed, and to his staff reverted to describing Noguès as "that goddamned son of a bitch." Patton angrily fired off a message to Eisenhower: "I believe it to be of the greatest importance that any [French] officer who has acted to assist this expedition shall be protected and upheld."

As a result of the intervention of many outraged American commanders, General Noguès agreed to "postpone any action" regarding General Béthouart, and on November 17 Béthouart and his pro-Allied officers were released quietly from jail.

Torch did not immediately bring American troops into contact with Axis ground forces, but it placed them in proximity to Germans and Italians on the field of battle. A confrontation would soon take place, as General Eisenhower promptly began moving Torch forces in Algeria and Morocco hundreds of miles eastward to Tunisia. The trek across the bleak north African terrain was slow and painful, made sluggish by a shortage of vehicles, pelting rains that turned roads into quagmires, and the inexperience of American commanders in moving large bodies of troops with their weapons and equipment.

Field Marshal Erwin Rommel, aware that Hitler had decided to fight it out in Tunisia, rushed to Berlin. Appealing to the Führer to withdraw the remaining forces from North Africa while there was still time, he spoke bluntly. "If our army is to remain in Africa, it will be destroyed."

Hitler flew into a rage. Rommel flushed as his mentor stopped just short of accusing him of cowardice. Not only would the Germans remain in North Africa, Hitler declared, but he intended to substantially reinforce Tunisia. In addition, Rommel was ordered to pull back his Afrika Korps remnants into Tunisia from in front of General Bernard Montgomery's pursuing British Eighth Army in Libya.

By January, there were 100,000 first-rate German troops and a similar number of Italian soldiers in Tunisia. At a time when General Eisenhower needed each available soldier in order to administer the coup de grace to the Axis in North Africa, four Torch divisions were sitting idle in French Morocco, more than a thousand miles west of Tunisia. Possibly through a German deception, Allied headquarters had become fixed in its view that Adolf Hitler would pour troops into Spain with the connivance of dictator Francisco Franco, leap the narrow Strait of Gibraltar into Spanish Morocco, and attack Torch forces from the rear.

So in bleak, inhospitable Tunisia, Eisenhower's Torch forces and Montgomery's Eighth Army slugged it out with the Axis for five violent, miserable, bloody months. The Germans and Italians were pushed back steadily until they were cornered in the northern tip of Tunisia. Field Marshal Rommel was not there with his men because Hitler, seeing the handwriting on the wall in North Africa, had quietly recalled him. Rommel's popularity on the homefront was beginning to rival the Führer's.

Finally, on May 13, Axis resistance collapsed. A human deluge of 130,000 German and 120,000 Italian soldiers—more prisoners than the Russians had taken at Stalingrad—streamed into Allied enclosures. But the victors had paid a heavy price. In the six months since the Torch landings, the Americans, British, and French had suffered 70,341 casualties, 10,290 of them killed, including 2,715 American dead. But Hitler had at last been driven out, and the Western Allies were now masters of the shores of North Africa.

Shortly after the war ended in Europe, in 1945, Maréchal de France Henri-Philippe Pétain, the World War I Hero of Verdun, age eighty-seven, was tried by his countrymen for treason. In 1940, after the German blitzkrieg had crushed the French army—reputedly the world's best—in only six weeks, Pétain had resolved that at all costs France must be spared needless suffering. So when asked to head the government in Vichy, Pétain felt duty-bound to accept the post to gain the best lot he could from the Germans for the French people. Now he was being forced to defend that decision and subsequent actions.

The mood of the French people at this time was one of vengeance and cruelty, and in this ugly climate the trial began. Pétain faced his ordeal with dignity, and some observers thought he seemed confused by the proceedings. The "Old Marshal" wore a plain uniform, devoid of medals except for the Medaille Militaire, and he refused to take his marshal's baton into court ("that would be too theatrical").

Predictably, Pétain was condemned to death. He accepted the verdict with no sign of emotion. On hearing of the court's judgment, thousands of French military officers wept for the revered Old Marshal, and for France. Later the penalty was reduced to life imprisonment.

In a final stroke of humiliation, the name of Marshal Henri Pétain was ordered stricken from the head of the Roll of Honor at Verdun.

The Old Marshal died in 1951.

Bibliography

BOOKS

Adams, Henry M. *Harry Hopkins.* New York: G. P. Putnam's, 1977.

Altieri, James. *The Spearheaders.* New York: Bobbs-Merrill, 1960.

Ambrose, Stephen E. *The Supreme Commander.* New York: Doubleday, 1970.

Ayer, Frederick J., Jr. *Before the Colors Fade.* Boston: Houghton Mifflin, 1964.

Bauer, Eddy. *Encyclopedia of World War II.* New York: Marshall Cavendish, 1970.

Bekkar, Cajus. *The Luftwaffe War Diaries.* New York: Doubleday, 1969.

Blumenson, Martin. *The Patton Papers.* Boston: Houghton Mifflin, 1974.

Brown, Anthony Cave. *Bodyguard of Lies.* New York: Harper & Row, 1975.

Bryant, Arthur. *The Turn of the Tide.* New York: Doubleday, 1957.

Butcher, Harry C. *My Three Years with Eisenhower.* New York: Simon & Schuster, 1946.

Churchill, Winston S. *The Grand Alliance.* Boston: Houghton Mifflin, 1950.

Clark, Mark W. *Calculated Risk.* New York: Harper & Brothers, 1951.

Deacon, Richard. *A History of the British Secret Service.* New York: Taplinger Publishing, 1969.

Davis, Kenneth S. *Experience of War.* New York: Doubleday, 1965.

——. *Soldier of Democracy: A Biography of Dwight Eisenhower.* New York: Doubleday Doran, 1945.

Eisenhower, Dwight D. *Crusade in Europe.* New York: Doubleday, 1948.

Ellsberg, Edward. *No Banners, No Bugles.* New York: Dodd Mead, 1949.

Essame, H. *Patton: A Study in Command.* New York: Charles Scribner's, 1974.

Farago, Ladislas. *Patton: Ordeal and Triumph.* New York: Ivan Obolensky, 1963.

Harmon, Ernest N. *Combat Commander.* New York: Prentice-Hall, 1970.

Harriman, W. Averell. *Special Envoy to Churchill and Stalin.* New York: Random House, 1975.

Ingersoll, Ralph. *Top Secret.* New York: Harcourt Brace, 1946.

Irving, David. *Hitler's War.* New York: Viking, 1977.

Ismay, Lord Hastings. *The Memoirs of General Lord Ismay.* New York: Viking, 1960.

Kahn, David. *Hitler's Spies.* New York: Macmillan, 1978.

Keitel, Wilhelm. *The Memoirs of Field Marshal Keitel.* New York: Stein & Day, 1965.

Kesselring, Field Marshal Albrecht. *A Soldier's Record.* New York: William Morrow, 1954.

Killen, John. *A History of the Luftwaffe.* New York: Doubleday, 1968.

King, Ernest J., and Whitehall, Walter M. *Fleet Admiral King.* New York: W. W. Norton, 1952.

Kirkpatrick, Lyman B., Jr. *Captains Without Eyes.* New York: Macmillan, 1969.

Lewin, Ronald, *Ultra Goes to War.* New York: McGraw-Hill, 1978.

Liddell Hart, B. H. *History of the Second World War.* New York: G. P. Putnam's Sons, 1971.

Maisky, Ivan. *Memoirs of a Soviet Ambassador.* New York: Scribner's, 1968.

Montgomery, Field Marshal the Viscount. *Memoirs.* London: Collins, 1958.

Moran, Lord Charles Wilson. *Churchill: The Struggle for Survival.* Boston: Houghton Mifflin, 1946.

Morison, Samuel Eliot. *The Two Ocean War.* Boston: Little Brown, 1963.

Murphy, Robert. *Diplomat Among Warriors.* New York: Doubleday, 1964.

Patton, George S. *War As I Knew It.* Boston: Houghton Mifflin, 1947.

Pogue, Forrest C. *George C. Marshall.* New York: Viking, 1965.

Pyle, Ernie. *Here Is Your War.* Cleveland: World Publishing, 1943.

Popov, Dusko. *Spy Counter-Spy.* New York: Grosset & Dunlap, 1974.

Roosevelt, Elliott. *As He Saw It.* New York: Duell Sloan, 1946.

Sanderson, James D. *Giants in War.* New York: Van Nostrand, 1962.

Secrets and Spies. Pleasantville, N.Y.: Reader's Digest, 1964.

Shapiro, Milton J. *Ranger Battalion.* New York: Messner, 1979.

Sherwood, Robert E. *Roosevelt and Hopkins.* New York: Harper Brothers, 1950.

Summersby, Kay. *Eisenhower Was My Boss.* New York: Prentice-Hall, 1948.

Tedder, Lord Arthur, *With Prejudice.* Boston: Little, Brown, 1966.

Toland, John. *Adolf Hitler.* New York: Ballantine Books, 1972.

Truscott, General Lucian K., Jr. *Command Missions.* New York: E. P. Dutton, 1960.

Whitehouse, Arch. *Espionage and Counterespionage.* New York: Doubleday, 1964.

Winant, John G. *Letter from Grosvenor Square.* Boston: Houghton Mifflin, 1947.

Winterbotham, F. W. *The Ultra Secret.* New York: Harper & Row, 1974.

Yarborough, General William P. *Bailout over North Africa.* Williamstown, N. J.: Phillips Publications, 1980.

Unit and Campaign Histories

Danger Forward, The Story of the 1st Infantry Division, Washington, D.C.: Society of the 1st Division, privately printed, 1947.

Howe, George F. *Northwest Africa: Seizing the Initiative in the West.* Washington, D. C.: Chief of Military History, 1957.

Taggart, Donald G. *History of the 3rd Infantry Division.* Washington, D. C.: privately printed, 1947.

Mittelman, Joseph B. *Eight Stars to Victory.* Washington, D. C.: privately printed, 1947.

Index

Rommel, Erwin:
in Battle of El Alamein, 57, 87–88, 93, 95, 96–97
as commander of Afrika Korps, 20, 86, 124, 239, 256, 257
Rooney, Thomas, 182
Roosevelt, Franklin D.:
Churchill and, 36, 62–63
"Darlan Deal" supported by, 253–254
Eisenhower and, 91
letter to de Gaulle from, 51
Operation Sledgehammer supported by, 3, 7
Operation Torch supported by, 7, 8–9, 12, 21, 37, 51, 107, 114, 190, 194, 210
Patton and, 66–67
security problems of, 62–63, 64
Roosevelt, Theodore, Jr., 122, 133–134, 135, 136, 229, 230
Rosenfeld, A. H., 167
Roubertie, Pierre, 159
Royal Air Force, 27, 29
"Rube Goldberg" mortar, 126, 130–132
Rundstedt, Karl Rudolf Gerd von, 20–21, 25, 29, 38
Russell, A. B., 168
Russia:
German campaign against, 7, 21, 37
Operation Torch and, 7, 18–20, 21
war effort of, 3, 257
Rutledge, John M., 211
Rutter, Operation, 5–6, 9, 23
Ryder, Charles W. "Doc," 158, 162, 170–171, 201, 225, 238

Safi, Allied assault on, 84, 175, 176–184, 202, 212
St. Amiel, 234
St. Cloud, 132–133, 217–219
St. George Hotel, 225, 226, 253
Samuel Chase, 166, 167
Santee, 183
Savannah, 219
Schnellboot squadrons, 94
Schwarze Kapelle, 60
scramblers, telephone, 62–63
Seafires, 148
Sebkra D'Oran, 151–155, 183, 215–216
2nd Armored Division, U.S., 65–66, 175, 199, 236–237
2nd Moroccan Infantry Regiment, French, 178

16th Tunisian Regiment, French, 132
60th Carrier Group, U.S., 47–48
60th Infantry Regiment, U.S., 190–192
68th African Artillery Regiment, French, 132
78th Infantry Division, British, 250
692nd Coast Guard Artillery, U.S., 192
Semmes, Harry H., 199, 219
Senegalese troops, 169, 170
Seraph, 73–75, 78, 79–80, 99–100
Services of Supply (SOS), 34, 49–50
Shark Bait, 148–149, 151, 215
"sibs" campaign, 57–58
Sladin, Fred W., 207
Sledgehammer, Operation:
British opposition to, 3–9, 21
U.S. support of, 3, 5, 7, 21
Smith, Walter Bedell "Beetle," 91, 98
snipers, 182, 184, 236
Spanish Morocco, 125, 150, 153, 256
Spey, 102–103
Spitfires, 216, 224–225
spotter planes, 206, 219, 220–221
Stalin, Josef, 18–20, 30, 63
Stark, Harold R. "Betty," 14
Starkweather, M. K., 232, 233–234
Stewart, Ollie, 82–83
Stimson, Henry, 21, 30
Stumme, Georg, 86–87
Summersby, Kay, 51–53
Swenson, Edwin T., 158–159, 167–170
Syfret, Neville, 92
Sympson, Gordon H., 179–180

Tafaraoui airport, paratroop assault on, 43–48, 118, 123, 147–156, 215–216, 219
tank warfare, 182–183, 184, 197, 199, 216, 219, 230–231
Telegraph Cottage, 51–52
Terminal, Operation, 158–159, 167–170
Tessier, Monsieur, 75, 76, 77, 78, 79
Third Army, U.S., 174*n*–175*n*
3rd Infantry Division, U.S., 175, 203–207, 211, 219–221, 238, 246–247
35th Infantry Division, U.S., 163
39th Infantry Regiment, U.S., 102
Thomas, Frank P., 14, 15
Thomas Stone, 102, 103*n*, 166
Tibbets, Paul, 72, 97–98
Times (London), 29
Titania, 182–183
Todd, John, 217, 230